ESSENTIAL OILS

ESSENTIAL
OILS

Penguin
Random
House

Editor Claire Cross
Senior Designer Collette Sadler
Design and Art Direction
  Emma Forge and Tom Forge
Managing Editor Angela Wilkes
Managing Art Editor Marianne Markham
Jacket Designer Harriet Yeomans
Senior Jacket Creative Nicola Powling
Producer, Pre-Production
  Catherine Williams
Producer Poppy Werder-Harris
Art Director Maxine Pedliham
Publisher Mary-Clare Jerram
Special Sales Creative Project Manager
  Alison Donovan

DK US
Editors Ann Barton, Jane Perlmutter,
Lori Hand
US Publisher Mike Sanders

First American Edition, 2016
This edition published in the United States by
DK Publishing 345 Hudson Street, New York,
New York 10014

Copyright © 2016, 2017
Dorling Kindersley Limited
DK, a Division of Penguin Random House LLC
17 18 19 20   10 9 8 7 6 5 4 3 2 1
004—296393—May/2017

A catalog record for this book is available from
the Library of Congress.

DISCLAIMER See page 256.

ISBN 978-1-4654-6811-6

Printed and bound in China

All images © Dorling Kindersley Limited
For further information see:
www.dkimages.com

A WORLD OF IDEAS:
SEE ALL THERE IS TO KNOW
www.dk.com

THE AUTHORS

Susan Curtis is a qualified homeopath and naturopath and is the Director of Natural Health for Neal's Yard Remedies. She is the author of numerous books, including *Looking Good and Feeling Younger* and several books on essential oils, and coauthor of *Natural Healing for Women*. Susan has two adult children and is passionate about helping people to live a more natural and healthy lifestyle.

Pat Thomas is a journalist, campaigner, and broadcaster. Her previous books include *Cleaning Yourself to Death, What's in this Stuff?,* and *Skin Deep*. Through her work she has led the way in exposing harmful chemicals in many everyday beauty products, as well as promoted natural alternatives that work. She is a former editor of *The Ecologist* magazine and is a trustee of the Organic Research Centre and editor of Neal's Yard Remedies' natural health website, *NYR Natural News*.

Fran Johnson is a passionate cosmetic scientist and aromatherapist, and has been part of the Product Development team at Neal's Yard Remedies since 2006, formulating therapeutic products for healing and well-being. She has written and teaches a number of Neal's Yard Remedies' courses that cover aromatherapy, natural perfumery, and making cosmetic products.

Contents

BASE OILS 146

ESSENTIAL OIL RECIPES 162

HEALING REMEDIES 214

Introduction

Aromatic essential oils have been used for thousands of years as traditional remedies to enhance **health** and **well-being.** The ability of **fragrances** to affect mood and atmosphere has long been recognized, and different cultures have made use of the **aromatic** plants available to them for spiritual rituals and personal use. The appeal of essential oils has endured, and today the practice of **aromatherapy** is well established in the lexicon of natural health.

Essential Oils **Today**

The essential oil trade emerged about 200 years ago for use in the perfumery and food industries. In recent years, an increased emphasis on holistic healing has led to a resurgence of interest in the traditional use of essential oils for health, well-being, and beauty.

Pleasurable and versatile, essential oils can be used as remedies for ailments, used in cosmetics and fragrances, and, increasingly, are used in the fast-growing trend for diffusing aromas to enhance living spaces and create a sense of well-being.

Therapeutic oil blends, scented candles, and nourishing skin products are just some of the ways to enjoy aromatic essential oils.

The growth of interest in essential oils also coincides with a rise in stress-related conditions associated with hectic modern-day living. With their ability to soothe body and mind, essential oils are especially helpful for combatting the effects of chronic stress.

At Neal's Yard Remedies, we have sold pure and natural essential oils since our first store opened in 1981, and have witnessed, and been part of, the growth of interest in essential oils, as more and more people look to natural ingredients to improve their lifestyle and enhance well-being.

A greater understanding There's an art and a science to using essential oils. In the past decades, the aromatherapy industry's understanding of how to use

Neroli essential oil, extracted from the delicate orange blossom, has an exquisite floral aroma.

oils and their properties has grown. The traditional use of oils in different cultures is being researched in laboratories, and clinical trials are being performed to enhance our understanding of how and why oils act as they do.

In this book, we impart some of this knowledge to help you learn how to enjoy oils in your daily beauty and health regimen. With a little knowledge and common sense, oils can be used by everyone. This book will help you become confident incorporating these wonderful essences into a more natural lifestyle. For serious or chronic health concerns, seek medical advice and see a professional aromatherapist.

Versatile and a pleasure to use, essential oils are natural healers.

Enjoying **Essential Oils**

At Neal's Yard Remedies, we believe an understanding of the plant that is the source of an oil is important to choose the best oil for your needs. The beautiful images in the A–Z section of this book, together with the plants' properties and suggestions for use, will help you develop an understanding and awareness of each plant and its oil.

Highly concentrated, essential oils are used in tiny amounts and need to be diluted before use in a base, or carrier, oil. A chapter on base oils guides you through some of the most popular oils and their properties.

We have developed a wide range of recipes and remedies for this book for health, beauty, and home. Simple instructions show you how to create blends and products, and tried-and-tested remedies will help you treat a range of common complaints.

So enjoy this introduction to essential oils and go on to create some wonderful products and experiences for you and your friends and family.

Susan Curtis, Director of Natural Health, Neal's Yard Remedies

With a range of properties, *the essential oil of thyme can be used cosmetically and therapeutically.*

Understanding
Essential Oils

Essential oils contain the **essence of nature.** Find out what exactly is in essential oils, how these complex substances work **holistically** to heal and balance body and mind, and how to ensure you are using the purest, **very best quality** products.

What Are Essential Oils?

Aromatic essential oils are the **highly concentrated** essences derived from plants. Used today in **aromatherapy** and fragrances, they have a long history in **natural healing**. The oils harness a plant's **therapeutic** properties to restore **balance** to the mind, body, and spirit.

The Plant's **Essence**

The aromatic compounds in essential oils are thought to help plants survive, for example, by attracting pollinators and warding off fungus and bacteria. Once extracted, essential oils contain the essence of a plant in a very concentrated form, which means the essential oils often smell delightful and retain the plant's unique therapeutic benefits for our use.

Essential oils in aromatherapy

Today, there are around 150 essential oils used in aromatherapy. Each has a unique chemistry and properties that produce a distinct therapeutic, psychological, and physiological effect. In addition to being anti-inflammatory, pain relieving, decongesting, and antiseptic, oils can ease anxiety and lift the spirits. Their powerful constituents can have a profound physiological effect, restoring balance and vitality.

A single essential oil contains as many as 100 different chemical components.

Essential Oil **Sources**

Each plant contains essential oils. In some plants, oil is extracted from the dried seeds, peel, or resin, while in others it is found in the leaves, roots, bark, or flowers.

Both dried and fresh seeds *can be pressed to extract the essential oils.*

The essential oils of citrus fruits *are concentrated mostly in the rinds.*

The cistus flower *yields its aromatic essential oil from the leaves and stems. In some plants, the oil is extracted from the petals, which can be a delicate process.*

12

What's in **an Oil?**

A single essential oil can contain as many as 100 chemical components, which work together to give the oil its unique properties and aroma. Each component plays a role, but some are more dominant and determine how an oil will act on the body and mind.

The chemistry of oils Oils are made up of major, minor, and trace components. Menthol is an example of a major component, making up around 40 percent of peppermint oil. These major components work with the more numerous minor and trace components and all contribute to an oil's aroma and therapeutic value.

Breaking oils down Each oil's component parts split into two further categories: oxygenated compounds and terpenes. Oxygenated compounds tend to be stronger smelling and longer lasting than terpenes. They include alcohols, which are antibacterial and found in oils such as ginger and juniper; esters, which can be antiseptic, found in oils such as basil and clove; and ketones, which regenerate cells, found in oils such as rose, camphor, and vetiver. Terpenes, found in oils such as myrrh, have a range of properties, but spoil quickly when exposed to air.

The amber-hued essential oil derived from the cistus plant is rich in oxygenated compounds.

The History of Essential Oils

Traditionally, highly concentrated oils from a variety of natural sources have been used to calm or stimulate the emotions and enhance well-being.

The use of scented oils in incense and candles has played a part in religious rituals throughout the ages, with many cultures believing the aromas could ward off evil or inspire us to new heights. The Egyptians used scented oils in burial rituals and as a symbol of status. The Greeks believed aromas connected them to the gods, while the Romans used scented oils for seduction.

The modern use of essential oils as a therapy began in the 1930s when the French chemist René-Maurice Gattefossé coined the term aromatherapy after finding that lavender oil helped heal his burned hand without scarring. In World War II, Dr. Jean Valnet, a French army surgeon, used oils on wounded soldiers, while Austrian beauty therapist and biochemist Marguerite Maury prescribed oils and is credited with the idea of using essential oils in massage.

Whether lifting the spirits or healing wounds, aromatherapy is a safe and effective traditional practice with real relevance to our lives today.

Plants such as ginger and plai produce a highly concentrated essential oil from the roots.

The resin from trees such as myrrh can be extracted and distilled into therapeutic oils.

Some plants, such as fragonia, hold essential oil in the branches, as well as the leaves.

How Essential Oils Work

Our sense of smell is more **sensitive** and immediate than any of our other senses, which is why aromas can be so evocative. Chemicals in a scent can trigger **physiological** responses and affect our mental state. These combined effects enable aromatic oils to work holistically on **mind**, **body**, and **spirit**, bringing **balance**, healing, and often a profound sense of well-being.

Mind

On the **Mind**

Essential oils can be used to help promote a state of mind. For example, stimulating oils can be used to enhance focus, while oils that are calming enable us to relax and help to combat the effects of stress.

Enhance well-being and mood

Essential oils have many components that affect the nervous system, helping to lift mood and enhance well-being. For example, studies show that the compound linalool in lavender and clary sage reduces anxiety, while limonene, found in many citrus oils, can ease anxiety and lift depression. Chamomile and bergamot essential oils contain the compounds alpha- and beta-pinene, which also work as antidepressants, helping lift the spirits and increase feelings of well-being.

When we feel anxious or depressed, it's not just our minds that are affected; our bodies can also suffer. For example, we tend to hold tension in our muscles when we are anxious. Many oils have both mood-enhancing properties and physiological effects so they treat

Well-being and mood

Chamomile is calming and can help to balance emotions.

Concentration and focus

Rosemary essential oil can clear the mind, enhancing focus.

Relaxation

Lavender has deeply relaxing properties.

Balance and energy

Geranium is uplifting and balances emotions.

Essential oils can both calm emotions and stimulate the mind.

both the mental and physical symptoms of stress and anxiety.

An aromatherapy massage adds the inherently relaxing benefits of touch to an oil's therapeutic effects, which can be profoundly calming and uplifting. Even without the benefit of touch, simply smelling a pleasant aroma, such as a tangerine or vanilla bean, can reduce stress-induced muscle tension.

Promote relaxation The relaxing effects of essential oils are well documented. How they help us relax is a complicated process thought to involve several parts of the brain. One theory is that linalool, found in oils such as lavender, regulates the neurohormone GABA (gamma-aminobutyric acid). This in turn regulates levels of adrenaline, noradrenaline, and dopamine.

Rose has an uplifting and calming aroma.

Improve concentration and focus Some oils clear and refresh. For example, inhaling rosemary oil has been shown to improve memory by up to 75 percent. The oil contains the compound eucalyptol, which acts in a similar way to dementia drugs by increasing a neurotransmitter called acetylcholine that helps regulate brain activity.

Balance energy Many oils can relax or stimulate as needed and are called *adaptogens.* These balance body systems in a process called homeostasis, calming or stimulating. Adaptogens help the body process stress by recharging the adrenal glands, which can be overstimulated or exhausted from stress. Lavender, rose, and geranium are examples of adaptogens.

How Oils Work Holistically

The concept of holistic healing involves treating the entire person so that the body, mind, and spirit are in harmony. This approach is very different from the conventional one that uses targeted drugs to tackle or suppress symptoms, but doesn't always address the root cause of a symptom.

Essential oils act on the mind and body to achieve deeper healing. For example, when relaxed, the body may be better at letting go of toxins and maintaining a healthy circulation. Inhaling black pepper oil gives physical and mental support to smokers trying to quit since the oil is decongesting and also helps reduce cravings.

Black pepper essential oil

Body

On the **Body**

Essential oils are natural healers, harnessing the medicinal properties that are traditionally associated with plants. For example, oils can be anti-inflammatory, antiseptic, and antifungal, and many essential oils are antimicrobial, helping to kill a whole variety of harmful microorganisms to protect us against disease.

Work as antiseptics Many essential oils have been shown to destroy the bacteria, viruses, and fungi that cause infection. One of the best known antiseptic essential oils, tea tree, is thought to be as effective as conventional treatments for athlete's foot, and recent research suggests that wounds infected with the *Staphylococcus aureus* bacterium heal faster when treated with tea tree oil than they do with conventional methods of treatment.

Chemical components, such as thymol found in thyme essential oil, menthol in peppermint, and eugenol in clove essential oil, to name but a few, have been shown to be powerfully antiseptic. Studies have demonstrated that inhaling these antiseptic essential oils can be as effective as applying them directly to the skin, and essential oil inhalation therapy has been used to treat the symptoms of bronchitis and acute sinusitis for many years.

In a world where many strains of bacteria are becoming resistant to conventional antibiotics, essential oils are beginning to be seen as a viable alternative.

Relieve pain and reduce inflammation Essential oils are often used for their mild anesthetic properties that can relieve localized pain. Oils such as thyme, rose, eucalyptus, clove, bergamot, and fennel have been shown to work on the body in a similar way to nonsteroidal anti-inflammatory drugs (NSAIDs) such as ibuprofen, by inhibiting the enzymes in the body that cause inflammation, swelling, and pain. This analgesic effect makes these essential oils especially useful for soothing muscle and joint pains and for providing localized pain relief, for example from tension headaches and from sprains and strains.

Pain is often accompanied by inflammation. Many essential oils have anti-inflammatory properties. One notable example is frankincense. Several varieties of frankincense essential oil have been shown to inhibit the production of inflammatory proteins called cytokines and to prevent white blood cells, known as leukocytes, from leaking into tissues, both of which cause inflammation.

Have a cleansing action When functioning properly, our lungs, liver, digestive system, kidneys, and skin all help to remove waste products and toxins from the body. Negative factors such as stress, anxiety, poor diet, and lack of sleep can all interfere with this process. Essential oils often have detoxifying properties that help to cleanse the body and support a healthy excretory system.

For example, a chemical called D-limonene, found in citrus fruits such as oranges, lemons, tangerines, limes, and grapefruits, supports the healthy functioning of the liver, as well as helping

Star anise has strong antiseptic properties.

Antiseptic

Tea tree essential oil is a well-established antiseptic.

Pain relief

Thyme has warming properties that provide gentle pain relief.

Cleansing

Orange essential oil helps to cleanse and detox the body.

Influence hormones

Basil can help to balance hormones.

Boost immunity

Sage can be used to help bolster the body's defences.

Therapeutic essential oils have powerful healing properties.

Influence hormones The endocrine system secretes hormones to regulate the body's processes. Essential oils can influence the action of hormones and smooth out imbalances. For example, relaxing rosemary has been shown to reduce levels of the stress hormone cortisol, and inhaling calming rose essential oil can help to decrease elevated levels of adrenaline. Several essential oils are thought to help regulate women's hormones during different stages of reproductive life. Lavandin essential oil is believed to help control hormone-induced mood fluctuations, and clary sage, fennel, basil, sage, cypress, and geranium have a similar balancing effect.

to regulate appetite and lower cholesterol. And juniper, grapefruit, rosemary, fennel, and cypress oils have a mild diuretic effect that helps to support the work of the kidneys by encouraging the elimination of excess water. Combining these oils with a gentle massage and body brush encourages the healthy circulation of blood and lymphatic fluid, and in turn the removal of waste.

Help boost immunity

Essential oils promote wellness by enhancing and strengthening our immune response to disease. Some essential oils actually stimulate the production of disease-fighting white blood cells, such as phagocytes, T-cells, and B-cells, which are vital to the body's defenses and immunity. In particular, eucalyptus and niaouli essential oils have been shown to encourage the process known as phagocytosis, where larger white blood cells called phagocytes engulf and then destroy, or deactivate, bacteria and viruses.

The compound linalool, which is found in high levels in essential oils such as lavender, sage, bay laurel, and eucalyptus, has also been shown to increase the efficiency of the body's white blood cells.

The Concept of Synergy

Blending oils can enhance their effects. For example, mixing an antiviral oil with one that is anti-inflammatory provides more effective relief from coughs and colds. This is sometimes called synergy, but the concept of synergy goes deeper than blending.

Often, the therapeutic benefit of an essential oil is attributed to one or two of its major components. But increasingly evidence shows that the benefits of oils come from the interaction of major and minor components. For example, thymol, a major component of thyme, is highly antibacterial. However, studies show that the whole essential oil has a greater antibacterial effect than the isolated component. There's still much to understand about how oils work synergistically, but it is clear that while science is geared toward using single compounds, whole oils have benefits that can't be replicated in the lab.

The components in a single oil work together to greater effect.

Essential oils work on the root cause as well as the symptom.

Spirit

On the **Spirit**

Essential oils have been used for thousands of years to enhance spiritual practice. From their use in traditional ceremonies to supporting personal spiritual practices such as meditation, essential oils help to support spiritual attainment.

Promote spiritual pursuit

Essentials oils have been used for millennia to support prayer. Historically, oils such as frankincense, myrrh, cinnamon, cedarwood, and rose have been used in religious ceremonies. A well-chosen fragrance can calm breathing, settle and focus the mind, and create a sense of intent.

Enhance mindful practices

Aromas that calm the mind or help to lift the spirits, found in oils such as lavender, elemi, and bergamot, can be used to enhance focus during practices such as meditation, yoga, and breathing techniques.

Energy and chi In some traditional practices, essential oils are used to clear blockages in the *chakras*, believed to be the energy centers in the body that relate to specific glands and organs. Chakras are said to be connected by meridians, which are described as channels through which vital energy, or *chi,* flows.

Blockages in these areas are thought to lead to poor health in the related part of the body. The illustration shows the position of the seven chakras. Specific essential oils are associated with different chakras, or centers, and are recommended to help bring balance and healing to these areas.

● **The crown chakra** at the top of the head governs the pineal gland and our "inner self." Oils such as frankincense, rose, jasmine, lavender, and elemi correspond with this area.

● **The brow chakra**, located just above and between the eyes, is connected to the pituitary gland and rules memory and mind. Oils such as myrrh, sandalwood, and jasmine can be used to treat blockages here.

● **The throat chakra** covers the area of the throat and the thyroid gland and relates to communication. Try lavender, chamomile, clary sage, cajuput, peppermint, geranium, and rosemary to treat this area.

● **The heart chakra**, located around the heart and upper body, affects well-being. Useful oils include rose, bergamot, lemon balm, chamomile, neroli, sandalwood, and palmarosa.

● **The solar plexus chakra** includes organs in the upper abdomen and is connected to self-esteem. Try ginger, helichrysum, manuka, coriander, lavender, marjoram, and orange.

● **The sacral chakra**, located in the lower abdomen, is linked to the reproductive system and responds to essential oils such as sandalwood, jasmine, rose, ylang-ylang, orange, and geranium.

● **The base chakra**, at the base of the spine, connects to our ability to feel grounded. Oils that help healing here include myrrh, cedarwood, patchouli, petitgrain, benzoin, carrot, and vetiver.

In some practices, *oils are used to clear blockages in the chakras, or energy centers, in the body.*

Cinnamon enhances meditation.

Chakras

The crown chakra

The brow chakra

The throat chakra

The heart chakra

The solar plexus chakra

The sacral chakra

The base chakra

17

How Essential Oils Are Extracted

A plant's essential oils are contained in tiny sacs on the surface of a leaf or flower, and sometimes within bark, seeds, and roots. When you scratch a piece of lemon peel and get a spray with an **intense lemon fragrance**, you are breaking open the sacs on the peel's surface and **releasing** the lemon oil. And when you rub the leaves of an herb between your fingers to produce a smell, you are **breaking the vessels** to release the oil. Producing essential oils involves one of several methods to burst open the sacs and collect the oil.

Methods of **Extraction**

The method used to produce an essential oil depends on the type of plant material that the oil is being extracted from. Most essential oils are produced by a process of steam distillation, but the oil in some flowers and plants is extremely delicate and would be destroyed by the heat used in this method, so these plants require a special method of oil production known as absolute extraction.

There are four main methods of production: **steam distillation**, the most widely used; **expression**, a simple method that is used to extract oil from rinds; **absolute extraction**, used for producing an oil from very delicate flowers; and **CO$_2$ extraction**, a new, evolving method.

Peppermint essential oil is extracted by steam distillation.

The surface of the peppermint leaf contains globular oil glands (shown in gray). These glands are broken open during the distillation process to release the aromatic essential oil.

The pale yellow essential oil that is extracted from the peppermint plant has a thin, almost watery texture.

The type of plant material determines which method of extraction is used to produce the essential oil.

Steam distillation The most popular method for extracting essential oils is steam distillation, a process used for herbs, roots, bark, and resins. This ancient method of extraction can be dated back around 5,000 years with the discovery of earthenware stills. Today, most stills are made of stainless steel or copper.

First, the plant material is put in a large container. Either steam is passed through the container, or water is added and heated to produce steam. As the plant material heats up, it gradually softens and pressure builds up on the surface of the plant, breaking open the tiny sacs that contain the plant's essential oil. The volatile oil rises up with the steam. The steam is then condensed, usually with cold water held in a coiling pipe, and collected in a vessel. Here, the oil and the water separate, with the oil rising and gathering on top of the water, ready to be drawn off and bottled.

3 Condensation occurs in connecting pipe

2 Extracted oil rises with the steam

4 Oil and water pass into a collecting vessel

5 The essential oil rises to the top, ready for collection

1 Steam or heated water combines with plant material

Steam distillation uses heat and condensation to extract and collect essential oils.

19

Expression The simplest way to extract an essential oil is to press the plant material and then collect the oil.

This method is used when the essential oils are found in the outer rind of a fruit and are easily released, as is the case with citrus peel. Citrus fruits, such as grapefruit, orange, lemon, and lime are mechanically pressed to extract their liquid, and then the watery juice is separated from the essential oil.

The outer rind of citrus fruits contains oil glands that can be pressed to extract the oil.

Absolute extraction The fragrance of extremely delicate flowers, such as jasmine or mimosa, is damaged by the heat involved in distillation, so these plants require a different method of extraction without steam or water. The result is a highly concentrated oil known as an absolute.

In Grasse, the perfumery capital of France, flower oils were traditionally hand extracted using a time-consuming process known as

The oil from the delicate jasmine flower is obtained by solvent extraction.

enfleurage. Framed glass plates were covered with lard, and the flowers placed on top. After a few days, the lard absorbed the fragrant oil from the flower, which was then extracted by alcohol to produce the absolute.

Modern methods involve blending flowers with a solvent. The solvent is then removed to leave the absolute oil.

CO_2 extraction A new method of extraction called supercritical carbon dioxide (CO_2) extraction uses gas rather than heat. This involves putting CO_2 under pressure to convert it from a gas into a liquid that can be used as a solvent. The solvent diffuses through the plant material and extracts its aromatic constituents.

This method tends to produce additional constituents, and so more research is needed before it becomes widely used. However, it does produce an aroma closer to that of the actual plants than that acheived by other methods, and so may grow in popularity.

Choosing Essential Oils

It is not always easy, especially as a novice, to know whether or not you are buying a **pure**, **natural**, good-quality, **sustainable** essential oil. Being aware of what to look for can help you make a worthwhile purchase. The following guidelines set out key factors to consider when purchasing oils, helping you to assess **quality** and **provenance** and to choose the best oils for you.

QUALITY CHECKS

A reputable company will rigorously test and analyze the quality of essential oils before supplying them to check that the oils are pure and haven't been adulterated with any other product.

The essence of a plant is present in a pure essential oil.

Natural versus **Synthetic**

A pure essential oil can be made up of a hundred or more individual chemical constituents, some of which are major constituents, others minor, which all work together synergistically. This means that when combined they create an overall effect that is greater than their individual parts (see p16). Synthetic fragrances, or isolated compounds such as menthol, are far cheaper than pure essential oils, and although these may have a pleasant scent, they have none of the therapeutic benefits that make essential oils so special and unique. To be sure that you are choosing a pure essential oil, try to avoid products that contain added ingredients and bulking agents, since these additions increase the volume but reduce the quality of the oil.

Recognizing **Quality**

Spend time researching companies and try to identify reputable ones that are likely to go to the most trouble to ensure their oils are of a high quality.

Company credentials Some companies have developed their own terminology to demonstrate that their oils are superior. For example, an oil may be described as being of "therapeutic" or "aromatherapy" grade, but ultimately these are marketing terms and not meaningful. It can be more helpful, though not a guarantee of quality, to check if a company is a member of a reputable association, such as the National Association of Holistic Aromatherapy (NAHA) in the US or the Aromatherapy Trade Council (ATC) in the UK. Another way to check a company's credentials is to find out if it runs aromatherapy courses and/or has links with qualified aromatherapy practitioners, which indicates that the company has a deserved reputation.

All in the name If an essential oil is authentic, the botanical name should appear on the label, and compounds called chemotypes (substances that

Make sure that you are buying a pure, natural, good-quality, sustainably produced essential oil.

link oils to a specific plant variety) may also be listed. For example, thyme will list its botanical name *Thymus vulgaris*, and the label might also mention linalool or thymol, to indicate that the oil is from one botanical species. The label, or a company website, may also cite a country of origin, which indicates that it is a true plant.

Checking **Sustainability**

Certain oils, such as sandalwood and rosewood, are now available only in limited amounts, or are unavailable, due to concerns about sustainability. Check the sustainability policy of a company before you buy an oil.

Endangered plants Some plants have been harvested almost to extinction. For example, spikenard (*Nardostachys jatamansi*) has a critically endangered status, and so this oil should be avoided unless the supplier can guarantee that it is cultivated. You can check a plant's status at www.iucnredlist.org/search.

Supporting fair trade Fair trade often ensures sustainability. Harvesting plants for oils can be an important source of income for some communities. With a conservation plan in place, plants are more likely to be protected as an important resource. Frankincense oil from Kenya, for example, is available as a FairWild source, a standard that protects the harvesting of wild species and ensures fair trading. When choosing oils, look

for Fairtrade or Fair for Life logos that suggest sustainability and help to ensure the benefits of producing an oil are felt by the people growing and harvesting the plants.

Choosing **Organic**

Organic essential oils and base oils have a higher therapeutic value because they contain the highest levels of antioxidants and are less likely to have potentially toxic residues from pesticides and chemical fertilizers. Organic production also benefits farmers, their families, and communities; is kinder to the soil; and generally provides a more positive outlook for future crops, wildlife, and water sources. Check company literature to see if they support organic farming practices.

What's on the Label?

Reading a label closely can help you to make an on-the-spot assessment of an essential oil. A label that has the following information suggests a high-quality oil:

The oils's botanical name and the part of the plant used.

The country of origin.

The distillation or packaging date and/or expiration date.

The batch number and, if applicable, a chemotype (such as thymol).

Assessing **Cost**

All essential oils require a large amount of plant matter to make just a small amount of oil. The price of an oil is connected to its yield from the plant matter, which can vary greatly, from less than 0.1 percent to 25 percent. For example, around 2,200 lb (1,000 kg) of hand-picked orange blossom produces just 2¼ lb (1 kg) of neroil oil —hence the high cost of exquisite neroli. In contrast, just over 1 ton of cloves produces up to 440 lb (200 kg) clove oil, making this a less expensive oil.

Any company that sells all of their oils for the same price, or has prices that seem too good to be true, should be avoided. The good news is that because essential oils are so highly concentrated, just a small amount goes a long way, and only a few drops are used at a time. To ensure freshness, buy a small amount regularly, rather than large amounts that might spoil before you use them.

21

Where Do Oils Come From?

Essential oils are extracted from a wide range of plants worldwide. Where plants grow depends on factors such as their **tolerance to frost** and if there's sufficient **rainfall** or irrigation. Many oils **thrive** in Mediterranean areas and in subtropical and tropical climates.

Europe

Europe is a major source of essential oils. The range of climates means that a variety of plants can be grown, from citrus fruit in the hot and sunny climates of Spain and Italy to more frost-tolerant plants in northern European countries.

Bosnia	Bay laurel
	Helichrysum
Bulgaria	Parsley
	Rose
	Valerian
France	Angelica
	Caraway
	Carrot
	Cedarwood
	Clary sage
	Cypress
	Fenugreek
	Juniper
	Lavender
	Lemon balm
	Mullein
	Oregano
	Pine
	Sage
	Tarragon
	Thyme
	Tuberose
	Violet
Germany	Chamomile (blue)
Hungary	Coriander
	Dill
	Fennel
	Roman chamomile
	Savory
	Yarrow
Italy	Bergamot
	Helichrysum
	Lemon
	Orange
Sweden	Birch
Spain	Cistus
	Eucal. globulus
	Lemon verbena
	Marjoram
	Rosemary
	Sage
United Kingdom	Lavender
	Peppermint
	Roman chamomile
	Yarrow

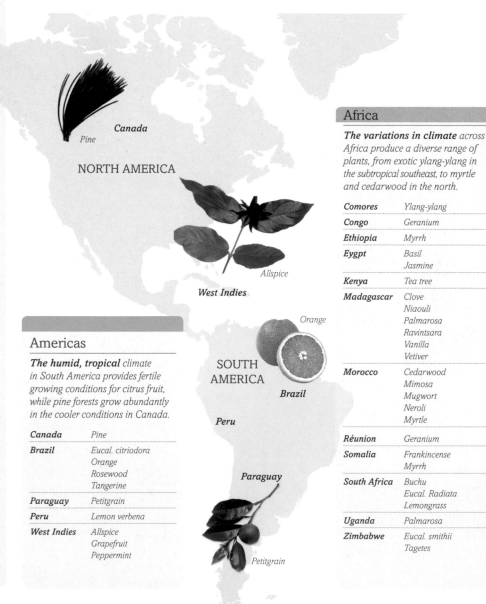

NORTH AMERICA

Canada
Pine

Allspice

West Indies

Orange

SOUTH AMERICA

Brazil

Peru

Paraguay

Petitgrain

Americas

The humid, tropical climate in South America provides fertile growing conditions for citrus fruit, while pine forests grow abundantly in the cooler conditions in Canada.

Canada	Pine
Brazil	Eucal. citriodora
	Orange
	Rosewood
	Tangerine
Paraguay	Petitgrain
Peru	Lemon verbena
West Indies	Allspice
	Grapefruit
	Peppermint

Africa

The variations in climate across Africa produce a diverse range of plants, from exotic ylang-ylang in the subtropical southeast, to myrtle and cedarwood in the north.

Comores	Ylang-ylang
Congo	Geranium
Ethiopia	Myrrh
Eygpt	Basil
	Jasmine
Kenya	Tea tree
Madagascar	Clove
	Niaouli
	Palmarosa
	Ravintsara
	Vanilla
	Vetiver
Morocco	Cedarwood
	Mimosa
	Mugwort
	Neroli
	Myrtle
Réunion	Geranium
Somalia	Frankincense
	Myrrh
South Africa	Buchu
	Eucal. Radiata
	Lemongrass
Uganda	Palmarosa
Zimbabwe	Eucal. smithii
	Tagetes

How Crops Are **Grown**

Traditionally, most essential oils were harvested from the wild, and this is still the case for some abundant species such as juniper. However, as aromatherapy grows in popularity, with markets expanding in the US, there is increased pressure on plants grown in the wild, and it can be a struggle to keep up with demand. To ensure a continuous supply of oils, many plants are specially cultivated, with suppliers creating the soil conditions and irrigation needed to grow crops.

Asia

Essential oils from Asia are mainly from the south of the continent, where tropical conditions provide ideal growing conditions for spices such as cardamom and nutmeg.

China	Camphor
India	Cardamom
	Cumin
	Patchouli
	Sandalwood
Indonesia	Benzoin
	Citronella
	Galangal
	Nutmeg
Iran	Rose
Nepal	Wintergreen
Oman	Frankincense
Philippines	Elemi
Sri Lanka	Black pepper
	Cardamom
	Cinnamon
	Citronella
	Ginger
	Lime
Thailand	Plai
Turkey	Rose
Vietnam	Cajeput
	Litsea
	Star anise

Sweden
Dill
Chamomile Roman
UK
Germany
France
EUROPE
Hungary
Bosnia Bulgaria
Spain
Italy
Turkey
Morocco
Rose
Egypt
Iran
ASIA
China
Oman
Nepal
India
Jasmine
AFRICA
Somalia
Ethiopia
Thailand
Star Anise
Vietnam
Philippines
Uganda
Kenya
Sri Lanka
Congo
Comores
Cardamom
Indonesia
Madagascar
Cedarwood
Zimbabwe
Réunion
South Africa

Australasia

Much of Australasia is semiarid, suitable for drought-resistant plants such as tea tree.

Australia	Eucal. globulus
	Fragonia
	Tea tree
New Zealand	Manuka

AUSTRALASIA
Australia
Manuka
New Zealand
Eucal. globulus

Using
Essential Oils

Healing and enhancing, aromatic essential oils are a joy to use and easily incorporated into **health and beauty regimens.** Discover all the ways to enjoy essential oils, how to take care of your oils, and how to safely use concentrated substances.

How Essential Oils Enter the Body

The quickest way to absorb essential oils is by **inhaling** their aroma, which has a direct effect on the brain. Oils can also be absorbed via the skin during a **massage**, in a **bath**, or in a cream. Both routes allow oils to enter the bloodstream, where their healing properties take effect.

FEELING THE BENEFITS

Once essential oils have entered the body, they impart psychological and physiological benefits by working on the nervous system and entering the bloodstream.

Inhaling Essential Oils

Humans are believed to have the ability to distinguish between more than 10,000 different aromas. Of all the senses, smell has the most direct connection to the mind and effect on our emotions. In fact, our ability to perceive odor is so connected to our sense of well-being that those who have lost their sense of smell can be more prone to problems such as depression and anxiety. The entire concept of aromatherapy is rooted in how aromas directly interact with our brains and body chemistry.

Processing aromas This involves complex pathways in the brain. When we inhale a scent, we take in aromatic molecules that bind to receptor cells in the nasal passage. Here they send messages to the olfactory bulb in the forebrain and these are interpreted as a smell. Molecules are also inhaled into the lungs where they enter the blood.

The effects on the body Studies show that inhaling a scent has an immediate effect on brain activity. Scents breach the blood–brain barrier (the brain's protective membrane), accessing centers in the brain linked to conscious thought, and also reaching the limbic system—the brain's emotional switchboard, where memory and emotions reside, and impulses such as "fight or flight," nurturing, hunger, and arousal are controlled. The limbic system is also linked to hormones.

How the Body **Inhales an Aroma**

When you inhale the aroma of an essential oil, it is processed rapidly by the brain so that you quickly receive the therapeutic benefits of the oil.

Olfactory receptor cells

Olfactory bulb

Lungs

1 Aromatic molecules travel up the nasal passage, where they bind to olfactory receptor cells in the nose. The cells send impulses to the olfactory bulb at the base of the forebrain.

2 The forebrain interprets the electrical impulses as a smell and rapidly processes and responds to the essential oil's unique aroma and properties.

Molecules are also inhaled directly from the nasal passages into the lungs, and from these enter the bloodstream, contributing to the healing effect of essential oils.

Essential oils impart their therapeutic effects on the body by being inhaled or absorbed into the skin.

Absorption into the Skin

Diluted essential oils can be absorbed into the bloodstream through the skin. Many factors influence how much oil is absorbed, including skin type, the temperature of the room and the oil, and whether the base that the essential oil is mixed with is easily absorbed.

Therapeutic touch When essential oils are combined with massage, it enhances the healing effects of the oils since massage in itself can induce a state of deep relaxation. When you are stressed, physically or emotionally, your body is flooded with hormones that keep you awake and aware. In this "fight or flight" state, other processes, such as immunity, cellular repair, and the assimilation of nutrients

from food are shut down. The relaxing effect of a massage helps the body systems to start working effectively again.

During an aromatherapy massage, you inhale the aroma of the essential oil. Studies using either a plain base oil or an essential oil blend in a massage have shown that those receiving the essential oil blend usually experience greater therapeutic benefits. For example, a footbath with lavender essential oil is more relaxing and healing than a footbath with just warm water. Likewise, a massage with essential oils chosen for specific healing properties has been shown more effective at healing and relieving pain, including postsurgical pain, cancer pain, and backaches, than a massage with plain vegetable oil.

Diluting Essential Oils

Concentrated essences *Essential oils are highly concentrated plant essences, so as a general rule they should always be used diluted in a base oil, lotion, ointment or balm, or bath oil. In addition, while diluted oils can be used as mouthwashes and gargles, they should never be swallowed without the advice of a medically trained practitioner.*

Even when diluted, most leave-on essential oil skin preparations should avoid delicate areas of the body, such as the eyes and mucous membranes. If you have sensitive skin, or suffer from allergies, it is always good to perform a patch test of your chosen oil first. Never apply undiluted essential oils on babies or children. See pages 36–37 for safety guidelines.

Exceptions to the rule *Some essential oils, such as rose absolute, ylang-ylang, jasmine, chamomile, lavender, and tea tree, are an exception to this rule and can be applied undiluted, as a scent. Likewise, tea tree can be used undiluted as emergency first aid for cuts, stings, and bites. Follow the guidelines in the A–Z section of this book.*

27

Oils can be absorbed into the bloodstream via application to the skin. During massage, you also gain therapeutic benefits from inhaling the aroma of oils.

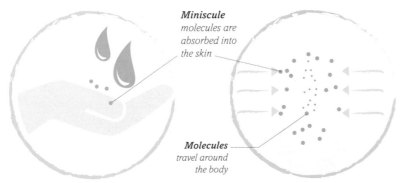

Miniscule molecules are absorbed into the skin

Molecules travel around the body

1 Tiny essential-oil molecules are absorbed through the pores of the skin where they enter the bloodstream and start to take effect.

2 Once in the bloodstream, the oils travel around the body via the circulatory system. The therapeutic effects of the oils act on the body systems and promote healing.

Always dilute *essential oils with a base oil before using, unless the oil's usage guidelines state otherwise.*

Applying Essential Oils

There are many ways to enjoy the benefits of essential oils. Languishing in a luxurious **aromatherapy** bath or enjoying an **oil-infused massage** are two popular methods. You can also disperse oils in the air, dab an oil balm on a **pulse point**, or sprinkle a few drops of oil on a tissue and **inhale** the scent deeply. Here are the main ways to enjoy your essential oils.

THE THERAPY OF TOUCH

Massage is one of the most popular and relaxing ways to enjoy the therapeutic effects of essential oils.

28

An aromatherapy massage helps relieve tension in the body while delivering the benefits of your chosen blend of oils.

Massage

An essential oil massage has the added benefit of soothing touch. A massage from a trained aromatherapist is a wonderful treat, but you can just as easily enjoy a massage from a partner, or practice self-massage, which is a great way to nurture yourself and can become part of a daily skin- and health-care routine.

Essential oils are concentrated so they need to be diluted in a base, or carrier, oil (see pp148–61). For normal skin, try a light base, such as almond, grape seed, coconut, sunflower, or canola. For dry skin, use heavier oils, such as avocado, olive, wheat germ, argan, or jojoba. Medicinal bases, such as calendula, neem, or St. John's wort, provide therapeutic properties.

Mix essential oils with the base oil that best suits your needs.

Mixing massage blends For a body massage, use a 2.5 percent (for sensitive or damaged skin) to 5 percent (for normal skin) dilution; for a facial massage, use a 1 percent dilution (see the dilutions chart on page 37). To make enough for a full-body massage, pour about 2 tablespoons base oil onto a saucer and add about 4–6 drops of your chosen essential oil, or oil blend.

Pulse point massage Pulse points are areas where blood vessels are close to the surface. Applying essential oils at these points speeds the oil's absorption.

When **to use**

Massage is ideal for addressing problems over a large surface area, for example, achy muscles and joints, digestive problems, and fluid retention. You can also home in on an area, for example, massaging the abdomen to relieve period pain or digestive upsets.

A therapeutic massage with essential oils is effective at creating a sense of calm and deep relaxation, and a feeling of being cared for.

To ease headaches, massage an essential oil balm onto the temples. You can also try massaging a balm into the pulse points on the wrist or neck to help you relax and unwind.

Inhalation

Inhaling an essential oil, or a blend of oils, is a quick and easy way to enjoy the oils' benefits, and forms the basis of aromatherapy, since an essential oil's aroma is inhaled whichever method of application you use.

Tissue inhalation The simplest way to inhale an essential oil is to sprinkle 2–3 drops of the oil onto a tissue and then inhale deeply. You can place the tissue in a plastic bag and carry it around with you to use as and when you want. Similarly, you can sprinkle a few drops of a soothing essential oil onto your pillowcase (or a tissue to avoid staining) at night to help you relax and induce restful sleep.

Making a steam inhalation
Make a therapeutic steam inhalation by adding about 4–8 drops of your chosen oil, or oils, to a bowl of just-boiled water. Lean over the bowl and place a towel over your head to contain the vapor; then, with eyes closed, breathe deeply for 10 minutes, or until there is no more steam. Alternatively, you can buy a special inhaler cup.

For epilepsy or asthma sufferers, or with young children, use caution. Instead of leaning over a bowl and covering the head with a towel, simply place the bowl of hot water nearby and capture the wafts of steam.

When **to use**

Respiratory conditions, such as hay fever, colds, congested sinuses, or a phlegmy cough, particularly benefit from inhalations. Steam inhalations also refresh and cleanse the skin.

Try an inhalation as a quick remedy to calm or invigorate the mind or lift the spirits.

A steam inhalation scented with essential oils can help to clear congestion and soothe the mind.

Baths

Whether you are enjoying a leisurely warm bath or a quick shallow hand, foot, or sitz bath (see below), adding essential oils to water is a hugely pleasurable and popular way to use them. The warmth of the water relaxes and soothes muscles, encouraging relaxation, and at the same time opens pores to help the essential oils penetrate the skin and enter the body more rapidly.

Adding oils to a bath Even though the essential oils will be diluted in the bath water, you still need to blend the oils in a base, or carrier, oil before adding them to the bath. This helps the oils to disperse in the water and also moisturizes the skin. For an average-sized bath, mix 4–6 drops of your chosen essential oil, or oils, with 1 tablespoon of a light base oil, such as sunflower, which contains waxes that act like an emulsifier, helping to disperse the oils evenly. You can also buy neutral, water-dispersing base oils, or

Soothing chamomile is perfect for baths.

mix the essential oils with 1 tablespoon of whole milk —the fat in the milk works in a way similar to the base oil, helping to disperse the oils evenly. Try to relax in the bath for at least 15 minutes. To get the full benefits of the oils, add them once the bath has been run since they can quickly evaporate in the heat.

Hand and footbaths Hand and footbaths are a great way to target smaller areas of the body quickly. A footbath can treat a specific condition such as athletes' foot, or soothe tired, sore feet. If your ankles are swollen, try following a hot footbath with a cool one to improve circulation. You can also use hot and cold baths for sore, swollen hands. Fill a bowl or basin (one large enough to fit both your feet, or hands) with hot water, and add 4–6 of drops of your chosen oil to a base oil or milk, as for a normal bath. Soak the hands or feet for 10 minutes.

Sitz baths A sitz (shallow) bath is an excellent way to treat conditions such as yeast infections, hemorrhoids, and urinary-tract infections, or to heal stitches after childbirth. A tea tree oil sitz bath is a classic treatment for yeast. To make the bath, fill the bath halfway with warm water. Use the same method of dilution as for a large bath, and sit in the water for 10 minutes.

When **to use**

Aromatherapy baths are deeply relaxing and reviving. Make sure you give yourself plenty of time to lie back and enjoy the therapeutic soak.

A sitz bath can bring immediate relief to conditions such as yeast infections or hemorrhoids, while a hand or footbath is best for aching, swollen, or tired hands and feet or athlete's foot.

Infuse your bath with your favorite blend of essential oils, then lie back and relax.

Adding calming oils to warm water soothes body and mind.

Compresses

A compress infused with therapeutic essential oils is a simple and effective way to treat local complaints such as bruises, burns and scalds, headaches, and varicose veins.

Hot or cold? Using hot or cold water can depend on your preference, but some conditions do require cooling while others respond to heat.

A hot compress is ideal for complaints such as skin infections, including abscesses and boils, and muscular or joint problems, including strains, backaches, rheumatism, and arthritis. For example, a hot compress with ginger, cypress, juniper, pine, and lavender essential oils is wonderfully warming and relieving for aching muscles and joints.

A cold-water compress is ideal for sprains and sports injuries, especially if the area already feels hot and inflamed, and for headaches. Using essential oils such as lavender, neroli, peppermint, and eucalyptus helps to enhance the cooling process.

Making a compress Add 3–4 drops of essential oil to a shallow bowl of hot or cold water. Disperse well. Soak a washcloth, wring out well, and apply to the relevant part of the body. For a hot compress, once the

Neroli has calming properties that work well in a compress.

washcloth is positioned, you can cover it with a towel or piece of plastic wrap to insulate it if you want. This also stops the water from dripping onto clothes. Leave the washcloth on the skin until it reaches body temperature, then repeat the whole process three times.

If you are using essential oils that can irritate the skin in a compress, it's important to always predilute the essential oils in a base, or carrier, oil, such as almond or sunflower, before adding the oils to the water.

When **to use**

Try a hot compress to relieve aching and tired muscles after an exercise workout or strenuous physical activity.

A cold compress works especially well for soothing eye strain brought on by staring at computer screens for long periods of time.

Showers and Saunas

Essential oils make a wonderful addition to saunas and steamy showers. Experiment with different blend combinations and aromas to suit your needs at different times. For example, if you want to have an energizing shower to kick-start the day, choose stimulating and invigorating oils such as basil and rosemary. Or to help lift the spirits and create a sense of positivity, try uplifting oils such as bergamot, lemon, and rose.

Using oils in the shower
For a steamy aromatherapy shower, put 5–8 drops of an essential oil, or oil blend, on a warm, damp washcloth, then put the washcloth in the shower area, but don't use the washcloth to

wash yourself. If possible, hang the washcloth at face level to enjoy the aroma fully. Make sure the shower is hot enough to produce steam. You can also add the essential oil drops to 2 tablespoons unscented shower gel.

Using oils in a sauna Add 20–40 drops of an essential oil, or oil blend, to the pitcher of water that is used to splash the coals during a sauna. Cypress, eucalyptus, and pine essential oils all work well in a sauna.

When **to use**

Adding essential oils to a sauna or shower is a great way to clear sinuses, relieve tension headaches, and soothe irritating hay fever and allergy symptoms.

Using oils in a shower or sauna also invigorates the mind and helps you to feel calm and relaxed.

The woody aroma of eucalyptus works well in a steamy sauna.

HEALING OILS

Using essential oils with healing properties in a compress is an efficient and effective way to target local complaints such as muscle pain and skin conditions.

Diffusion

This increasingly popular way to use essential oils disperses tiny molecules of the oil into the air in a fine vapor or mist. Traditionally, oil burners have been used to diffuse oils. Today, there are several types of diffusers, including ultrasonic ones, vaporizers that use a small fan or warm water, electronic aromastones, and reed diffusers. Room sprays can also be used to disperse oils.

Using a diffuser, vaporizer, or oil burner To use an oil burner, pour a little warm water on the hot plate before adding the oil drops to stop the oil from burning too quickly. To use electronic diffusers or vaporizers, add the oils and use according to the manufacturer's instructions.

Making a room spray A room spray is a type of diffusion that releases a more concentrated amount of oil into the air very quickly. To make a room spray, combine 20–30 drops of essential oils with 2 tablespoons each of mineral water and vodka, and transfer the solution to a sterilized atomizer bottle.

Most essential oils can be used to scent a room, but citrus oils are particularly refreshing. Essential oils that have antiseptic properties, such as cedarwood, eucalyptus, lavender, and tea tree, are ideal for fumigating rooms, while lemon, lemongrass, and citronella can be used in a spray to repel insects.

When **to use**

Diffusers can deodorize or fumigate a room, or simply create a special atmosphere.

Sitting near to a burner or vaporizer is an effective way to inhale the vapors of the oils and to benefit from their therapeutic properties.

Use a room spray to change the mood in a room, either to create a feeling of calm, to invigorate, or perhaps to add a little romance.

Room sprays are also useful for disinfecting and deodorizing an area such as a sickroom and for repelling insects.

Cedarwood oil can be added to a diffuser to clear stale air.

Personal Scents

While some oils, such as lavender, rose otto, chamomile, jasmine, vanilla, and ylang-ylang, can be worn on their own as a scent, most need to be diluted in a base—perfumes are usually a mixture of fragranced oils in an alcohol base. You can use a single oil or several oils in a blend to create a scent that may have different "notes." When you smell a perfume, the top notes are typically the first thing you smell, followed by mid- and then base notes (see p164).

Creating a scent Don't be afraid to experiment with blends to find your favorite scent—see page 164 for blending guidelines. Essentially, try to keep blends to no more than 4–7 oils, and try a blend for a day or so to let it settle to get a better idea of its true aroma. To make your own personal scent, see the recipe on page 184.

When **to use**

Adding essential oils to a base solution is a great way to create your own personal fragrance. You can tailor the scent to suit your unique style and preferences and to create daytime and evening perfumes.

Mouthwashes and Gargles

Although essential oils should not be swallowed, you can dilute them in water or a base of aloe vera juice to make an effective mouthwash or gargle that can be used to support good oral health and hygiene.

Homemade mouthwashes are cost-effective and can be tailored to your needs. They also avoid a range of synthetic ingredients that are often found in commercial mouthwashes.

Making a mouthwash To make a basic mouthwash or gargle solution, dilute 4–5 drops of essential oil (clove, fennel, ginger, lemon, mint, rosemary, and sage are all good antiseptic choices) into a tablespoon of base oil. Further dilute this blend into a glassful of hot water and use as needed. Do not swallow the mixture.

When **to use**

Mouthwashes and gargles are ideal for mouth sores, gum disease, and throat infections, and to help combat bad breath.

Peppermint has a fresh, menthol aroma.

Dab a small amount of cream on irritated or itchy skin.

Ointments, Balms, and Creams

Using oils in ointments, balms, and cream bases is an effective way to promote skin healing and to nourish skin. Ointments tend to be oil based, while balms and creams contain extra ingredients for a creamier texture. Treat localized areas, applying a balm or ointment where needed, to encourage healing or to combat skin dryness.

When **to use**

Use for skin conditions such as eczema, psoriasis, bruising, and varicose veins, and apply to wounds to encourage healing.

Essential oils in a cream can form part of a daily skincare regimen.

Use ointments with tea tree and manuka as first-aid remedies.

Hair Care

Combining essential oil blends with herbal infusions, or creating conditioning hair oils by mixing essential oils with nourishing bases such as coconut oil, are great ways to enjoy a hair-care regimen using natural products. See pages 202–03 for essential oil hair products that can help to restore shine and luster to hair while avoiding the many added ingredients in commercial products.

When **to use**

Use nourishing essential oil hair treatments to revive dry and dull-looking hair.

Enriching balms can be used to heal and soothe irritated skin and to nourish and hydrate dry skin.

Storing Essential Oils

Essential oils are **volatile** substances, which means they evaporate and deteriorate more quickly when exposed to light, air, and heat. Sunlight is especially harmful to the oils since it can cause chemical reactions that degrade them. To get the complete **therapeutic** benefits from your essential oils, store them correctly so that they remain as **fresh** as possible.

Taking Care of
Your Essential Oils

Following the guidelines below will help you to maximize the life span of your essential oils and fully enjoy their benefits.

● **Avoid storing your essential oils** in plastic containers. Plastic is not recommended since it is not totally inert, which means that over time the essential oils will interact with the plastic and may become contaminated by potentially toxic ingredients that leak out of the plastic.

● **Store your essential oils** and essential oil blends in sterilized glass (or stainless steel) bottles with lids that seal tightly. Bottles with dark-colored glass are best since ultraviolet rays of light can taint oils by reacting with chemicals in the oil. Amber, dark blue, or deep violet glass bottles offer the best protection for your essential oils, keeping them as fresh as possible.

● **Store bottles in a cupboard** out of direct light and away from heat. Some oils, such as citrus oils, should be stored in the fridge (see opposite).

● **Make a note on the bottle** of the date it was opened, or label made-up blends that you've bottled with the names of the oils that were used and the date the blend was made.

● **Essential oil bottles** should have a dropper insert, which makes them harder to spill (see p36), and easier to measure out. This is also a good safety device if a child gets ahold of a bottle.

Disposing of Essential Oils Safely

If you have essential oils that are past their best or that you no longer need, contact your local authority's waste disposal department, or check their web page, for advice on how to dispose of them, and follow their recommendations.

If there is no specific advice, dispose of essential oils at your local household waste recycling center in the same way as you would for unused paints and solvents.

● **Keep oils away from children.** Though safe if properly diluted, essential oils are highly concentrated and can irritate the skin or the eyes if they are rubbed in, and can be toxic if taken internally (see page 36 for what to do if an oil is ingested).

● **Essential oils, like alcohol,** are flammable, so should never be left near sources of ignition, such as fires, stoves, candles, or open flames.

Small, dark-colored bottles *help to protect oils from the damaging effects of light and air.*

Follow the storage advice to ensure oils stay as fresh as possible so that you fully enjoy their benefits.

Shelf Life of **Essential Oils**

The following chart is a useful guide to how long you should keep your essential oils before they are past their best. These guidelines are based on an oil being relatively fresh when you buy it from your supplier (check the batch number or use-by date), being opened and therefore exposed to air, and on their being stored under ideal conditions (see opposite). As such tiny amounts of essential oils are used at any one time, the oils usually come in small bottles that can be replaced as needed.

If you are in any doubt about how fresh an essential oil is, avoid using it on the skin (some oils that are nonirritant when fresh may irritate the skin when oxidized) or for therapeutic use. Instead, use the oil around the house, in a diffuser perhaps, or added to a household cleanser.

9–12 months

Citrus oils *such as grapefruit have the shortest shelf life. This is because they have a lot of the highly volatile components terpenes, which are prone to oxidization. Store in the fridge.*

12–18 months

The melaleuca family *(tea tree, niaouli) and pine and cypress essential oils have a fairly short shelf life due to relatively volatile components in their chemical composition.*

2–3 years

Most of the essential oils *that are steam-distilled have a shelf life of 2–3 years. Some resinous oils, such as sandalwood or myrrh, may last longer than this.*

3–5 years

Absolutes*, such as rose absolute and jasmine, have the greatest longevity of all the oils and can last for up to five years.*

Shelf Life of **Base Oils**

Base oils generally have a shorter shelf life than essential oils. Unlike essential oils, they become rancid when they spoil. Your nose should tell you that something is wrong, and at this point the oil is unsuitable for use on the skin.

Store base oils in dark glass bottles too, away from light and heat.

12–18 months

Most base oils *have a shelf life of 12–18 months once opened.*

2–3 years

Coconut and jojoba oils *last the longest and should keep well for 2–3 years.*

10–12 months

Borage, grape-seed, and evening primrose oils *tend to oxidize at 10–12 months.*

Using Essential Oils Safely

Since essential oils are **highly concentrated,** they need to be used sensibly and **diluted** properly. Follow advice on what to do if oils are spilled or misused, using oils on infants, and oils to avoid in pregnancy, when breastfeeding, and for some conditions.

SAFELY USING **OILS**

Essential oils are perfectly safe if used sensibly. Before using an oil, carefully check the safety advice and make sure you follow the recommendations for dilution.

Spillage and **accidents**

Many essential oils irritate the skin if applied neat, without being diluted in a base or carrier, oil, or other lotion. If you spill an essential oil, it can strip away varnish on furniture and stain fabrics such as carpets and bedding. Here are some tips for dealing with essential oil spillages and accidents and for cleaning diffusers and burners:

Accidentally ingesting oils Drink milk to dilute the oil and get medical advice quickly (see the box, below, for general information on ingesting essential oils).

Spilling oil on skin Quickly pour on a vegetable oil to dilute the essential oil: use sunflower, olive oil, or any other cooking or base oil. Once you've diluted the oil, gently wash the area with soapy water. If you don't have vegetable oil on hand, rinse the area with plenty of cold water.

Ingesting Essential Oils

Never take an essential oil internally without the supervision of a suitably qualified medical practitioner. Some essential oils that are totally nontoxic when applied to the skin are highly toxic when taken internally, and there can be a risk of irritation to the throat or stomach, or even liver or nervous system damage.

Splashing oil in the eyes Rinse the eye with milk or, if you don't have milk, flush the area with plenty of cool water, then seek urgent medical advice.

Spills on furniture Wearing gloves, mop up spills immediately with paper towels, then wash the area with soapy water. If a surface is damaged, you may need to repair or revarnish. Put bottles on saucers or tubs, not directly on furniture.

Spills on soft furnishings and bedding Apply a stain remover for oil stains and then wash with detergent.

To clean an essential oil burner or diffuser Wipe with a cloth soaked in mineral spirits or white vinegar, then use a cloth dipped in soapy water to get rid of the vinegary smell. Rinse out the cloth; give the diffuser or burner a final wipe to remove any soapy residues.

Medical **Conditions**

Essential oils are generally safe to use with medical conditions, but there are some cases where caution is needed. There have been concerns that oils should be avoided with **hypertension,** but there is no evidence for this.
● **If you have asthma**, avoid directly inhaling vapor in a steam inhalation (use a diffuser instead) and use essential oils well diluted.
● **If you have epilepsy**, avoid hyssop and wormwood oils.
● **For atopic children** (with a tendency

to allergic reactions or a family history of allergic responses), or those with hypersensitive skin, use no more than 1 percent essential oils in a blend and do a patch test first (see opposite).
● **For other contraindications**, check safe usage for each oil in the A–Z section of this book (see pp38–145).

Safe Usage Terms

In the A–Z entries of the book, individual safe usage advice is given for each oil. All the recommendations are based on the essential oil being properly diluted in a suitable base oil when used on the skin (see the table, opposite). Note that though many oils are safe for most people to use and are considered nontoxic and nonirritant in general, an individual reaction or allergy to an oil is possible. If you react to an oil, or oil blend, stop using it immediately. The following terms are used in the guidance for safe usage throughout the A–Z section:

***Nontoxic** An oil does not represent a hazard when used as directed and an adverse reaction is unlikely.*

***Nonirritant** Is unlikely to cause irritation or an adverse skin reaction.*

***Sensitizing** Repeated use may cause irritation or an adverse reaction in some individuals.*

***Phototoxic** May cause the skin to be more susceptible to damage on exposure to the sun's UV rays.*

Pregnancy and **Breastfeeding**

There are a few essential oils that should be avoided in pregnancy and when breastfeeding. They may be too stimulating in the early weeks of pregnancy, as is the case with sage, or an oil may have a level of toxicity, as is the case with basil. The skin can be hypersensitive in pregnancy, so oils such as cinnamon bark oil should be avoided. Check the A–Z entries for advice on each oil.

Essential Oils for Pregnancy

The following essential oils are safe to use in pregnancy and when breastfeeding. Check the botanical name on the label since different varieties of a plant may not be safe in pregnancy. Also check the safe usage advice for each oil in the A–Z entries on pages 38–145.

Refreshing thyme is soothing in pregnancy.

- *Anthemis nobilis*—**Roman chamomile**
- *Boswellia carterii/sacra*—**Frankincense**
- *Cananga odorata*—**Ylang-ylang**
- *Cedrus atlantica*—**Cedarwood**
- *Citrus aurantifolia*—**Lime**
- *Citrus aurantium, Citrus aurantium amara*–**Neroli/Petitgrain**
- *Citrus aurantium bergamia*—**Bergamot (bergaptene-free)**
- *Citrus limonum*—**Lemon**
- *Citrus paradisi*—**Grapefruit**
- *Citrus reticulata*—**Mandarin**
- *Citrus sinensis*—**Orange**
- *Coriandrum sativum*—**Coriander**
- *Cupressus sempervirens*—**Cypress**
- *Cymbopogon martinii*—**Palmarosa**
- *Elettaria cardamomum*—**Cardamom**
- *Eucalyptus globulus/radiata*—**Eucalyptus**
- *Helichrysum italicum*—**Helichrysum (Immortelle)**
- *Lavandula angustifolia*—**Lavender**
- *Matricaria recutita*—**Chamomile (blue)**
- *Melaleuca quinquenervia*—**Niaouli**
- *Origanum marjorana*—**Marjoram**
- *Pelargonium graveolens*—**Geranium**
- *Piper nigrum*—**Black pepper**
- *Pogostemon cablin*—**Patchouli**
- *Rosa centifolia*—**Rose absolute**
- *Thymus vulgaris CT linalool*—**Thyme**
- *Vetiveria zizanoides*—**Vetiver**
- *Zingiber officinale*—**Ginger**

Babies and **Children**

Be cautious about using oils on young infants as their skin is sensitive and very permeable, and babies can struggle to deal with adverse effects. Diffusers can be the best way to use oils with infants.

Guidelines for Babies and Children

Premature babies and infants up to 3 months old Essential oils aren't recommended on the skin. Use simple base oils such as olive and grape seed.

3–6 months old Use only lavender or Roman chamomile. Dilute at 0.25 percent: 2 drops of essential oil to 2 tablespoons of base oil.

6–12 months old Use only chamomile, Roman chamomile, lavender, neroli, mandarin, or rose absolute. Dilute at 0.5 percent: 4 drops of essential oil to 2 tablespoons of base oil.

1–6 years old Use only oils listed in the A–Z as nontoxic and nonirritant. Dilute at 1 percent: 8 drops of essential oil to 2 tablespoons of base oil.

7–15 years old Use only oils listed as nontoxic and nonirritant. Dilute at 1.5 percent: 12 drops of essential oil to 2 tablespoons of base oil.

Use olive oil to moisturize the skin of young babies.

Doing a **Patch Test**

If you have sensitive skin or you have never used a particular essential oil, or blend of essential oils, before on your skin, do a patch test before using the oil the first time to check that you won't have an adverse reaction.

To do a patch test, make up the oil blend using the blending guidelines in the table, right. Apply a small amount to the inside of your elbow and wait for 24 hours. If no redness or irritation occurs, you can then try using the blend on a larger area of skin.

Blending Essential Oils and Base Oils

Use this table as a guide to essential oil and base oil quantities for oil blends.

	Number of drops of essential oils for base oil quantities:			
	2 tsp/10 ml	*15 ml/1 tbsp*	*2 tbsp/30 ml*	*3½ fl oz/100 ml*
Adults with delicate skin or for a facial blend (less than 1 percent)	2 drops	3 drops	6 drops	20 drops
Massage blend for adults with no skin sensitivities (2.5 percent)	5 drops	7 drops	15 drops	50 drops
Bath oil or therapeutic blend for applying to small area of the body, for example, a joint (5 percent)	12 drops	18 drops	40 drops	130–150 drops

A–Z of
Essential Oils

Discover the unique properties of over 80 **essential oils**. Ordered alphabetically by their botanical names, each profile details a plant's **origin and properties**, the oil's appearance and aroma, and suggests some of the **best ways to use** each essential oil.

BATH OIL FRAGRANCE

Mimosa

Acacia dealbata

Warming and **relaxing**, mimosa is a popular addition to perfumes. In skincare products, its nourishing and **soothing** properties provide a softening balm for sensitive skin, and its **calming action** helps to ease tension and lift spirits.

What is it **good for?**

Soothes skin The nourishing properties of mimosa essential oil help to soften the skin, and the oil's calming effect is useful for soothing inflamed and sensitive areas. Used as part of a daily beauty regimen, mimosa oil helps to balance and tone combination skin and oily complexions.

Enhances well-being The deeply calming and relaxing properties of mimosa have a naturally uplifting effect on both body and mind. In addition to being relaxing and soothing, the oil simultaneously energizes, and it is this ability that makes the oil a natural aphrodisiac.

Best **uses**

As a bath oil Indulge the senses and enjoy some relaxing time out by combining a few drops of mimosa in a base oil or 1 tablespoon milk and dispersing in a warm bath.

As a fragrance Mimosa essential oil is a good "fixative" for perfumes, helping to set the blend and make it last longer. It is often used as a "base note" in expensive scents.

Safe usage Nontoxic and nonirritant.

The plant

A member of the acacia family, mimosa is native to southeastern Australia. With its cheerful, yellow, popcorn-shaped flowers, it is now widely cultivated as an ornamental plant in warm, temperate regions around the world.

The essential oil

Mimosa essential oil is an "absolute," which is solvent-extracted from the tree's flowers and twigs. The thick oil is pale yellow to brown in color with a sweet floral scent that carries slight woody undertones.

The nectar-rich clusters of bright yellow blossom make mimosa a popular choice for bees.

MASSAGE OIL   STEAM INHALATION

Yarrow

Achillea millefolium

Revered by the ancient Greeks and Egyptians, yarrow is derived from the Greek *hieros*, meaning **"sacred."** Its traditional use as a **skin healer** still holds today, and its clearing properties can relieve sinus-related headaches.

What is it **good for?**

Soothes aches and pains
Massage this natural anti-inflammatory into stiff joints to reduce pain and inflammation, or try a gentle abdominal massage to ease menstrual cramps.

Eases sinus pain
Yarrow loosens congestion, relieving sinus-related headaches and breathing problems.

Heals skin
Its antiseptic properties help treat minor cuts and wounds, and its potent healing action works on scar tissue, ulcers, slow-to-heal cuts, and itchy skin complaints such as eczema.

Balances oily skin
Add a few drops of the oil to face creams or toners to balance oily skin and help keep acne under control.

Relieves stress
With its soothing action, yarrow is an effective oil for stress-related conditions, such as hypertension or insomnia.

Best **uses**

In a massage oil
Mix 2–3 drops with St. John's wort oil and rub into sore, inflamed joints for pain relief.

In a steam inhalation
To relieve the symptoms of hay fever and alleviate nasal congestion, add a few drops of yarrow essential oil to a bowl of hot water, place a towel over your head, and inhale the steam deeply for 2–3 minutes.

Safe usage Nonirritant in dilution. Avoid during pregnancy and breast-feeding.

The plant

A grassland plant from the daisy family and a native of Europe and Western Asia, yarrow is now found worldwide. The oil of the Green Yarrow (*Achillea nobilis*) should be avoided for use in aromatherapy.

The essential oil

The herb is dried then steam-distilled to release the pale to dark blue or greeny-blue oil, with a powerful, herbaceous and slightly sweet smell reminiscent of chamomile.

DIFFUSER   OINTMENT

STEAM
INHALATION   MASSAGE OIL   COMPRESS

Buchu

Agathosma betulina

One of South Africa's best-known **medicinal** plants, buchu is a versatile essential oil that treats a wide range of ailments. Its **antiseptic, anti-inflammatory**, and detoxifying properties help to **soothe** and facilitate healing and calm digestive upsets.

What is it **good for?**

Heals skin With a potent antiseptic effect, buchu essential oil is ideal for treating skin infections.

Aids detox Buchu essential oil encourages the removal of toxins such as uric acid, which in turn relieves inflammation and sore joints. Its strong detoxifying action also helps to reduce water retention and to tackle areas of cellulite.

Eases digestive upsets Added to a massage blend, the essential oil helps to calm and soothe an irritable stomach and can also stimulate a sluggish digestion.

Acts as an insect repellent The sharp aroma of buchu oil makes this a natural insect repellent. Keep some of the oil on hand when traveling to instantly ward off pesky flies, mosquitoes, and fleas.

A
PERFECT
BLEND

Ideal blends include mugwort, camphor, caraway, clary sage, lavender, geranium, patchouli, wintergreen, vanilla, and fennel.

Best **uses**

In a diffuser Add a few drops of buchu essential oil to an oil burner, vaporizer, or diffuser to help freshen stale air, or dilute in water in a spray bottle and use as an insect spray.

In an ointment Add 2–3 drops to an ointment base to create an antiseptic skin treatment.

Safe usage Use very well diluted (less than 1 percent). Avoid in pregnancy and when breast-feeding.

The plant

Buchu leaves *are collected while the plant is flowering and fruiting, and then dried. The pungent aroma of the leaves increases as the plant dries out.*

The essential oil

The golden oil *is extracted from the dried leaves and flowers by steam distillation. The oil has a sweet, medicinal aroma with hints of black currant and peppermint.*

Fragonia™

Agonis fragrans

Relatively new to aromatherapy, Fragonia has a reputation for working at a deep level to restore **physical** and **emotional balance.** In particular, it's thought to help regulate the body clock and to boost immunity by encouraging efficient lymph circulation.

What is it **good for?**

Soothes aches and pains Reviving for tired joints and muscles, Fragonia also acts as a mild analgesic, helping to ease joint and muscle soreness and pain, mild toothache pain, and menstrual cramps.

Balances emotions The essential oil is an effective stress reliever. Deeply soothing, it helps release emotional blockages.

Regulates the body clock Its ability to help keep body systems in sync makes the essential oil an ideal remedy for overcoming the confusion and exhaustion caused by jet lag and dealing with the demands of shift work.

Helps fight infection Its broad-acting antibacterial and antifungal properties help fight skin infections, and its antiviral action is a first-line defense against colds.

Strengthens immunity Fragonia aids lymph circulation and drainage, strengthening the immune system.

Best **uses**

In a steam inhalation Add 3–4 drops of the essential oil to hot water to create a steam inhalation to relieve respiratory and throat infections, break up mucus, and fight infection.

In a massage oil Use in a massage blend to stimulate lymph circulation.

As a compress Add a few drops to warm water and make a compress to relieve pain, congestion, cramping, and swelling and tenderness in the breasts.

Safe usage Nontoxic and nonirritant.

The plant

A native of Australia, the small shrub fragonia is commonly called "coarse tea tree" by the cut-flower industry. Although the petite white flowers are fragrant, the healing essential oil is concentrated in the branchlets and leaves.

The essential oil

Steam-distilled from the leaves and branches, Fragonia oil is a clear to pale yellow with a similar scent to tea tree, but milder, with citrus, spicy, and floral notes.

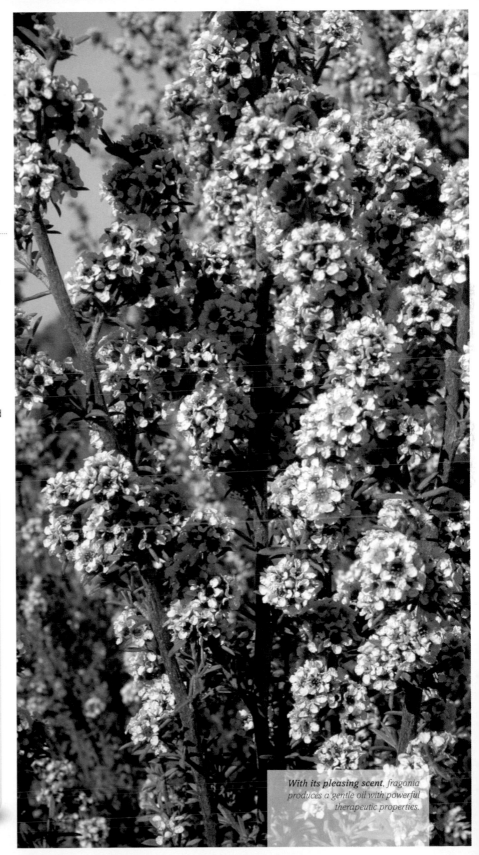

With its pleasing scent, fragonia produces a gentle oil with powerful therapeutic properties.

DIFFUSER   MASSAGE OIL   SKIN CARE

Lemon Verbena

Aloysia triphylla

Behind the sunny, **uplifting** scent of lemon verbena lies some serious healing properties. It has a toning and **strengthening** effect on the nervous, digestive, respiratory, and immune systems. Its **antiseptic** action aids healing, while **anti-inflammatory** properties restore tired postworkout muscles.

A
PERFECT
BLEND
Ideal blending partners include lemon, elemi, neroli, lavender, rose, bergamot, cedarwood, juniper, eucalyptus, and palmarosa.

What is it **good for?**

Relieves anxiety and aids focus Lemon verbena has a wonderfully calming, sedative effect. In addition to easing feelings of panic, it also aids focus, concentration, and retention when studying or reading.

Acts as an aphrodisiac The soothing effect of lemon verbena on breathing and heart rates lies behind the claim that it can be an effective aphrodisiac for both sexes.

Supports immunity In addition to supporting liver function, lemon verbena helps bring down a fever by encouraging perspiration.

Fights colds and flu With its fresh citrus scent and antiseptic action, the oil relieves cold and flu symptoms, easing irritating coughs and loosening congestion in the sinuses and lungs.

Soothes aches and pains Massaging with lemon verbena after a workout tones muscles and reduces the buildup of lactic acid. The oil also encourages the repair of weak connective tissue and speeds up the healing process of joint-related injuries. It has an anti-inflammatory effect that can help lessen the pain of arthritis and improve overall mobility.

Soothes digestion and relieves menstrual cramps A gentle massage with a lemon verbena blend eases stomach upsets and nausea. Its antispasmodic properties act on menstrual cramps, and it's thought the oil helps regulate menstrual cycles.

Best **uses**

In a diffuser Dispersed into the air, the oil helps calm nervous conditions, and can also be used to bolster the spirits when dealing with periods of stress, or when feeling down and depressed.

In a massage oil Blended into a base oil, lemon verbena provides skin benefits and supports health at a deeper level by lowering breathing and heart rates and boosting immunity and liver function.

In a lotion Add a few drops to a lotion base to help soften and tone the skin. The oil is also useful for reducing skin puffiness and inflammation.

Safe usage Use well diluted (less than 0.5 percent). Avoid on sensitive skin, children under 15 years old, before exposure to the sun, and during pregnancy and breast-feeding.

The plant

A native of Chile and Peru, lemon verbena now grows in many tropical areas worldwide. With its pointed pale green leaves and stems bearing tubular flowers, the plant has a strong and distinct lemon aroma.

The essential oil

The leaves and stalks are steam-distilled for the oil, which is a yellowish-green color. It has a fresh lemony smell described as simultaneously hot and bitter. Its extremely subtle aroma has proved difficult to reproduce synthetically.

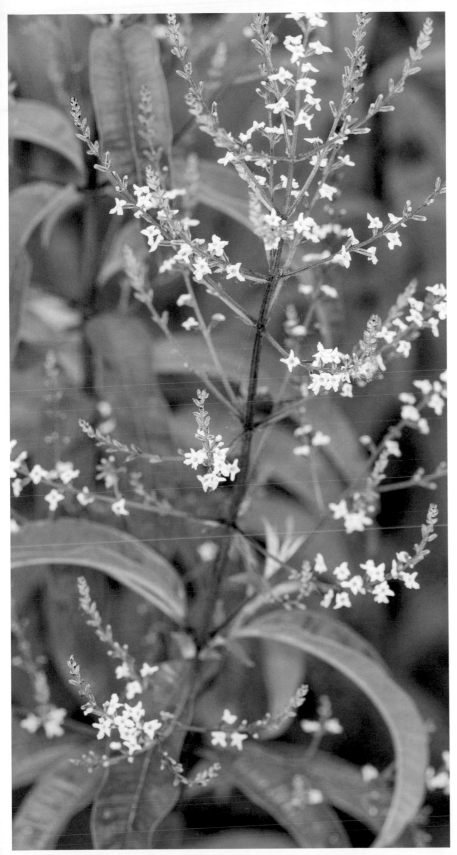

The oil's fresh, lemony aroma brings a feeling of calm and helps to enhance concentration.

This aromatic shrub flowers in the summer months, producing stems of delicate white or pale lilac flowers.

INHALATION   BATH OIL

MASSAGE OIL   BATH OIL

Galangal

Alpinia officinarum

This previously little-known essential oil is rapidly rising in popularity thanks to its **warming**, stimulating, and **antiseptic** properties. It can relieve nausea and motion sickness, has a natural **deodorant** quality, and also helps fight fungal infections.

What is it **good for?**

Helps fight infection The combined antibacterial and antifungal properties of galangal essential oil make it an especially useful oil in the treatment of skin eruptions. It also protects wounds, keeping them clean, and brings fungal infections such as athlete's foot under control.

Eases digestion and soothes stomach upsets Warming and soothing, galangal essential oil aids digestion and the assimilation of nutrients and helps to release uncomfortable trapped gas. If you suffer from motion sickness and nausea, this is a useful remedy to carry on long trips.

Acts as a deodorant The antiperspirant action of galangal helps reduce body odor, to keep you feeling fresh.

Energizes and lifts mood In addition to fighting fatigue and jet lag, galangal has a long history as an aphrodisiac because of its warming, stimulating aroma and ability to ease anxiety.

Best **uses**

In an inhalation To relieve motion sickness, add 2–3 drops to a tissue, keep in a plastic bag, and sniff as needed.

As a bath oil Mix with a base oil, 2 tablespoons of milk, or bath oil and add to a bath to heal dry, cracked skin.

Safe usage Nontoxic, nonirritant in dilution. Avoid near the face or nose of children under seven years old.

The plant

A native of Indonesia, galangal belongs to the same family as ginger and looks similar. The root (see above) is also a popular cooking ingredient and can be used like ginger.

The essential oil

The pale yellow to olive-brown oil is obtained by the steam distillation of the dried galangal root. Its aroma is reminiscent of ginger, but milder.

Dill

Anethum graveolens

For centuries, dill has been renowned for its impressive **healing** powers. It **stimulates** digestion, **calms** frazzled nerves, and has **antibacterial** properties that help speed the healing of cuts and wounds. It has a mild diuretic effect that makes it a natural aid to detox.

What is it **good for?**

Supports digestion Dill has a calming, anti-inflammatory effect on the digestive tract, so has long been used as a treatment for stomach upsets and bouts of colic.

Fights infection Dill is a natural antibacterial and diuretic that can be used to relieve the symptoms of cystitis and bladder infections.

Heals skin Dill is highly effective in promoting the quick healing of cuts, scrapes, and wounds, and helps protect them from infections.

Aids restful sleep Sedating and calming on the nerves, dill essential oil helps promote a deep sense of relaxation. This makes it a useful oil for relieving feelings of anxiety, tension, anger, and depression, and it can even ease hypertension, all of which helps to combat insomnia.

Aids detox The diuretic properties of dill essential oil aid the processes of perspiration and urination, helping to prevent a buildup of fluids and toxins.

Best **uses**

In a massage oil Add a few drops of the essential oil to an oil blend to support a detox regimen and create a state of calm.

As a bath oil Disperse a few drops of the oil in a base oil and add to the bath. Relax in the bath and inhale the steam deeply.

Safe usage Nontoxic, nonirritant in dilution.

The plant

The feathery leaves of the dill plant are commonly used to flavor food. The tiny flowers eventually give way to oil-rich seeds (see above).

The essential oil

The pale yellow essential oil is extracted through steam distillation of both the dried seeds and the whole plant. The oil has an appealing grassy aroma and blends well with lime, lemon, and other citrus oils.

This tangy herb has a spindly appearance with umbels of tiny yellow flowers in midsummer.

MASSAGE OIL   COMPRESS

Angelica

Angelica archangelica

A **warming** oil, angelica is fondly referred to as the "oil of the angels" because its **uplifting** effect promotes calm, positivity, and restful sleep. It is also soothing and **clearing**, relaxing muscles and relieving congestion.

What is it **good for?**

Aids detox A mild diuretic, angelica also encourages perspiration, which promotes health by aiding the removal of toxins from the body.

Soothes aches and pains Angelica's warming properties help to boost the circulation to aching joints and muscles, and provide effective relief from menstrual cramps.

Relieves congestion Used in a chest massage-oil blend or added to a steam inhalation, angelica essential oil can help break up stubborn congestion.

Enhances well-being Reputed to lift flagging spirits, angelica essential oil is thought to help you "discover" your true self and can be useful during periods of upheaval or in times of transition.

Best **uses**

In a massage oil Used in a complementary massage blend, angelica provides a detoxifying massage that lifts the spirits and improves well-being.

In a compress Add 2–3 drops to warm water, dip a cloth in, squeeze out, and use to ease menstrual pain.

Safe usage Nontoxic, use well diluted (less than 1 percent). Avoid use on skin for 12 hours prior to sun exposure.

The plant

*A **native of** northern Europe, the dramatic umbrella-like flower heads of the angelica plant produce a vast number of seeds. The seed oil is considered safest for aromatherapy since it contains less of the phototoxic chemical bergapten than is found in the root oil.*

The essential oil

***Both the roots** and seeds can be dried and then steam-distilled to produce a pungent oil with a sweet, spicy aroma. Oil from the seed is clear, while the oil from the roots is a pale yellow.*

The seed heads of the majestic angelica plant are harvested and dried before the oil is extracted.

BATH OIL   DIFFUSER

49

Rosewood

Aniba rosaeodora

Rosewood, also called **bois de rose**, is a member of the laurel family—a relative of cinnamon and bay. A **grounding** and centering oil, it works on the mind and emotions.

A PERFECT **BLEND**

Match rosewood with geranium, patchouli, lavender, rose, bergamot, neroli, black pepper, cinnamon, and other spicy oils

What is it **good for?**

Conditions skin This oil has tissue-regenerating properties that can help slow signs of premature aging, making this an effective treatment for dull, dry, or mature skin. Rosewood also has a healing action on wounds, making this an excellent first-aid remedy for cuts and insect bites.

Tones and calms skin Rosewood essential oil balances the levels of oil in combination or oily skins, and so helps to control pimples, acne, and blackheads.

Acts as a hair tonic As with the skin, rosewood has a balancing effect on the scalp, helping to regulate excessively dry or oily hair.

Acts as a mild pain reliever The mild analgesic action of this oil means rosewood can alleviate headaches and muscle and joint pain.

Balances emotions Thought to bring emotional stability and to create a sense of calm and empowerment, the essential oil of rosewood is also considered an aphrodisiac since it helps you to relax.

Best **uses**

As a bath oil Add to a bath and enjoy a restorative, steamy soak.

In a diffuser Diffuse this spicy, woody, floral aroma to calm emotions.

Safe usage Nontoxic and nonirritant.

The plant

This native Brazilian tree grows up to 130 ft (40 m). Now endangered, harvesting is strictly controlled. Oil from the heartwood should be avoided. A more sustainable oil from the leaves and twigs may be available.

The essential oil

The light yellow oil is steam-distilled from the wood chippings of the tree and has a spicy, sweet, floral aroma.

MASSAGE OIL   FOOTBATH

DIFFUSER   MASSAGE OIL

Tarragon
Artemisia dracunculus

A popular kitchen herb, tarragon also has a long history of use as a **medicinal** herb. The oil yields a warming massage, helping to **improve circulation** to the extremities, and is mildly **analgesic**. It also offers **emotional support** in times of upheaval.

What is it **good for?**

Eases digestion In a massage blend, tarragon oil stimulates appetite and has a pronounced effect on sluggish digestion, helping food move more efficiently through the digestive tract. It also helps calm flatulence, hiccups, and nervous indigestion.

Aids detox Its mild diuretic and laxative action helps to eliminate toxins.

Eases aches and pains Tarragon contains a natural anesthetic, eugenol, also found in clove. Like clove, it is a traditional toothache remedy. It also has a warming action that helps increase circulation to muscles, joints, and extremities, eases menstrual pain, helps regulate periods.

Acts as a deodorant The oil's spicy scent acts on body odor, inhibiting the growth of microbes on the skin, thus reducing stale, unwelcome smells.

Provides emotional support Tarragon is said to ward off feelings of despair and provide emotional support in times of change by alleviating fear and feelings of being "stuck."

Best **uses**

As a massage oil A gentle massage with tarragon oil eases digestive discomfort and menstrual pains.

In a footbath A tarragon-infused footbath boosts circulation, warms the body, and inhibits foot odor.

Safe usage *Use extremely well diluted (less than 0.1 percent). Avoid during pregnancy and breast-feeding, and on children under seven years old.*

The plant

In both Latin and Arabic, the name tarragon means "little dragon," thought to be a description of the way the root seems to coil up like a dragon.

The essential oil

The oil is steam-distilled *from the leaves and the flowering tops to produce a clear to pale green oil with an herbaceous aroma, somewhere between celery and aniseed.*

Mugwort
Artemisia vulgaris

A **powerful** oil that should be used sparingly, mugwort can nevertheless have **profound** effects. Used in massage or simply dispersed in the air, it has a pleasant **warming** quality that stimulates circulation, clears the airways, and relaxes the mind.

What is it **good for?**

Eases aches and pains Useful for arthritis and other inflammatory joint conditions. Mugwort eases stiff muscles and improves circulation.

Fights colds The oil works as a decongestant, loosening phlegm and mucus to ease bronchitis and colds.

Supports women's health With gentle massage, the oil eases cramps, relaxes abdominal tension, and encourages blood flow when periods are delayed or very light.

Provides emotional support Uplifting and relaxing, a drop on a pillow is said to bring pleasant dreams.

Best **uses**

As a diffuser Try blending a few drops of mugwort essential oil with lavender essential oil in an diffuser,

Pungent mugwort produces small clusters of white to yellow flowers in midsummer.

vaporizer, or oil burner to produce pleasant feelings of peace and tranquillity.

As a massage oil For aching joints and muscles, massage with a warming mugwort blend for deep relief.

Safe usage *Use well diluted (less than 1 percent). Avoid in pregnancy and if breast-feeding, on children under seven years old, and with epilepsy.*

The plant

A shrubby herb, mugwort is found in temperate regions, in meadows and on roadsides. The name is derived from the Old English mucg wyrt, meaning "marsh plant." In Chinese medicine, the dried, compressed leaves (moxa) are burned and briefly held close to the skin to provide warmth.

The essential oil

The oil is extracted by steam distillation of leaves, buds, and the flowering tops of the mugwort tree to produce an amber oil with a sweet, almost floral, citrusy scent.

HAIR CARE   MASSAGE OIL

Birch (leaf)

Betula alba

In Scandinavia, birch leaves and twigs are bound together and used in saunas to **tone skin** and **boost circulation**. White birch oil is **stimulating** and **detoxifying**, helping the kidneys to function efficiently and promoting perspiration to hasten the removal of toxins.

What is it **good for?**

Aids detox Birch oil facilitates both perspiration and urination that hasten the removal of toxins and impurities from the body. Added to a massage oil blend, it helps to improve a sluggish circulation.

Soothes aches and pains

A natural anti-inflammatory and analgesic, birch essential oil can help to ease sore muscles and joints after a workout and numb pain locally. These same properties also help to ease the discomfort caused by arthritis and rheumatism.

Acts as an antiseptic The

antiseptic properties of birch essential oil make it a useful remedy for skin eruptions such as cold sores. The oil is also an effective healer for irritating skin conditions, such as eczema and psoriasis, but make sure it is well diluted before using.

Tones skin and hair Birch has a balancing effect on combination skin, and can soften and tighten skin, giving mature skin a youthful appearance. Used in a hair rinse, it helps promote shine and tackles stubborn dandruff.

Best **uses**

In a hair rinse Add a few drops to water and use as a final rinse to combat dandruff and add shine.

In a massage oil Use in an all-over body massage to help improve circulation and remove toxins.

Safe usage *Use well diluted (less than 2 percent). Avoid in pregnancy and if breast-feeding; on children under 15 years old; if on anticoagulants or sensitive to salicylates.*

The plant

European white birch or silver birch is native to the Northern Hemisphere. The distinctive papery bark can be distilled into a highly antiseptic birch tar oil, unsuitable for aromatherapy. The young leaves produce the milder white birch oil.

The essential oil

The oil, which has a slightly spicy, woody aroma, is steam-distilled from the leaf buds and is pale yellow in color.

OINTMENT   SKIN CARE   DIFFUSER   MASSAGE OIL

Frankincense (Olibanum)

Boswellia carterii, B. sacra, B. frereana, et al

This is an important oil for **toning** and **invigorating** the complexion, particularly for mature or sun-damaged skin. Frankincense can be used as both an antiseptic and anti-inflammatory, and its distinct aroma helps to **soothe** and **calm** frayed nerves, making it useful for treating anxiety.

A PERFECT BLEND

Natural blending partners include citrus and spice oils, basil, cedarwood, chamomile, myrrh, neroli, pine, sandalwood, and vetiver.

What is it **good for?**

Soothes aches and pains The potent anti-inflammatory action of frankincense has been found to ease arthritis and rheumatic pain.

Tones skin The oil helps close pores and tone skin. Its rejuvenating qualities make it an excellent choice for mature skin, helping to minimize wrinkles and fine lines and reduce the appearance of blemishes and long-term sun damage.

Acts as an antiseptic Diluted, frankincense oil can be used topically to heal cuts and skin ulcers.

Fights colds Frankincense essential oil helps to soothe the mucous membranes, calming and deepening breathing, and easing coughs, bronchitis, and laryngitis.

Relieves anxiety This calming oil lifts the spirits, increases energy and focus, and aids meditation, ideal when feeling stressed, tired, or overwhelmed.

Best **uses**

In an ointment The powerful anti-inflammatory properties of frankincense essential oil make it an effective ointment to use on sore joints, helping to reduce pain and increase movement.

As a facial toner Mix 2 teaspoons aloe vera juice, 6 tablespoons water and 4 drops of frankincense.

In a diffuser Add a few drops to a diffuser, vaporizer, or oil burner.

In a massage oil Add a few drops to a base oil for a toning massage.

Safe usage Nontoxic, nonirritant in dilution.

The plant

Frankincense trees grow wild in northeast Africa and Oman. They produce an aromatic sap that, when dried, is called the "pearl of the desert," and is traditionally burned as incense.

The essential oil

The rich fragrant oil is steam-distilled from the tree resin (above). It produces a pale yellow or greenish oil with a sweet, spicy, resinous scent.

Frankincense promotes feelings of positivity, enhancing well-being.

SKIN CARE   HAIR CARE   FRAGRANCE   MASSAGE OIL   BATH OIL

The bright yellow petals of the ylang-ylang yield an exceptionally floral essential oil.

Ylang-Ylang

Cananga odorata

With its **exotic**, highly floral aroma, ylang-ylang is **uplifting** and **arousing**, and at the same time eases feelings of anxiety. A key constituent of the traditional hair preparation, macassar oil, its **balancing** properties make it suitable for all skin types.

What is it **good for?**

Improves complexion Ylang-ylang has a balancing action on the secretion of sebum, helping to regulate its production, making it an ideal skin cleanser for both oily and dry skin types. It is a particularly effective tonic for acne-prone complexions.

Tones skin With its stimulating effect, ylang-ylang helps to improve the structure and appearance of tired or sagging skin, restoring a youthful glow.

Nourishes hair The oil has a long history as a treatment for dry hair. It nourishes and stimulates the scalp, and conditions dry, brittle hair. It is even reputed to promote hair growth.

Aids relaxation Stimulating and calming, ylang-ylang essential oil is well placed for increasing feelings of well-being. Its calming properties have demonstrable effects, helping to lower blood pressure and breathing rates, in turn reducing feelings of anxiety.

Acts as an aphrodisiac The arousing aroma of ylang-ylang and its renowned relaxing effect make this oil a popular aphrodisiac, since it helps to release inhibitions and ease tension, while arousing the olfactory senses. Traditionally, petals were scattered on the beds of newlyweds to help dispel anxiety.

Treats depression The sedating and calming properties make it useful support in the treatment of depression and tension.

Best **uses**

As a skin toner Add 1–2 drops of the oil to 0.3oz (10ml) witch hazel and 1.7oz (50ml) water. Dab on with cotton ball.

As a hair tonic For a dry scalp, add 1–2 drops ylang-ylang oil to 1 teaspoon olive oil and massage into the scalp before bed. Brush through the hair with a natural-bristle brush, and wash out in the morning.

As a perfume The essential oil can be used neat as a simple perfume. Or you can mix 1–2 drops in a teaspoon of a base oil, such as apricot kernel, and apply it to the pulse points.

In a massage oil For a skin-toning and relaxing massage, add 1–2 drops of ylang-ylang oil to a base oil blend.

As a bath oil Add 1–2 drops of the oil to a base oil or 1 tablespoon of milk and disperse in the bath.

Safe usage *Nontoxic and nonirritant. Because it has a powerful scent, use well diluted, unless using neat as a perfume.*

The plant

A native of Asia, ylang-ylang means "flower of flowers," the waxy petals have been used in medicines and skin creams for millenia. Now grown mainly in Madagascar and the Comoros, it is a base of high-end Asian scents and a key ingredient in Chanel No.5.

The essential oil

The pale yellow oil *is steam- or water-distilled from the flowers to create an oil with an intensely sweet, exotic floral scent. The scent can be overpowering, so use sparingly at first to discover how strong you like it.*

The large drooping flowers of the tropical ylang-ylang tree have an intensely heady scent.

SKIN CARE   STEAM INHALATION

MASSAGE OIL   SKIN CARE

Elemi

Canarium luzonicum

Elemi has a long history in skin care, traditionally used in **healing** skin salves in the Middle East and Europe. Today, its ability to **tone** and **firm** skin makes it a favorite ingredient in high-end beauty products. It also helps to relieve congestion in the lungs.

What is it **good for?**

Combats signs of aging Elemi is ideal for dry or sun-damaged skin. It accelerates skin-cell renewal and supports collagen synthesis, helping to prevent sagging and the appearance of premature fine lines. In skincare products, elemi helps to harmonize both dry and oily skin types.

Heals skin The healing properties of elemi can help to reduce scarring, and its effective antiseptic action helps prevent infection in cuts and wounds.

Eases respiratory problems With expectorant and antiviral properties, a few drops of the oil added to a steam inhalation brings relief to respiratory problems such as chest infections, mucus, sinusitis, and bronchitis.

Lifts moods Calming and uplifting, this a good oil to choose when stressed, or suffering from nervous exhaustion.

Best **uses**

In a cream Add a few drops of elemi essential oil to an unscented cream or lotion base and apply before bedtime as part of an evening skin-care regimen for a revitalizing skin treatment.

In an inhalation Breathing in steam infused with elemi essential oil can help to bring welcome relief from the symptoms of hay fever, as well as ease the congestion that leads to coughs and sinus-related headaches.

Safe usage *Nontoxic, use well diluted (less than 0.5 percent).*

The plant

A relative of frankincense and myrrh, the elemi tree is native to the tropical forests of the Philippines and neighboring nations. The name means "above and below" in Arabic, suggesting that it was valued both spiritually and physically.

The essential oil

Steam-distilled from the resin of the elemi tree, the essential oil is pale yellow and has a distinctive sharp, citrusy, pine aroma.

The honey-colored resin produces the oil.

Caraway

Carum carvi

This **warming** essential oil works on both mind and body, **relieving** mental strain and emotional fatigue. It also supports the digestive and urinary systems, helps **clear** the respiratory system, and can be used to treat stubborn skin and scalp conditions.

What is it **good for?**

Soothes nerves Caraway oil is a natural tonic for frayed nerves, calming the mind and soothing mental fatigue. It also settles nervous digestion, colic, flatulence, and gastric spasms.

Helps fight infection Its expectorant action means that caraway can help to clear bronchitis, bronchial asthma, and irritating coughs. It also helps to soothe sore throats and laryngitis, supports the healthy function of the urinary system, and helps to flush out toxins.

Heals and soothes skin The tissue-regenerating qualities of caraway essential oil can be harnessed to help disperse bruises, reduce boils, and clean infected wounds. The oil is used to combat oily skin, help clear acne and flaky scalps, and relieve itching.

A PERFECT **BLEND**

Try blending with basil, chamomile, coriander, frankincense, ginger, lavender, or orange.

Best **uses**

In a massage oil Blended into a base oil, caraway makes a soothing massage that can relieve abdominal discomfort.

In a cream Add 2–3 drops to a cream base and use to relieve dry, itchy skin and scalp.

Safe usage Nontoxic. Use well diluted (less than 1 percent).

The plant

A native of southeastern Europe, caraway now grows in the wild and is cultivated all over Europe and temperate Asia. A member of the Umbelliferae family, it is related to cumin, fennel, and dill.

The essential oil

Caraway oil is extracted by steam distillation from the dried ripe seeds. It produces a clear to pale yellow oil that boasts a sweet and spicy aroma with a hint of pepper.

The aromatic caraway herb produces delicate white flowers in the early summer months.

HAIR CARE   FRAGRANCE   OINTMENT   MASSAGE OIL

Cedarwood

Cedrus atlantica

A long-established essential oil, cedarwood has an impressive range of benefits. Both **antiseptic** and **astringent**, it balances and tones complexions and facilitates healing in infections and skin eruptions. Its **uplifting** aroma makes it a perfect pick-me-up, helping to release tension and lift feelings of lethargy.

A PERFECT BLEND

Blends well with rose, black pepper, bergamot, jasmine, neroli, juniper, cypress, clary sage, frankincense, and mimosa.

What is it **good for?**

Soothes skin Cedarwood contains the highest level of the anti-inflammatory substances, known as sesquiterpenes, of any essential oil. This makes it helpful for easing itchy, irritated skin, especially in cases of acne, dandruff, or athlete's foot.

Relieves pain Cedarwood essential oil has a warming, regenerative effect, making it a useful treatment for chronic degenerative conditions, such as arthritis.

Tones and heals skin The astringent properties in this essential oil can help balance oily or acne-prone skin and make it an effective tonic for oily hair. It also promotes healing of wounds and skin ulcers.

Supports women's health The stimulating effect of cedarwood can help regulate the menstrual cycle and is a useful antiseptic treatment for unwanted vaginal discharges.

Aids detox Cedarwood helps to stimulate the flow of lymph, reduce water retention, and aid the removal of toxins from the body.

Fights colds and coughs Used as an inhalation or in a diffuser, the oil can help break up excessive mucus, and soothe coughs and bronchitis.

Lifts moods Grounding and calming, cedarwood can combat feelings of negativity. Its uplifting qualities treat nervous tension, anxiety, depression, and fatigue, as well as aid focus. For men, it is considered an aphrodisiac.

Best **uses**

As a hair treatment Added to shampoos or conditioners, the oil combats dandruff and hair loss.

As a room fragrance Use in a diffuser, vaporizers, or oil burner to help cleanse the air and lift anxiety, depression, and feelings of exhaustion.

In an ointment Add a few drops of the oil to a base oil or ointment base and apply several times a day to provide fast relief and healing for itchy, irritated skin conditions.

In a massage oil Add 2–3 drops cedarwood essential oil to 1 tablespoon base oil for an uplifting and skin-soothing massage.

Safe usage Nontoxic, nonirritant in dilution.

The plant

The sacred Cedars of Lebanon in the Atlas Mountains are large imposing trees that can live for up to 2,000 years. As a symbol of protection and power, they have been so highly prized and sought after over the years that they are becoming an endangered species, so make sure the oil you buy is sustainably harvested.

The essential oil

The tree bark is the source of a thick, pale, yellow to amber essential oil with a sweet, mild, balsamic–woody scent that becomes gradually more woody while the oil dries out.

The oil from the cedarwood tree works therapeutically to treat feelings of anxiety and depression.

MASSAGE OIL   OINTMENT

FOOTBATH   DIFFUSER

Camphor

Cinnamomum camphora

With its **medicinal** aroma, camphor is a very useful oil. It has a dual action on skin, at first **cooling** then deeply **warming**, and stimulates the circulation, metabolism, and digestion. It's an effective pain reliever and also helps to clear the head and calm the mind.

What is it **good for?**

Improves circulation The stimulating effect of camphor essential oil helps to boost a sluggish circulation and digestion, and also balances the metabolic rate.

Soothes aches and pains A natural anesthetic, camphor can provide relief from nerve pain and inflammation. It is also an effective antispasmodic and eases cramps and muscle spasms.

Fights colds and flu Camphor helps clear blocked sinuses and respiratory complaints, making breathing easier.

Best **uses**

In a massage oil If you are feeling chilly or achy, a massage blend with camphor essential oil warms and instills a sense of well-being.

In an ointment Add a few drops to an ointment base and use as a rub to relieve pain and ease sore muscles.

Safe usage *A strong oil, use well-diluted, and use only "white" camphor essential oil.*

The plant

The camphor tree *is native to Taiwan, China, and Japan and grows to a great age. It must be at least 50 years old to produce the oil, which is present in all parts of the plant.*

Ho Sho, or Ho Leaf, *oil is distilled from the leaves of the camphor tree and is a much milder oil that is soothing for the skin and mind. It is nontoxic and nonirritant in dilution.*

The essential oil

When the wood, *branches, and leaves of the camphor plant are steam-distilled, they produce a brown oil that must be distilled twice more before it becomes the clear oil, known as "white camphor" that is safe to use in aromatherapy.*

Cinnamon

Cinnamomum zeylanicum

This spicy, **warming** oil was used by the ancient Egyptians as an aromatic foot massage. It is used in very small amounts in cosmetics for its antiseptic properties, and its **energizing** and **stimulating** aroma makes it ideal for lifting flagging spirits.

What is it **good for?**

Soothes aches and pains Cinnamon is warming if you feel particularly chilly, because it helps boost circulation to the extremities. It's especially effective for reviving and soothing sore joints aggravated by cold, damp weather.

Aids digestion Massaged over the abdomen, cinnamon oil can stimulate circulation, improve sluggish digestion, and relieve constipation. It also has an antispasmodic action that helps to calm stomach cramps and spasms.

Acts as an antiseptic Cinnamon is effective against a wide range of bacteria, viruses, and parasites, especially lice and scabies.

Balances emotions An uplifting room scent, the oil can help counter exhaustion and depression.

BATH OIL   MASSAGE OIL

Best **uses**

As a footbath Warm cold feet by adding 1–2 drops of cinnamon oil to a relaxing footbath.

In a diffuser Use in a diffuser to disinfect and clear the air in a sickroom or to dispel unpleasant smells.

Safe usage *Use very well diluted (less than 0.5 percent), and use only cinnamon leaf oil on the skin (not cinnamon bark).*

The plant

The cinnamon tree *is a member of the laurel family and native of Sri Lanka. The name "cinnamon" refers to its medium brown color.*

The essential oil

The yellow or brownish-yellow *essential oil is obtained through steam distillation of the inner bark and leaves of the cinnamon tree. It has a warm and spicy aroma. The leaf oil is considered milder and is therefore safer for use in aromatherapy.*

Cistus

Cistus ladaniferus

Derived from the flowering plant also known as rockrose, rose of Sharon, and labdanum, **fragrant** cistus has powerful **skin-toning** and **healing** properties. It is a useful immune stimulant, and its antiseptic properties fight infection. It also helps center the mind.

What is it **good for?**

Aids detox Used in massage oils, blended with a favorite base oil, cistus helps to encourage effective lymphatic drainage, improves circulation, and boosts immunity.

Heals skin Known for its healing properties, cistus oil can help to speed up tissue healing in wounds. Its astringent properties also make it useful for treating bleeding gums, bruises, and mouth ulcers.

Tones skin Rich in antioxidants, cistus essential oil is beneficial for your skin and brightens tired-looking complexions. A good astringent, it can help tighten and tone mature skin.

Acts as an antiseptic Cistus oil has an effective antiviral action that is especially useful in the treatment of respiratory congestion caused by colds and flu and other infections.

Helps balance emotions The oil has a centering effect that facilitiates meditation and contemplation. Its earthy aroma stimulates the senses and supports and strengthens the emotions after loss or trauma.

Best **uses**

As a bath oil Blend in a base oil or in 1 tablespoon of milk and disperse in a bath for a refreshing, toning soak.

In a massage oil Add to a base oil for a toning and detoxifying massage that helps eliminate a buildup of toxins.

Safe usage *Nontoxic, nonirritant in dilution.*

The plant

In addition *to the oil, the mature branches of cistus, a Mediterranean native, produce labdanum, a sticky gum, used as a fixative in fragrances.*

The essential oil

Steam-distilling *the leaves and twigs yields an amber oil that has a warm, earthy aroma with honey overtones.*

The simple five-petaled flowers
*of the cistus plant come in an array
of hues from white to pink to lilac.*

SKIN CARE   DIFFUSER

Lime

Lime

Citrus aurantifolia

Stimulating and **refreshing,** lime can be relied on for its **cleansing** properties, and its fresh aroma calms and clears the mind. Like its relatives, grapefruit and lemon, it is a key oil for reducing water retention and puffiness. It also balances oily skin and hair.

What is it **good for?**

Aids detox Lime's strong detoxifying action helps tackle cellulite and the puffiness linked to water retention. As with grapefruit oil, inhaling lime oil has been shown to help weight loss by boosting the metabolism.

Balances oily skin and hair Lime has a toning effect that helps clear oily and acne-prone complexions. Added to a hair rinse, it conditions and removes excess oil to refresh the scalp. Treat dandruff by mixing lime juice in water and use it as a final rinse.

Has a cooling effect Lime oil "turns down the heat," helping to calm cold-related fevers. It also boosts the immune system, and eases bronchitis, coughs, sinusitis, and asthma.

Acts as an antiseptic The oil's soothing and antiseptic properties help to heal cold sores, insect bites, and cuts. Treat cuts by putting two drops of the oil in a cold compress and pressing on the affected area.

A stress reliever The refreshing and stimulating scent relieves stress, exhaustion, and anxiety, and its ability to calm promotes creativity and focus.

Best **uses**

As a lotion Added to a skin cream or lotion, lime essential oil clears and brightens dull, congested skin.

In a diffuser Used in an oil burner, vaporizer, or diffuser, the fresh scent lifts spirits and keeps the mind sharp.

Safe usage Nontoxic, use very well diluted (less than 1 percent). Avoid use on skin 12 hours prior to sun exposure.

The plant

The lime tree, grown widely in tropical and subtropical areas, produces an acidic green fruit that is a popular food and drink flavoring.

The essential oil

Lime oil, which is cold-pressed from the rind of the fruit, has a sharp citrus scent and is either pale yellow or light olive in color.

DIFFUSER

SKIN CARE

FRAGRANCE

Neroli

Citrus aurantium

The blossom of the bitter, or Seville, orange tree is the source of a **calming,** refreshing, and uplifting oil that has long been considered a treatment for anxiety and depression. It is intense, yet **refreshing** and light, and a component of eau de cologne.

What is it **good for?**

Relieves stress Neroli has a long history as a remedy for anxiety. Its power to balance and revive makes it a first choice in cases of acute shock. It alleviates the effects of chronic stress on the adrenal, circulatory, and digestive systems.

Hydrates and tones skin Mixed in an oil-based elixir or cream, the oil balances moisture levels in the skin, helping to reduce fine lines caused by dehydration. Its gentle toning action makes it ideal for fine skin, helping to maintain elasticity, and for oily and acne-prone skin.

Promotes healing The oil's antiseptic and antibacterial properties speed the healing of cuts and wounds.

Improves digestion A gentle massage with a neroli blend soothes stomach cramps and diarrhea.

Neroli blossom

SKIN CARE   MASSAGE OIL

Best **uses**

In a diffuser If you are suffering from anxiety, disperse neroli in the air with an oil burner, vaporizer, or in a room spray to induce a feeling of calm.

As a skin toner Make a simple toning facial spritz by combining 2 tsp aloe vera juice with 6 tbsp water and 4 drops of neroli in a spray bottle.

As a perfume Neroli has sufficient complexity to be worn neat as a scent in its own right, a trait it shares with rose and jasmine.

Safe usage Nontoxic and nonirritant.

The plant

This species of orange tree is native to China, but has been cultivated for hundreds of years in the countries bordering the Mediterranean. It takes at least 1000 lb (450 kg) of orange blossom flowers to make just 1 lb (450 g) of neroli oil.

The essential oil

With delicate blossoms, the best-quality oil is water, rather than steam-distilled. The pale yellow oil darkens with age, and its sweet floral smell is powerful yet refreshing.

Petitgrain

Citrus aurantium amara

Another **beneficial** oil from the bitter orange tree—the other being neroli from the flowers. One of its most valuable properties is its **balancing** and toning effect on oily skin and hair. The relaxing aroma of petitgrain helps calm body and mind.

What is it **good for?**

Tones skin and hair Added to lotions and toners, petitgrain balances oily skin by inhibiting overproduction of oil, helping to brighten and lift a dull complexion. Added to a rinse, it helps manage oily hair.

Acts as an antiseptic Petitgrain oil helps to calm acne outbreaks and other skin eruptions. Its antiseptic action keeps wounds clean while they go through the healing process.

Acts as a deodorant Its astringent properties help to regulate perspiration, and its antibacterial action helps to control unwelcome body odor.

Calms body and mind Petitgrain's woody aroma has a relaxing sedative effect on body and mind. It counters nervous exhaustion and stress-related conditions, especially anger and panic, and helps to calm a rapid heartbeat.

A PERFECT **BLEND**

Petitgrain blends especially well with bergamot, frankincense, lavender, palmarosa, geranium, rosemary, and sandalwood.

Best **uses**

As an acne treatment The essential oil is a useful addition to a skin toner or lotion to control oily skin and to help clear up existing pimples and acne outbreaks.

In a massage oil A gentle massage with a petitgrain oil blend restores calm and balance when you are feeling angry or anxious.

Safe usage Nontoxic, nonirritant in dilution.

The plant

In the past, the oil was extracted from the cherry-sized unripe oranges, hence the name "petitgrain," meaning "little grains."

The essential oil

Petitgrain oil is extracted from the green twigs and leaves to produce a pale yellow to amber oil whose floral aroma has woody and green undertones.

MASSAGE OIL   COMPRESS

Bergamot

Citrus aurantium bergamia

An aromatherapy favorite, this oil has a balancing effect on body and mind. Soothing and **cooling,** bergamot is ideal for dry or itchy skin conditions, and its fruity aroma helps to **elevate** a low mood, enhancing well-being.

What is it **good for?**

Soothes skin Bergamot essential oil is useful for balancing combination and oily skin and improving skin tone. Its strong soothing effects help to calm dry, itchy skin, and its natural healing properties can reduce the appearance of scars over time.

Enhances well-being The sweet aroma of bergamot acts as an antidepressant by balancing mood and easing anxiety. It is a popular ingredient in colognes.

Cools fevers Bergamot has a cooling action that can help the body fight fever.

Acts as an antiseptic The oil has antibacterial and antiviral properties. Dab, diluted, on cold sores (it is active against the herpes virus) and pimples.

Best **uses**

In a massage oil To promote feelings of relaxation and help ensure a restful sleep, make a refreshing blend by mixing 1–2 drops of bergamot oil with a base oil, and massage your feet before bedtime.

In a compress Add 2–3 drops to cool water and add to a compress, then apply directly to the skin to help relieve heat stroke or a fever.

Safe usage *Nontoxic, nonirritant in dilution. Make sure you buy bergaptene- free (also called Bergamot FCF), or it will be phototoxic.*

The plant

Named after *the Italian city of Bergamo, these oranges are very sour, but with a deeply scented rind. The familiar aroma is used, among other things, as an ingredient in Earl Grey tea and Eau de Cologne.*

The essential oil

The rind *of the bergamot fruit is cold-pressed to produce either a light yellow or pale green oil that carries an extremely rich, sweet, fruity smell.*

The bumpy-skinned bergamot fruit *has a distinctly sour flavor with fresh floral overtones.*

MASSAGE OIL   COMPRESS

Lemon

Citrus limonum

Fresh and **invigorating**, lemon stimulates the senses and clears the mind. **Detoxifying** and **toning**, the oil lends itself naturally to massage blends and skin products, and its citrus aroma and antiseptic properties make it a natural deodorizer.

What is it **good for?**

Tones skin Lemon boosts circulation, helping to reduce varicose veins and prevent chilblains. It cleanses oil-prone skin and hair, and tones, helping to ward off wrinkles and spider veins.

Acts as an antiseptic Lemon acts as an antiseptic, stimulating the defenses against bacteria and viruses and killing germs. Use in a compress for boils and skin eruptions, or apply neat to warts and plantar warts.

Aids detox A lemon oil massage supports the liver, aids lymphatic cleansing, and reduces cellulite and fluid retention.

Eases digestion It stimulates the digestive system, helping to combat obesity and loss of appetite.

Lifts moods A cheerful, deodorizing scent, lemon is great for busy days when you need mental focus and positivity.

Best **uses**

In a massage oil Add to a blend for a detoxifying body massage that can reduce water retention.

In a compress Dilute a couple of drops of lemon oil in almond oil or calendula tincture, and add to water to use as a compress.

Safe usage *Nontoxic, use well diluted (less than 2 percent). Avoid using for 12 hours prior to sun exposure.*

The plant

The lemon tree *is native to India, but arrived in Europe with the crusaders in the 12th century. In addition to being a natural remedy, the rind is used in baking and cooking, and the essential oil, expressed from the rind of the fruit, has a long history of use in perfumery.*

The essential oil

The clear oil *with its fresh, citrus smell, is pressed from the peel of the lemon fruit.*

A PERFECT BLEND

For a simple but relaxing massage, mix equal amounts of bergamot and lavender in a base oil of your choice. Also blends well with cypress, neroli, lemon balm, and black pepper.

MASSAGE OIL   FRAGRANCE   BATH OIL

DIFFUSER   MASSAGE OIL

Grapefruit

Citrus paradisi

Grapefruit has an **energizing** and stimulating effect on body and mind. It makes an **uplifting** room spray, and in a massage blend boosts circulation, aids detox, and reduces water retention. Gently antiseptic and astringent, it is useful for controlling oily skin and hair.

What is it **good for?**

Aids detox The oil aids lymphatic drainage, helps boost metabolism, and assists weight loss. Massaged into skin, its diuretic and cleansing properties combat cellulite and water retention, and it stimulates, boosting circulation.

Tones skin and scalp The oil's gently antiseptic and astringent effects makes it ideal for oily complexions, open pores, helps acne, as well as oily hair. It helps to tone and tighten skin.

Combats fatigue With its fresh, zesty scent, grapefruit oil can help lift emotions and is revitalizing if you are suffering from mental exhaustion or are recovering from a late night.

Soothes aches and pains Add a few drops of the oil to a favorite base oil and use as a massage blend to help provide relief from muscle and joint pain, and tension headaches.

Acts as an air freshener Its uplifting, zesty aroma can help eliminate unpleasant odors in kitchens and bathrooms.

Best **uses**

In a massage oil Use as part of a blend to cleanse skin and aid detox.

In a room spray Clear stale air by adding a few drops to water in a spray bottle. Shake well before use.

As a bath oil Add a few drops to a base oil and disperse in a bath, or use in a shower gel.

Safe usage Nontoxic, nonirritant in dilution (less than 3 percent). Avoid using 12 hours prior to sun exposure.

The plant

Unlike other citrus fruits, grapefruit originates from the Caribbean, and not Southeast Asia. Its name comes from the grapelike cluster in which the fruits grow.

The essential oil

The oil, which is cold-pressed from the peel of the fruit, can be yellow, pale green, or pale orange, with a zesty, sweet, citrusy smell.

Mandarin

Citrus reticulata, Citrus nobilis

Mandarin (also known as tangerine) has **antiseptic** and antifungal properties, similar to other citrus fruits. It has a tonic effect on the digestive system, nourishes the skin, and its sweet, **cheerful** aroma is almost instantly **uplifting**.

What is it **good for?**

Tones skin Mandarin essential oil nurtures skin. It can help reduce the appearance of stretch marks and tone areas of flabbiness.

Aids detox In a massage oil, mandarin encourages lymphatic drainage and helps improve circulation. Its diuretic action helps combat water retention and cellulite.

Heals skin This stimulating oil helps regenerate skin cells. Its antiseptic and gently astringent properties make it useful for combating oily skin and outbreaks of acne.

Aids digestion Mandarin has a tonic effect on the digestive system. It helps food move along the digestive tract and eases indigestion and constipation, especially if these are stress related. If you feel nauseous, it can calm your stomach.

Enhances well-being A gentle, relaxing, and uplifting oil, mandarin is especially good for calming restless children and is safe to use in pregnancy.

Best **uses**

In a diffuser Add to a diffuser or vaporizer to freshen air or calm nerves.

In a massage oil Add 2–3 drops to a base oil for a soothing massage.

Safe usage Nontoxic, nonirritatant in dilution.

The plant

A native of China and the Far East, the mandarin tree was introduced to Europe in the nineteenth century. From Europe, the tree was shipped to the United States, where it was renamed tangerine.

The essential oil

An orange or amber color with a tangy sweet, floral aroma, the oil is cold-pressed from the rind of the fruit.

Synonymous with the tangerine, the small, easy-to-peel mandarin is renowned for its sweet, juicy fruit.

BATH OIL   MASSAGE OIL   DIFFUSER

Orange

Citrus sinensis

Sometimes called sweet orange, this **versatile** oil is widely used for its **uplifting** and **detoxifying** effects. It is also **calming** and may help ease tense muscles, and its **rejuvenating** properties help skin maintain a youthful appearance. Cheering and familiar, its aroma acts as a reviving tonic.

What is it **good for?**

Aids detox Orange essential oil has a detoxifying and cleansing effect throughout the body. Used as part of a massage blend, the oil helps to improve the circulation, stimulates the lymphatic system, and supports the action of the bladder and kidneys, facilitating the removal of toxins and waste from the body.

Tones skin Used in skincare products, orange essential oil helps to promote the production of collagen and supports the skin's natural repair process. The oil has inherent healing properties that are attributed to the aromatic compound limonene, also an effective antiseptic.

Revitalizes and brightens skin Orange essential oil has toning and slightly astringent properties that can help clarify oily skin and revitalize a dull or tired-looking complexion.

Boosts immunity Orange essential oil helps support the body's immune system, and the oil's cooling and refreshing properties can also help to relieve the symptoms of a feverish cold or flu virus.

Improves digestion As with other citrus oils, orange calms the digestive system, helping food to move efficiently through the digestive tract, and in turn relieves constipation and trapped gas, and eases indigestion.

Relieves anxiety Orange essential oil has a sweet, uplifting scent that can calm nervous tension, lift feelings of depression, and promote restful sleep in cases of insomnia.

Best **uses**

As a bath oil Enjoy a relaxing bath that smoothes and tones by blending a few drops of orange oil in a base oil or 1 tablespoon of milk and dispersing in a warm bath.

In a massage oil If you've overindulged, try a gentle orange massage blend over the abdomen to relieve nausea and indigestion and release trapped gas.

In a diffuser Used in a diffuser or room spray, the oil can help clear the air and mind. Its disinfectant action is useful in sickrooms, while its calming aroma can aid restful sleep for both adults and children.

Safe usage Nontoxic, nonirritant *in dilution.*

The plant

Like most citrus trees, the sweet orange tree originated in China. Today, however, most of the commercial production of orange essential oil takes place in Brazil, the US, and Cyprus.

The essential oil

Orange oil is cold-pressed from the rind of the fruit. A fine oil, it is a pale orange-greenish color with the same sweet, fresh, and fruity smell you get when you peel an orange.

Sweet-smelling citrus oil is reviving and uplifting, enhancing feelings of well-being.

The sweet orange tree grows abundantly in warm, temperate climates around the world.

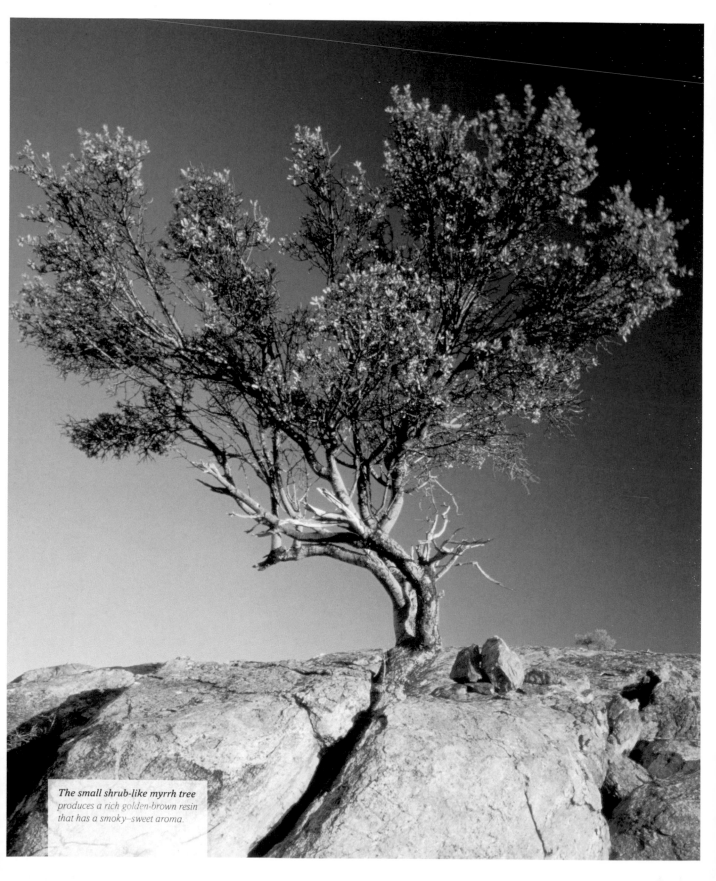

The small shrub-like myrrh tree produces a rich golden-brown resin that has a smoky–sweet aroma.

SKIN CARE   MOUTHWASH

Myrrh

Commiphora myrrha, C. molmol

The **antiseptic** properties of myrrh make it a popular remedy for healing cuts and wounds. As a well-established **anti-aging** treatment, it is added to skincare products to help prevent the premature appearance of fine lines. A grounding and centering oil, it both stimulates and **fortifies** the emotions.

A PERFECT BLEND

Make a spicy blend by combining with oils such as cedarwood, cypress, frankincense, lemon, patchouli, and sandalwood.

What is it **good for?**

Heals skin Myrrh has an established history treating various types of skin eruptions, such as acne, athlete's foot, weeping eczema, and cold sores. Its healing properties make it useful for cuts, burns, and wounds. A nonirritating oil, myrrh can be applied neat to skin.

Tones skin Its ability to preserve skin tone helps delay wrinkles and other signs of aging. It is also ideal for healing chapped and broken skin.

Cares for teeth and gums As part of a mouthwash, the antiseptic properties of myrrh help tackle infection and inflammation, soothing ulcers, sore throats, bleeding gums, bad breath, and oral thrush.

For coughs and colds Myrrh makes an excellent expectorant, particularly when coughs and colds produce thick, white mucus. Try using myrrh in a steam inhalation to ease chronic lung conditions, coughs, colds, and bronchitis.

Enhances well-being The aromatherapeutic properties of myrrh are purported to help strengthen confidence in overcoming difficulties and to enhance focus and provide a strong sense of purpose.

Best **uses**

As a skin toner Adding a few drops of myrrh essential oil to facial lotions and toners can improve skin tone and quality, especially for mature and sun-damaged skin.

In a mouthwash Add a few drops of the oil to water for a mouthwash to fight gum disease and bad breath.

Safe usage *Nonirritant in dilution. Only use extremely well diluted (less than 0.2 percent) in pregnancy and when breast-feeding.*

The plant

The myrrh tree *belongs to a family of small spiky shrubs and bushes native to the Middle East, North Africa, and northern India. The resin is gathered by making incisions in the tree that allow it to flow freely.*

The essential oil

Dried lumps of resin *are steam-distilled to produce the essential oil, which is pale orange to amber in color.*

Strengthening and healing, myrrh has a rejuvenating effect on skin.

MASSAGE OIL   MOUTHWASH

Coriander

Coriandrum sativum

This highly **aromatic** oil has a long history of medicinal use, especially in Ayurvedic and Chinese medicines. Its **antiseptic** action helps clear pimples and fungal infections, and when used in a mouthwash, the oil freshens breath. Its light, **herby aroma** is a natural tonic for flagging spirits and helps fight exhaustion.

What is it **good for?**

Relieves pain Coriander has a warming effect that helps stimulate circulation and relieve stiffness and pain in muscles and joints. The oil's analgesic properties help relieve general headaches and localized neuralgia pain, and can ease menstrual cramps.

Acts as an antiseptic Coriander essential oil is useful for dealing with occasional pimples, and fungal infections. The oil's strong antiseptic and deodorizing effect also makes it especially helpful for dealing with the bacteria that cause smelly feet, bad breath, and gum disease.

Enhances well-being Used as a room spray, coriander's soothing herbal aroma has an energizing effect that helps lift apathy and feelings of nervous exhaustion.

Best **uses**

In a massage oil Add to a suitable carrier oil to make a warming and deodorizing massage oil.

In a mouthwash Mix 1–2 drops of the essential oil in a teaspoon of glycerine or calendula tincture and add to water before using as a gargle or mouthwash to treat gum infections.

Safe usage Nontoxic and nonirritant.

The plant

Both the leaves and seeds of the coriander plant produce useful oils. When the oil is distilled from the leaves it is known as cilantro essential oil. The leaves are also a popular culinary ingredient.

The essential oil

Steam distillation of the crushed ripe seeds produces a clear to pale yellow oil with a sweet, spicy, slightly fruity, warm herbaceous scent that is warming, uplifting, and calming.

Warming coriander makes a gently stimulating and soothing oil, perfect for lifting the spirits.

The seeds produced from the flowering coriander plant are used to make the aromatic essential oil.

MASSAGE OIL   COMPRESS

Cumin

Cuminum cyminum

The use of cumin can be traced back to the ancient Egyptians and Assyrians. This **warming** essential oil helps to **relax** muscles and relieve aching joints. It stimulates circulation and helps **calm** the nerves and **lift** the spirits. It is also a useful antiseptic that can support healing.

What is it **good for?**

Aids detox The detoxifying action of cumin makes this a useful massage oil for fighting stubborn cellulite. Cumin also supports liver function, aiding the removal of toxins.

Boosts circulation Cumin has a tonifying effect on the body. It helps to boost the general circulation and can also be useful for helping to control high blood pressure.

Eases pain and digestive discomfort Cumin helps to fortify the digestive tract, relieving nausea, bloating, and constipation. It brings relief to mild headaches.

Heals skin Added to skin preparations, cumin essential oil has an antiseptic action that helps to heal dry or cracked skin, reduce bruising, and control acne, eczema, and psoriasis. It also revitalizes mature and tired-looking skin.

Fights fatigue The stimulating aroma provides a welcome lift if you feel lethargic, weak, or unable to focus.

Best **uses**

In a massage oil Add to a base oil to make a warming oil that helps relieve joint and muscle pain.

In a compress Add 2–3 drops to some glycerine or almond oil, add to cool water, and use as a compress to relieve itchy skin and bruises.

Safe usage Dilute very well (less than 0.5 percent). Avoid using for 12 hours prior to sun exposure.

The plant

Found from the eastern Mediterranean *through to east India, cumin is a member of the parsley family. It has delicate leaves and tiny white flowers that produce aromatic, oil-rich seeds.*

The essential oil

The crushed seeds *of the cumin plant are steam-distilled to produce a pale yellow oil that darkens with age. The oil has a pungent spicy–woody aroma that is musky and sensual as well as stimulating.*

This relaxing oil is ideal for easing and soothing muscular pains.

COMPRESS   MASSAGE OIL   FRAGRANCE

Cypress

Cupressus sempervirens

With a well-deserved reputation as a **warming** and **uplifting** oil, cypress also soothes and relaxes, making it a useful remedy for relieving muscular aches and pains. It helps to **stimulate** circulation and its strong **toning** action works on skin and veins. The fresh, woody aroma creates a feeling of **positivity**.

A PERFECT BLEND

Clary sage, bergamot, lemon, lavender, ginger, juniper, pine, and geranium essential oils are all natural blending partners for cypress.

77

What is it **good for?**

Improves circulation Cypress oil has a powerful toning action on the veins and helps to regulate blood flow. This makes it especially useful for treating spider veins, varicose veins, and troublesome hemorrhoids.

Tones skin The oil's balancing properties make it ideal for evenings out oily and puffy complexions and also for toning areas of loose skin, for example, after weight loss.

Aids detox Strongly astringent, cypress oil is useful in combating water retention and cellulite. It also supports healthy circulation and helps flush out toxins.

Acts as a deodorant Its astringent quality makes the oil an effective antiperspirant and deodorizer. Added to a footbath, it helps control perspiration and foot odor.

Supports women's health The soothing action of cypress helps ease menstrual discomfort and cramping.

Soothes aches and pains Diluted in a base oil and massaged over

affected areas, cypress can relieve rheumatism and osteoarthritis, as well as general muscle and joint pain. It can help control spasms, relieve menstrual cramps, and may be used for injury rehabilitation.

Heals wounds A popular ingredient in antiseptic lotions and creams, cypress essential oil has antiseptic properties that help heal wounds. Its astringent properties can slow bleeding, such as nosebleeds.

Calms nerves Refreshing and mentally toning, cypress oil helps to ease stress-induced nervous strain and tension and to lift weariness.

Best **uses**

As a compress To stem nosebleeds, apply a few drops to a cold compress. Keeping your head level, gently press your nostrils together.

In a massage oil Dilute with a base oil for a warming massage that helps relieve rheumatism, arthritis, menstrual cramps, and varicose veins.

As a cologne The masculine notes suit men's colognes and aftershaves.

Many women also enjoy using this essential oil as an alternative to heavy floral scents.

Safe usage Non-toxic, nonirritant in dilution.

The plant

This coniferous evergreen tree *can grow up to to 115 ft (35 m) tall and live for more than 1000 years. A native of the Mediterranean regions, cypress has long been an important ingredient in incense for ritual uses as well as being a source of the therapeutic healing oil.*

The essential oil

The clear to very pale yellow *oil has a woody, nutty aroma with a hint of spice. It is produced by steam-distilling the fresh leaves and cones.*

SKIN CARE   DIFFUSER   FIRST AID

Lemongrass

Lemongrass

Cymbopogon citratus,
C. flexuosus

This essential oil works on body and mind to **refresh** and **stimulate**. It has antiseptic and astringent effects that work on oily or acne-prone skin. Lemongrass is **deodorizing**, **antibacterial**, and makes an effective **insect repellent**.

What is it **good for?**

Acts as an antiseptic Its astringent and antiseptic effects cleanse skin: a few drops in a facial steam work on open or blocked pores, and the oil relieves acne, eczema, and athlete's foot. Its antiseptic properties and fresh scent also help control sweating and the bacteria that cause body odor.

Acts as an insect repellent Lemongrass is one of the key active ingredients in natural insect repellents.

Aids digestion Lemongrass is a natural appetite stimulant. It is also a good remedy for gastric infections.

Eases aches and pains Diluted in a blend, a lemongrass massage strengthens muscle tone and slack tissues, ideal for a presports massage or to treat aching muscles or muscle strain. It can also soothe headaches.

Enhances well-being Lemongrass calms and fortifies nerves and eases depression and stress.

Best **uses**

As a toner Add a few drops to witch hazel or a light lotion to refresh and tone skin.

In a diffuser Disperse into a room to raise spirits and lift exhaustion.

As an insect repellent Dilute 2–3 drops in witch hazel or another flower water for use in a spray bottle, or mix with a lotion and dab on the skin.

Safe usage Use only very well diluted (less than 0.5 percent). Avoid use on hypersensitive skin and on children less than seven years old.

The plant

Lemongrass is a native of India. Its oil is used in cosmetics and scents. There are two main types: West Indian (Cymbopogon citratus) and East Indian (Cymbopogon flexuosus), both with similar properties. After distilling the oil, the grass is used as cattle feed.

The essential oil

The essential oil is produced by steam distillation of the chopped grass. The liquid is pale yellow to amber in color, and has a fresh, herbaceous, lemony aroma.

BATH OIL   MASSAGE OIL   DIFFUSER

Palmarosa

Cymbopogon martinii

Palmarosa comes from a wild grass native to India. The pleasant floral aroma has hints of rose. Its **balancing** action makes it a popular skin-care product: it **hydrates** dry skin, **rejuvenates** tired or mature skin, and helps controls sebum secretions in oily skin.

What is it **good for?**

Nourishes and tones skin Palmarosa hydrates and balances. By stimulating cell regeneration and controlling sebum, it helps keep skin supple and elastic and improves the appearance of scar tissue and stretch marks. A natural toner, the oil helps to reduce the appearance of wrinkles and fine lines and to brighten tired complexions. In a facial steam, it can unclog pores and tone sagging skin.

Aids recuperation A gentle tonic, the oil helps to hasten recovery after illness. It aids digestion and boosts poor appetite. Diluted and massaged over the abdomen, it may also relieve symptoms of diarrhea.

Acts as an antiseptic Its antiseptic properties are specifically active against the bacteria that cause acne. It can also treat athlete's foot, dermatitis, and minor skin infections.

Enhances well-being A palmarosa massage helps relieve stress, anxiety, and tension, and is a mild aphrodisiac, countering strong negative emotions that interfere with sexual fulfillment.

Best **uses**

As a bath oil Mix in a base oil or 1 tablespoon of milk and disperse in a bath to fortify yourself if recuperating, tired, or to relieve digestive problems.

In a massage oil Add to base oils or body lotions to improve skin elasticity.

In a diffuser Diffuse to freshen air, fight fatigue, and focus the mind.

Safe usage *Nontoxic, nonirritant in dilution (less than 5 percent).*

The plant

Also called Indian or Turkish geranium, palmarosa grass is a relative of lemongrass, but has a floral, rather than citrus, scent. Native to India, it is now cultivated in Indonesia, East Africa, the Comoro Islands, and Brazil.

The essential oil

The thin, pale yellow essential oil can be steam- or water-distilled from the fresh or dried grass. It has a sweet floral aroma with a subtle hint of rose.

DIFFUSER   SKIN CARE

Citronella

Cymbopogon nardus

Best known as an **insect repellent** used in a variety of candles, potpourri, and lotions, citronella has other important uses. As a room scent it helps to **clear** and **refresh** the mind, and its antiseptic properties make it effective in deodorants.

What is it **good for?**

Tones skin The toning properties of citronella help balance skin that is prone to oiliness.

Acts as an insect repellent This popular insect repellent is a very useful travel companion. Carry a citronella-infused tissue to help keep annoying bugs at bay.

Freshens and clears air The antiseptic properties of citronella help to clear the air of viruses, which is especially useful during the cold and flu season or to clear the air in a sickroom. Its antiseptic effect also makes it a useful ingredient in deodorants.

Enhances focus Citronella essential oil can lift the emotions when you feel dejected and also helps you to keep a clear head and maintain focus.

A PERFECT BLEND

Try blending citronella essential oil with bergamot and other citrus oils. It also blends well with geranium, lavender, pine, and peppermint.

Best **uses**

In a diffuser Add to oil burners, vaporizers, or room sprays to make an effective insect repellent.

In a lotion Make a foot lotion that will combat unpleasant odors by adding a few drops of citronella oil to an unscented lotion base.

Safe usage *Nonirritant in dilution (less than 15 percent). Avoid using on hypersensitive skin.*

The plant

A hardy grass, native to Sri Lanka and Java, citronella is distinguishable from its cousin, lemongrass, by its reddish-colored stems.

The essential oil

Citronella oil is steam-distilled from the finely chopped fresh, dried, or partly dried grass. It is a pale to dark yellow oil with a sweet, lemony scent.

DIFFUSER   SKIN CARE

Carrot seed

Daucus carota

This unusual oil has a **rejuvenating** effect on many body systems. A **grounding** oil, it can relieve feelings of stress and lift exhaustion. It also has a mild diuretic action that helps to eliminate toxins, and its **healing properties** can be harnessed to **revitalize** problem complexions and nourish dry and mature skin.

What is it **good for?**

Aids detox The mild diuretic effects of carrot essential oil help to reduce excess fluid retention. This detoxifying oil also supports the efficient functioning of the liver, and strengthens the digestive system.

Relieves stress The earthy aroma of carrot essential oil is grounding and calming, helping to relieve feelings of stress and give the body stamina to fight feelings of exhaustion and general lethargy.

Soothes aching muscles As part of a massage oil blend or diluted in the bath, carrot seed oil is deeply warming, helping to ease aches and pains and boost the circulation.

Repairs skin Highly valued in cosmetics, carrot essential oil is added to face and body creams to nourish, tighten, revitalize, tone, and rejuvenate tired-looking skin. Its calming properties also make it suitable for itchy and irritated skin.

Best **uses**

In a diffuser Unlike some oils, which can be overpowering, adding carrot seed oil to an oil burner or diffuser imparts a very subtle, grounding aroma to the air.

In a cream Add a few drops of the essential oil to a cream or lotion base to help soften dry skin, and also encourage healthy cell growth and skin rejuvenation.

Safe usage Use in dilutions of less than 2 percent. Avoid using during pregnancy or while breast-feeding.

The plant

Wild carrot, also known as "Queen Anne's lace," is a European native with hairy leaves and delicate white lacy flowers with purple centers that spread out in a distinctive umbrella shape. Though wild carrot bears little resemblance to the root vegetable, it does share the same carrot-like aroma of the commercial vegetable.

The essential oil

Steam distilling the dried seeds of the wild carrot plant produces a yellow–brown oil that has a fairly viscous texture. The oil has an understated, mildly sweet, dry, and distinctly earthy aroma with some noticeable herbaceous undertones.

With its subtle aroma, carrot oil holds potent healing properties.

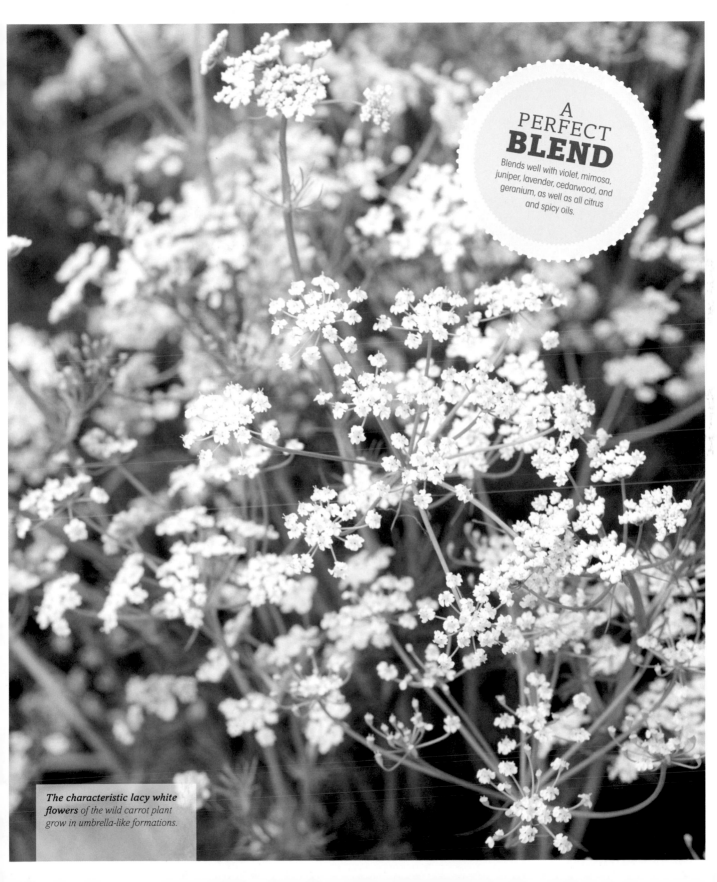

A
PERFECT
BLEND

Blends well with violet, mimosa, juniper, lavender, cedarwood, and geranium, as well as all citrus and spicy oils.

The characteristic lacy white flowers of the wild carrot plant grow in umbrella-like formations.

MASSAGE OIL   MOUTHWASH

Cardamom

Elettaria cardamomum

A natural **diuretic** and digestive stimulant, cardamom **boosts** the metabolism and helps the body to metabolize fat efficiently. It is also an effective **antiseptic**, making it a popular component of natural mouthwashes and deodorants.

What is it **good for?**

Acts as a deodorant Cardamom essential oil is a good addition to deodorants, helping to eliminate the bacteria that cause body odor.

Cares for teeth and gums Its antiseptic properties are useful for treating bad breath and for helping heal sore, bleeding gums.

Aids detox Diluted with a base oil, cardamom makes a stimulating massage blend, helping to boost circulation. Its mild diuretic action also helps facilitate the removal of toxins.

Soothes digestive upsets Cardamom has a calming action ideal for an upset stomach and nausea. It also relieves heartburn.

Combats fatigue The oil relieves stress and refreshes, helping combat fatigue. A reputed aphrodisiac, especially if you are overly tired.

Best **uses**

In a massage oil Add to a light base oil to make a refreshing, detoxifying all-over body massage.

In a mouthwash Mix 1–2 drops in a teaspoon of glycerine or calendula tincture; add to water for a mouthwash.

Safe Usage Nontoxic and nonirritant. Avoid using in children under seven years old.

The plant

A native of India, cardamom seeds and pods have been used for centuries as a culinary spice and a healing remedy. Cardamom is also used in traditional Chinese medicine.

The essential oil

The essential oil is extracted by steam distillation from the seeds and produces a colorless to pale yellow oil that has a sweet–spicy aroma with woody notes.

The seeds of the aromatic cardamom plant are used as a sweet and spicy culinary flavoring.

MASSAGE OIL

STEAM INHALATION

DIFFUSER

Eucalyptus

Eucalyptus globulus

This **warming** and **antiseptic** oil is great for relieving aches and pains as well as healing mouth ulcers and insect bites and stings. The oil **tones** and balances the skin, and its sharp aroma helps **increase concentration** and lift feelings of depression.

83

What is it **good for?**

Acts as an antiseptic Dab onto skin to heal bacterial and fungal infections and wounds and soothe bites. In a bath, it can relieve cystitis. The oil makes a good sickroom spray.

Tones skin A facial steam with a few drops of the oil helps to cleanse and tone oily or acne-prone skin.

Eases aches and pains Add the oil to a base oil or an ointment to warm and loosen tight muscles and joints.

Improves focus Eucalyptus refreshes the mind, banishing headaches and improving concentration.

Best **uses**

In a massage oil Blend 2–3 drops in an ointment to rub on the chest to clear sinuses and aid sleep when congested.

In an inhalation Add a few drops to hot water and use as a facial steam to unclog pores, cleanse, tone, and leave you clear headed and refreshed.

In a diffuser Add a few drops to a diffuser to combat fatigue.

Safe usage *Nontoxic externally; nonirritant in dilution (less than 20 percent). Avoid near nose or face on children under seven years old.*

The plant

The blue gum eucalyptus, a tree native *to Australia, is the most widely cultivated of hundreds of species of eucalyptus.*

Several other *varieties are used in aromatherapy, notably the slightly gentler Eucalyptus radiata and the more cooling Eucalyptus citronella.*

The essential oil

This oil is steam-distilled *from the leaves of the tree. It has a clear to pale yellow hue and has a strong, camphorous, woody smell.*

MASSAGE OIL   MOUTHWASH

Fennel (sweet)

Foeniculum vulgare

With a long history as a sacred and medicinal herb, fennel is a **cooling** and **cleansing** essential oil. Its main action is to **unblock**, where it works on both body and mind, easing constipation and other complaints and providing the courage to express held-in emotions.

What is it **good for?**

Aids detox Fennel has a diuretic effect and helps to stimulate circulation. Diluted in a base oil, it provides a good detoxifying massage that helps tackle stubborn cellulite.

Cares for teeth and gums Well diluted, fennel essential oil can be gargled in a mouthwash to help fight the bacteria that causes tooth decay and bad breath.

Soothes digestion Fennel has unblocking properties. A massage blend containing fennel helps relieve flatulence, bloating, digestive cramps, and constipation. The oil also stimulates appetite, and eases nervous indigestion brought on by a rushed meal or emotional distress.

Fights colds A mild expectorant, fennel essential oil helps loosen phlegmy coughs. Blend with a base oil for a chest rub, or add to a diffuser, vaporizer, or oil burner.

Best **uses**

As a massage oil For indigestion, blend fennel oil in a light base and gently massage the abdomen in a clockwise direction.

In a mouthwash Mix 1–2 drops in a teaspoon of glycerine or calendula tincture and add to water to use as a mouthwash.

Safe usage *Dilute well before use (less than 2 percent). Avoid during pregnancy and if breast-feeding. Not suitable for children under seven years old.*

A PERFECT BLEND

To relieve indigestion, blend with ginger, nutmeg, and peppermint oils. Also blends well with geranium, lavender, marjoram, and rose.

The plant

The fennel plant *grows up to 6 ft (2 m) high. Its green feathery leaves and golden-yellow flowers attract insects and bees and eventually produce the oil-rich seeds.*

The essential oil

The essential oil *is steam-distilled from crushed fennel seeds. It is pale yellow with a sweet–spicy smell that is reminiscent of aniseed.*

COMPRESS

DIFFUSER

OINTMENT

Wintergreen

Gaultheria procumbens, G. fragrantissima

A pungent **medicinal** oil, wintergreen should be used sparingly. Its strong minty aroma can clear the head and even small amounts applied topically can provide **pain relief**.

What is it **good for?**

Relieves pain The oil is a popular ingredient in muscle ointments and rubs. It contains a natural aspirin-like analgesic that can help to relieve pain locally. Used in a compress, the oil can alleviate headaches, muscle cramps, joint pain, and tendonitis, and can also bring some relief to pain caused by chronic conditions such as arthritis and rheumatism.

Aids digestion Once absorbed through the skin, the oil can stimulate the digestive process by triggering the release of digestive juices.

Tones skin and hair Arguably too strong for use on the face, when well diluted, wintergreen's astringent and antiseptic action is useful for treating acne on the body. Its antifungal properties also help prevent dandruff and can work to clear up athlete's foot.

Clears the head A few drops of wintergreen essential oil in a vaporizer or diffuser aids breathing and helps relieve stress and tension.

Best **uses**

In a compress Try blending with lavender oil for an effective hot or cold compress to relieve localized aches and pains.

In a diffuser Used in a diffuser or vaporizer, the oil can help to open up the nasal and respiratory passages.

In an ointment Add 1–2 drops to an ointment base to relieve pain locally.

Safe usage Dilute well before use (less than 2 percent). Avoid during pregnancy and if breast-feeding. Not suitable for young children. Avoid if on anticoagulant medication and if sensitive to aspirin.

The plant

A shrubby evergreen, wintergreen is native to North America. It has glossy, green, oval leaves and abundant white blooms in the summer, which turn into bright red berries during the winter, often lasting through to spring. The berries were used traditionally in herbal medicine to help relieve muscular aches and pains.

The essential oil

Steam-distilled from the chopped-up leaves, wintergreen essential oil has a sweet, fresh, and pleasant minty aroma. The oil is pale yellow or pinkish-yellow in color. Wintergreen blends well with other minty oils, such as peppermint, and also complements bergamot, basil, lavender, and lemongrass essential oils.

This essential oil has strong antibacterial and antifungal effects.

FIRST AID

COMPRESS

STEAM INHALATION

DIFFUSER

SKIN CARE

A
PERFECT
BLEND

For a balancing aroma, try blending with chamomile, geranium, and lavender oils. Also blends well with rose, rosewood, clary sage, bergamot, and other citrus oils.

Helichrysum (Immortelle)

Helichrysum italicum

Also known as immortelle, or **"everlasting" oil**, this is a fantastic, **regenerative** oil that **cools** and soothes the skin. Its antiseptic and **anti-inflammatory** properties help heal scars and skin eruptions. Deeply **de-stressing,** it's perfect for relieving anxiety, nervous exhaustion, and feelings of depression.

What is it **good for?**

Enhances well-being The oil's therapeutic properties help treat tension, depression, exhaustion, and other stress-related conditions. Uplifting, it curbs negativity and promotes a feeling of safety, helping to heal old emotional wounds.

Relieves pain An effective anti-inflammatory, it's a good choice for joint pain, arthritic conditions, and general strains and sprains.

Heals wounds and fights infections Helichrysum can be applied in a cream to wounds to help reduce swelling, disinfect, and promote healing through tissue regeneration. It has demonstrated antibacterial properties.

Heals and protects skin The anti-inflammatory and regenerative properties of helichrysum oil make it useful for treating skin problems such as acne, dermatitis, bruises, boils, and abscesses. It can also help to fade scars, stretch marks, and blemishes. The oil's antioxidant properties protect the skin from harmful free radicals that cause premature skin aging.

Soothes skin The oil's calming action helps soothe allergic skin breakouts and numbness and tingling in nerve-related conditions.

Boosts circulation The oil stimulates circulation. It can also help to control blood pressure and provide relief from conditions such as varicose veins.

Relieves coughs and colds The oil has an antispasmodic effect that relieves asthma and persistent coughs. It may act as a decongestant in cases of sinusitis and phlegm, especially when these are allergy- or stress-related.

Best **uses**

As first aid The oil can be applied in a cream as an effective emergency treatment for burns, scrapes, or cuts.

As a compress Add a few drops to a cool compress and hold over skin flare-ups and bruises.

As an inhalation Add a few drops to a steam inhalation to help clear blocked sinuses.

In a diffuser Add 3–4 drops to a diffuser to create a calming ambience.

As a skin toner Added to facial spritzers, toners, or lotions, helichrysum essential oil leaves skin feeling fresh and toned and helps to reduce the appearance of fine lines and skin blemishes.

Safe usage Use well diluted (less than 0.5 percent).

The plant

A Mediterranean herb, helichrysum's small, cheerful flowers are popular with florists. Part of the sunflower family, the oil's names, "everlasting" and "immortelle," come from the reputation of the flowers for retaining their brilliant color even when dried.

The essential oil

This watery yellow essential oil that occasionally has a tinge of red is steam-distilled from the flowers. It has a distinctive straw-like aroma with hints of fruit, tea, and honey.

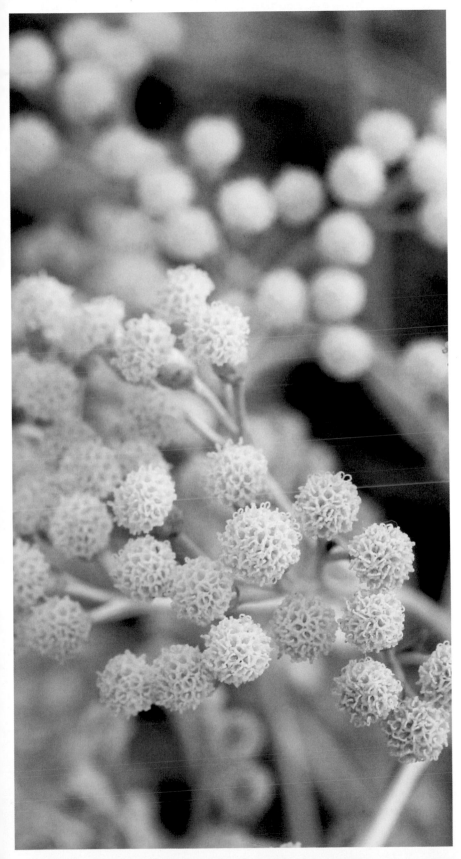

This cooling and soothing oil nourishes, rejuvenates, and heals skin.

This fragrant evergreen shrub produces clusters of bright yellow flowers in the summer months.

STEAM
INHALATION

MOUTHWASH

Star anise

Illicium verum

Star anise has been in use since ancient times in Europe, the Middle East, and Asia, favored for both its **therapeutic benefits** and distinctive flavor. With its sharp aroma, the essential oil acts as a mild **pain reliever** and also makes an effective **antiseptic**.

What is it **good for?**

Relieves aches and pains Star anise has pain-relieving properties that provide localized relief from muscular aches and pains, and help to ease rheumatism and arthritis.

Acts as an antiseptic The essential oil has a strong antibacterial action. It also has potent antifungal properties that can help heal skin infections such as athlete's foot, and it can be used to treat head lice and mites.

Acts as a deodorant Star anise is often added to soaps to combat body odor, and the oil makes a natural breath freshener.

Tones skin Its skin-balancing properties are useful for calming oily and combination skin.

Promotes restful sleep The oil has a sedative action that helps to calm, slowing the heart rate and aiding sleep, making it especially useful for anxiety-related sleep problems.

Best **uses**

In an inhalation Add a few drops of star anise oil to a steam inhalation to provide temporary relief from bronchitis, cold, and flu symptoms.

In a mouthwash Add 1–2 drops to a teaspoon of glycerine or calendula tincture. Add to a glass of water and rinse in the mouth to fight the germs that cause bad breath. Do not swallow.

Safe usage Use well diluted (less than 1 percent). Avoid during pregnancy and if breast-feeding. Not suitable for children under seven years old.

A PERFECT **BLEND**

Star anise blends well with vetiver, palmarosa, orange, and other citrus oils, as well as neroli, frankincense, lavender, ylang-ylang, and tea tree.

The plant

An evergreen tree from China and Vietnam, star anise produces distinctive star-shaped fruits that are commonly used in Asian cooking as well as in traditional medicine.

The essential oil

The pale yellow oil has an aroma similar to black licorice and is steam-distilled from the fresh and partly-dried fruits.

FRAGRANCE　　SKIN CARE

Jasmine

Jasminum officinale

The heady aroma of jasmine is highly prized by perfumers. The essential oil is one of the most **uplifting**, and its deeply **relaxing** effects account for its reputation as an aphrodisiac.

What is it **good for?**

Soothes skin Added to skin lotions, the oil can be a calming treatment for sensitive and inflamed skin that feels hot to the touch.

Tones skin Naturally toning, jasmine improves skin elasticity. Diluted in a massage blend and used regularly, it can help to fade stretch marks and scars.

Enhances well-being The warm, floral aroma of jasmine has a powerfully uplifting effect, helping to increase feelings of alertness, relieve tension, stress, and anxiety, and disperse feelings of negativity. It is traditionally regarded as an aphrodisiac for men and women.

Fights coughs and colds
A few drops of jasmine oil added to a steam inhalation can help to soothe irritating coughs and hoarseness and relieve laryngitis.

Best **uses**

As a perfume Jasmine oil can be applied neat as a perfume, creating a sense of relaxation and imbuing the wearer with a feeling of enjoyment.

As a toner Make a simple facial toner by adding 2–3 drops of jasmine absolute to a teaspoon of glycerine or witch hazel, then add to water. Soak a cotton ball in the solution and apply to the skin.

Safe usage Nontoxic and nonirritant.

The plant

*A **native** of northwest India, the name "jasmine" is derived from the Persian "yasmin," which means "fragrant flower." The waxy flowers are esteemed in perfumery for their exotic, intensely floral aroma.*

The essential oil

*The **flowers** are too delicate to be steam-distilled, so solvent extraction is used to create a thick orange–brown oil known as an absolute.*

Fresh and floral, the sweet aroma of jasmine is instantly uplifting.

In full flower, the prolific blossoms of the jasmine plant exude a heavenly aroma.

MASSAGE OIL   DIFFUSER   COMPRESS

Juniper

Juniper

Juniperus communis

A distinctive, crisp-smelling oil that stimulates and **strengthens** the nerves and **bolsters spirits**. It has a mild diuretic effect that helps relieve water retention, a **warming** action that **soothes** aching muscles and joints, and a toning and **balancing** effect on the skin.

What is it **good for?**

Tones skin and hair Juniper oil is stimulating, astringent, and detoxifying. It helps unblock pores, and balances oily skin and skin prone to blackheads and acne. Diluted, it can be applied to eczema and psoriasis, and in a hair rinse it helps treat dandruff.

Aids detox Juniper's purifying action reduces water retention. As a diuretic, it helps to dispel toxins, making it useful for gout, rheumatism, and arthritis.

Treats urinary infections A few drops in a warm, shallow bath can ease symptoms of cystitis. Try as a massage or compress on the lower back to ease kidney stone discomfort.

Eases aches and pains Juniper essential oil soothes rheumatic and arthritic pain. Its tonic effect helps regulate the menstrual cycle and can ease cramps.

Relieves varicose veins Its gentle astringent action can help to shrink varicose veins and hemorrhoids.

Relieves anxiety Juniper eases tension and mental exhaustion. It is reputed to dispel negative emotions such as insecurity, loneliness, and guilt.

Best **uses**

As a massage oil Add to a base oil: one of the best ways to enjoy the full range of juniper oil's holistic benefits.

In a room freshener Add 2–3 drops to a diffuser or spray to clear stale air.

In a compress In a cool compress the oil can soothe skin eruptions.

Safe usage Nontoxic, nonirritant in dilution.

The plant

Evergreen juniper trees produce seed cones called berries. While oil can be distilled from the needles and twigs, the sweetest oil comes from the berries.

The essential oil

Steam-distilled from the berries, the colorless or pale yellow oil has a fresh, warm, woody, herbaceous smell. If it smells like a cocktail, that's because the berries also flavor gin.

STEAM INHALATION   MASSAGE OIL

Bay laurel

Laurus nobilis

The same bay leaves that flavor cooking can, when distilled in an essential oil, produce a remedy that is **warming** and **pain relieving** and that can lift spirits and **relax** the mind. The oil is an effective **antiseptic**, especially useful in the cold and flu season.

What is it **good for?**

Soothes aches and pains With a mild analgesic action, bay laurel can relieve sore muscles and lower backaches and bring relief to tension headaches and migraines.

Fights colds and flu An effective expectorant and decongestant, bay laurel essential oil is an excellent choice for treating congested lungs and blocked sinuses and for disinfecting sickrooms.

Acts as a sedative Try putting a drop or two of the essential oil on your pillow or a tissue before bedtime to promote relaxation and aid a restful night's sleep.

Enhances well-being Bay laurel has long been associated with peace, wisdom, and inner confidence, and is thought to help you to maintain courage and focus when dealing with challenges in life.

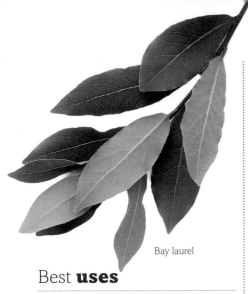

Bay laurel

Best **uses**

In an inhalation Add to a steam inhalation to ease sinus congestion, ease breathing, and soothe coughs.

Massage Dilute 1–2 drops of the oil in a teaspoon of base oil and massage into the temples to relieve headaches.

Safe usage *Use well diluted (less than 0.5 percent). Not suitable for hypersensitive skin or for children under seven years old.*

The plant

The tree, *with its familiar deep green, swordlike leaves, originates from Asia Minor, but is established throughout the Mediterranean. Both the fruit and leaves are used medicinally and as food flavorings.*

The essential oil

The leaves are steam-distilled *to produce a clear oil with a spicy, floral aroma, popular in colognes and aftershaves.*

BATH OIL   MASSAGE OIL

Lavender

Lavandula angustifolia

A versatile and popular essential oil, lavender has a **calming** fragrance and is particularly renowned for its ability to relax and promote restful sleep. Its **rejuvenating** and **soothing** effects make it an effective skin treatment and a good skin healer.

What is it **good for?**

Soothes skin Lavender oil has a softening and conditioning effect on the skin. Try adding to creams, base oils, and bath preparations.

Heals skin Lavender is regenerative, making it useful for wounds and mouth ulcers. Applied neat, the oil makes an effective first-aid remedy for cuts, burns, bites, and stings. Its healing effects can ease acne, eczema, acne rosacea, and psoriasis, and reduce scarring.

Promotes restful sleep Deeply relaxing, lavender helps reduce stress levels and anxiety and is a popular remedy for promoting restful sleep.

Acts as a pain reliever Mild analgesic properties make lavender a good treatment for headaches and migraines, as well as muscular and nerve pain. As an antispasmodic, it eases menstrual cramps.

Acts as an antiseptic It keeps wounds, ulcers, and sores clean. In a shallow bath, its antibacterial and anti-inflammatory properties make it excellent for infections such as cystitis.

Freshens the air It makes an ideal deodorizing and antiseptic room spray.

Best **uses**

As a bath oil Combine with a base oil or 2 tablespoons of milk and disperse in a relaxing bedtime bath.

As a massage oil In an oil blend, it is restorative and de-stressing.

Safe usage *Nontoxic and nonirritant. Can be used neat on small areas.*

The plant

Lavandula augustifolia *is commonly used for essential oils.* ***Lavandin*** *or spike lavender is a hybrid with a medicinal aroma and antiseptic and tonic properties.*

The essential oil

Colorless *or pale yellow, lavender oil has a floral, slightly harsh, sweet aroma. Some oils have synthetic compounds. Check the label for the name Lavandula angustifolia.*

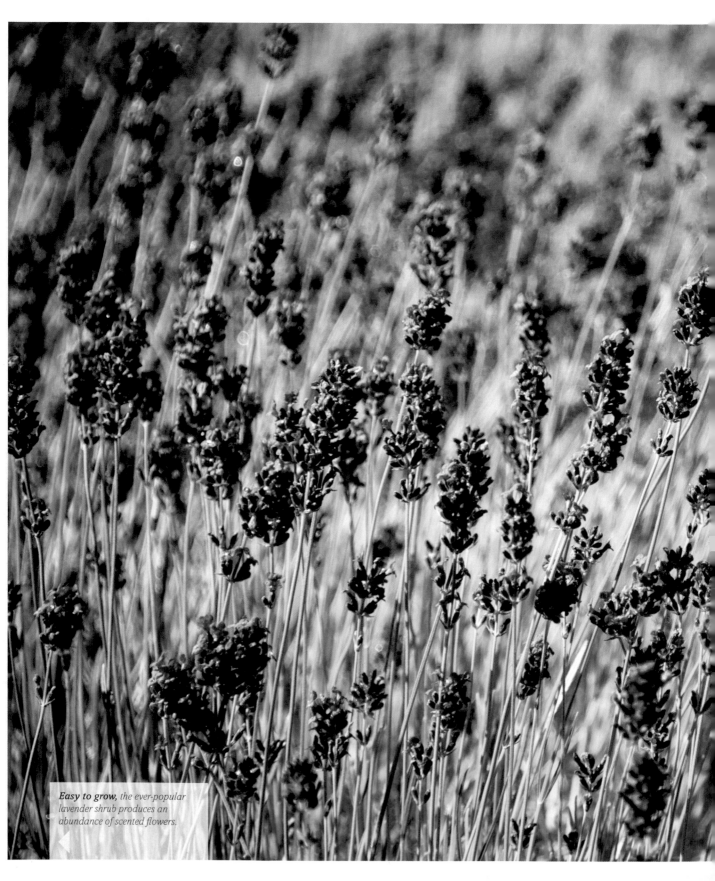

Easy to grow, the ever-popular
lavender shrub produces an
abundance of scented flowers.

HAIR CARE   FIRST AID

Manuka

Leptospermum scoparium

Strongly **antiseptic**, manuka is ideal for use on cuts and wounds. It also contains a natural **antihistamine** that can bring welcome relief to hay fever sufferers. A sharp, **earthy aroma** clears the mind and dispels anxious or angry feelings.

What is it **good for?**

Heals skin The powerful antiseptic action of manuka speeds the healing of cuts and abrasions, as well as insect bites and stings. The oil is also strongly antifungal and can be added to ointments to treat athlete's foot, and to hair rinses to treat dandruff.

Fights colds and flu Added to a steam inhalation, manuka oil's antibacterial action makes it a good remedy for colds and coughs.

Acts as a deodorant Well diluted, manuka can control perspiration and the bacteria that cause body odor.

Soothes aches and pains An anti-inflammatory, the oil relieves joint and muscle pain and stomach cramps.

Soothes allergies Manuka contains a natural antihistamine that can calm reactions to pollen, dust, and irritants of the respiratory tract and the skin.

Enhances well-being If you suffer from anxiety or feelings of anger, use the oil to ground yourself, promote calm and relaxation, and help clear emotional and mental blockages.

Best **uses**

In a hair rinse Add a few drops to warm water and use as a final rinse to balance excessively dry or oily hair.

As first aid A powerful antiseptic, a few drops in an ointment help to kill bacteria and speed healing of cuts.

Safe usage Nontoxic, nonirritant in dilution.

The plant

Manuka is a shrubby tree, native to New Zealand. Its copious pink, dark-red or white flowers attract the bees, but it's the understated leaves that produce the aromatic essential oil.

The essential oil

Steam-distilled from the leaves and twigs, the yellow to light brown oil has a sharp, earthy aroma with honeylike and herbaceous undertones.

Vividly colored, the flowers of the manuka plant are irresistible to honeybees.

MASSAGE OIL   SKIN CARE

Litsea

Litsea cubeba

Also known as May Chang, litsea is a warming, refreshing, uplifting oil that helps to calm and **soothe** frayed nerves. Its antiseptic and **skin-balancing** properties are particularly valued in skincare preparations.

What is it **good for?**

Tones skin Astringent and anti-inflammatory, litsea helps control acne and assists healing in existing breakouts, and also balances oily and combination skins.

Aids digestion The oil stimulates digestion and eases nausea. A good remedy for those with a poor appetite.

Acts as a deodorant In a body spray or footbath, the oil helps control perspiration and the bacteria that lead to body odor.

Relieves stress Litsea helps lift depression and calm the rapid heartbeat that comes with panic or stress, enabling you to think more constructively about a situation.

Soothes aches and pains The oil has a warming effect that boosts circulation and reduces inflammation in sore, tired muscles.

Best **uses**

As a massage oil A gentle massage with a litsea oil blend leaves you feeling warm, relaxed, calm, and balanced.

As a toner Add to a toner to leave skin feeling clean and refreshed.

Safe usage *Use well diluted (less than 0.5 percent). Not suitable for children under seven years old or for hypersensitive skin.*

The plant

Litsea is also *called mountain, or Chinese, pepper, because its berries resemble peppercorns. All the parts of the plant contain oil, but it is the hard berries that yield the highest quality. In spite of its lemony scent, it is a relative of cinnamon and other fragrant members of the laurel family.*

The essential oil

The fruit *is steam-distilled to produce a yellow oil with a complex and refined lemony scent.*

BATH OIL   MASSAGE OIL   COMPRESS   SKIN CARE

Chamomile (blue)

Matricaria recutita

Popular as a herbal tea, chamomile essential oil makes an effective skin treatment thanks to its **calming** and **toning** properties. It has a strong **anti-inflammatory** action that penetrates the skin's layers to **soothe** and repair, useful for skin conditions such as eczema and for healing.

What is it **good for?**

Soothes skin A deeply soothing and calming oil, chamomile has anti-inflammatory properties that make it ideal for treating allergic skin conditions and sensitive skin and scalps. It helps to relieve the itchy, inflamed skin caused by rashes, cracked nipples, and conditions such as chicken pox. Its efficacy in treating eczema rivals treatments such as hydrocortisone.

Heals and cleanses skin A repairing oil, chamomile helps heal scratches and wounds, and also has been shown to promote faster tissue regeneration than corticosteroids. Its mildy astringent properties help to clean blocked pores.

Acts as a mild pain reliever The anti-inflammatories present in chamomile, bisabolol and apigenin, work in a similar way to analgesics such as ibuprofen, providing effective mild pain relief and helping ease conditions such as arthritis.

Soothes digestion Chamomile is a natural soother and a popular remedy for calming digestive upsets. It can be used to treat a range of digestive complaints such as indigestion, peptic ulcers, and bouts of colic.

Strengthens immunity Use chamomile as a first line of defense against viruses and infection. It boosts immunity by stimulating leucocyte (white blood cell) production.

Promotes restful sleep Chamomile helps to calm irritability, nervousness, and tension headaches, helping promote relaxation and sleep.

Best **uses**

As a bath oil Mix with 1 tablespoon of milk to disperse the oil in a bath. The heat and fragrant steam can relax muscles and help calm anxiety.

In a massage oil A gentle massage with a chamomile oil blend helps ease insomnia, back pain, stomach upsets, and menstrual pain, boosts immunity, and lifts depression.

In a compress Add a few drops of chamomile essential oil to a wet, wrung-out cloth to make a cool compress that can help heal sores and calm allergic skin reactions.

In a skin cream Add a few drops to a cream base for a healing skin cream.

Safe usage Nontoxic, nonirritant in dilution.

The plant

Also known as German chamomile, the plant, which has delicate feathery leaves and simple daisy-like white flowers on single stems, is cultivated widely throughout northern and Central Europe.

Roman Chamomile (Anthemis nobilis) is a milder, sweeter oil with similar anti-inflammatory properties that is particularly suitable for infants and children.

The essential oil

A deep ink-blue viscous liquid, the oil is steam-distilled from the flowers. The heavy, herbaceous sweet smell has a fruity note. Roman chamomile makes a paler oil.

Also known as "scented mayweed," chamomile's dainty flowers blossom throughout the summer.

FIRST AID   FOOTBATH

Tea Tree

Melaleuca alternifolia

Best known for its powerful **antiseptic** properties, tea tree essential oil is great to keep in your first-aid kit, ready to use on wounds and sores. Studies show it is effective against a range of bacteria and fungi that can lead to infection. It also has a strong **deodorizing** action that can combat body odor.

A PERFECT BLEND

Try blending tea tree with clove, eucalyptus, lavender, lemon, pine, rosemary, or thyme essential oils.

What is it **good for?**

Boosts immunity Tea tree has immune-stimulating properties that help the body fight off infection. A massage with a tea tree blend can aid recovery during convalescence.

Fights skin infections The oil acts as a barrier against bacteria, viruses, and fungi. It can be added to an ointment to treat athlete's foot and ringworm, or can be dabbed on neat to cold sores, warts, and plantar warts.

Heals cuts, scrapes, and bruises Tea tree promotes the formation of scar tissue to aid healing.

Helps to control acne A popular ingredient in skin remedies, the oil can be applied to pimples as an immediate treatment.

Acts as a hair tonic A tea tree scalp massage can help bring dandruff under control, and used in a rinse, tea tree can restore the balance of oils to combat oily hair.

Mouth and gum care Use well diluted to treat bad breath, mouth ulcers, and gum infections.

Fights body odor A natural deodorizer, tea tree can be added to baths, body sprays, or creams to combat body or foot odor.

Fights cold and flu symptoms This antiseptic is effective in warding off colds and flu. Once a cold has set in, a steam inhalation with the oil eases congestion and breathing.

Eases urinary-tract infections Tea tree can help to fight cystitis and other genital infections, including yeast, herpes, warts, pruritus, and trichomonas.

Best **uses**

As first aid Use tea tree essential oil in a dilution of 10 percent (1 part tea tree to 10 parts witch hazel) to rinse and clean infected cuts and sores.

In a footbath For tired, hot, smelly feet, or for athlete's foot, add 20 drops of tea tree oil to a small basin of warm water and soak feet for 15 minutes. Dry thoroughly.

Safe usage Nonirritant in dilutions of less than 10 percent. Nontoxic externally.

The plant

A hardy tree, native to New South Wales in Australia, tea tree was an important medicine in Aboriginal tribes. Similar to the cypress in appearance, it has needlelike leaves with white flower heads.

Two close relatives also produce essential oils: niaouli, also native to Australia, is primarily used to treat skin complaints and respiratory illnesses, and cajuput, native to Indonesia and the Philippines, is used to treat respiratory conditions.

The essential oil

Steam-distilled from the leaves of the tree, the essential oil is a clear liquid with a medicinal scent reminiscent of eucalyptus.

The branches of the tea tree *have an abundance of feathery, brush-like white flowers.*

This healing essential oil, commonly used for its antiseptic effect, has a distinctive medicinal scent.

MASSAGE OIL   DIFFUSER

Cajeput

Melaleuca cajeputi

A PERFECT BLEND

Good blending partners for cajeput include angelica, bergamot, geranium, lavender, clary sage, geranium, pine, rosemary, and ylang-ylang.

A member of the tea tree family, cajeput has a **milder** and less overpowering aroma, but many of the same benefits. Its **antiseptic** properties are useful for fighting respiratory and urinary-tract infections, and, as a natural **pain reliever**, it can ease headaches and muscle and joint pain.

What is it **good for?**

Acts as an antiseptic Its broad antiseptic properties make cajeput useful for fighting cold and flu viruses, bacterial urinary tract infections, and fungal infections, such as athlete's foot. Diluted, the oil can also be applied to cuts and wounds to keep these clean and infection free.

Acts as a decongestant Cajeput makes an excellent decongestant and expectorant that helps to clear blocked sinuses and congested lungs.

Acts as a pain reliever Cajeput has soothing analgesic properties that can provide local pain relief from tension headaches and muscle and joint aches and pains.

Tones skin The oil helps to brighten oily or combination skin and keeps the bacteria that cause acne at bay.

Aids detox By promoting sweating, cajeput aids the removal of toxins from the body and also provides a pleasant cooling sensation that is especially helpful for soothing fevers.

Aids focus Cajeput helps to clear the mind and to fight mental exhaustion and apathy.

Best **uses**

In a massage oil Dilute cajeput essential oil in a massage oil blend and massage into achy, painful areas.

In a diffuser Add a few drops of the oil to a diffuser, vaporizer, or oil burner to relieve sinusitis and a blocked nose and to clear germs in the air. Or add a few drops to a steam inhalation.

Safe usage Nonirritant, nontoxic externally. Avoid use near the nose of children under seven years old.

The plant

Also called white tea tree, cajeput is a native of Malaysia now found throughout Southeast Asia and parts of Australia. From the Malaysian "kayu-puti" (white wood), its name describes its white bark. The oil is concentrated in its pointed leaves.

The essential oil

The clear to pale yellow essential oil is steam-distilled from the fresh leaves and twigs. Cajeput has a penetrating, slightly sweet aroma with hints of camphor.

This relatively mild oil has many therapeutic benefits.

BATH OIL · FIRST AID · MASSAGE OIL · STEAM INHALATION

Niaouli

Melaleuca viridiflora, M. quinquenervia

Chiefly a **disinfectant** and astringent, niaouli helps to fight a range of infections. **Stimulating** the body and mind, it increases concentration, clears the head, and lifts the spirits. Think of niaouli as a gentler version of tea tree—suitable even for sensitive skin.

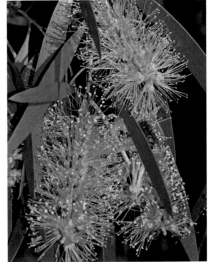

A large evergreen, niaouli has clusters of yellow flowers amid distinctive pointed leaves.

What is it **good for?**

Heals wounds Niaouli's disinfectant properties make it valuable for cleaning wounds, cuts, and applying to ulcers. Use it to help calm acne and balance oily skin.

Reduces the appearance of scars Niaouli encourages tissue regeneration, which in turn helps to minimize the appearance of scars, including the marks left by acne, pimples, or chickenpox.

Fights cold and flu symptoms A decongestant and expectorant, the oil helps to break up congestion in the lungs, bronchi, and nasal passages. Its antiviral and immune-boosting properties make it an important oil in the treatment of colds and flu.

Aids detox Niaouli stimulates the release of digestive juices as well as the circulation of blood and lymph, aiding the absorption of nutrients and encouraging the healthy excretion of waste and toxins.

Acts as a pain reliever An effective analgesic, niaouli can provide localized pain relief by numbing sensitive areas. It's useful for headaches, migraines, muscle and joint pain, and pain due to sprains.

Aids focus The sharp aroma of niaouli essential oil clears unwanted thoughts from the mind and enhances focus. This quality makes it a useful aid to meditation and helpful for concentration.

Best **uses**

As a bath oil If you feel as though you might be coming down with a cold, add a few drops to a bath oil blend to help fight the infection.

As first aid Dilute a few drops in a glassful of water and use as an antiseptic wash for cuts and other minor skin irritations.

In a massage oil Add to a base oil and use for an all-over body massage to strengthen the whole body, or use specifically, for example to help fight an infection, relieve pain, or stimulate a sluggish circulation.

In a steam inhalation Add 2–3 drops to a steam inhalation (or add to a diffuser or vaporizer) and inhale for several minutes to help you fight cold and flu symptoms, bronchitis, whooping cough, sinusitis, mucus, and other respiratory conditions.

Safe usage Nontoxic and nonirritant.

The plant

A popular tree for planting on streets and in parks, naiouli has fluffy spikes of flowers and a papery bark that periodically peels. It is native to New Caledonia, Papua New Guinea, and Australia and belongs to the same family as tea tree and cajeput.

The essential oil

Niaouli oil is extracted from the young leaves and twigs by steam distillation. It has a mildly sweet, fresh, camphorous smell and its color varies from clear to a pale yellow-green hue.

SKIN CARE   MASSAGE OIL

Lemon Balm

Melissa officinalis

Lemon balm, also known as melissa, is often added to **skin-care** products because of its calming, **anti-inflammatory** action on irritated skin. Its antiseptic effect makes it useful to have on hand for treating bee and wasp stings, and its cheerful **"feel-good"** aroma ensures it is a popular choice in aromatherapy.

What is it **good for?**

Soothes skin Lemon balm helps to calm inflamed skin and allergic skin conditions. It can be used, well diluted, to treat skin ulcers and eczema, especially when stress related, and to reduce redness and irritation from insect bites and stings, and sunburns.

Tones skin With a stimulating action on the circulation, the oil brightens dull-looking complexions and has a tightening and toning effect on the skin. Lemon balm is exceptionally high in the antioxidants that help fight aging caused by free radical damage.

Heals skin This antibacterial oil can be useful for treating acne and other skin eruptions such as cold sores.

Relieves headaches Uplifting and soothing, lemon balm can be a useful remedy for headaches and migraines, especially when a headache is associated with stress and held-in tension in the neck and shoulders.

Acts as an antiseptic Lemon balm has an antiviral action that works on the cold-sore virus. If used at the first sign of a cold sore, it can limit its impact.

Aids digestion Added to a gentle abdominal massage blend, the essential oil can help relieve gas, colic, and dyspepsia, and is also useful for treating feelings of nausea.

Eases breathing Lemon balm has a mild antihistamine effect, helpful for hay fever and asthma. It also calms anxiety-induced respiratory problems.

Reduces anxiety A sedative action makes lemon balm especially useful in cases of panic. It can calm a racing heartbeat and help lower blood pressure. The oil makes a soothing massage when you feel overwhelmed.

Cools fevers A cooling action makes lemon balm useful for relieving heat exhaustion and soothing fevers.

Best **uses**

As a skin toner To tone skin, add 20 drops of lemon balm to 1 tablespoon witch hazel or 1 teaspoon glycerine. Add to 3 tablespoons water and put in a spray bottle for a cooling spray.

In a massage oil Use 2–3 drops in 1 tablespoon base oil for a massage oil that counters the effects of overindulgence, such as indigestion, trapped gas, and nausea.

Safe usage *Nontoxic externally. Sensitization possible. Use well diluted (less than 1 percent).*

The plant

A native of Central and southern Europe, lemon balm is a member of the mint family. Its leaves are a similar shape to mint, but when you rub them between your fingers, they release a tart sweet smell, like lemons.

The essential oil

This pale yellow oil with a pleasant lemony, fresh, sweet, and herbaceous smell can be steam-distilled from the fresh leaves and flowers. Because the plant yields very little oil, lemon balm is often adulterated with other lemon-scented essential oils. Pure lemon balm oil is very expensive.

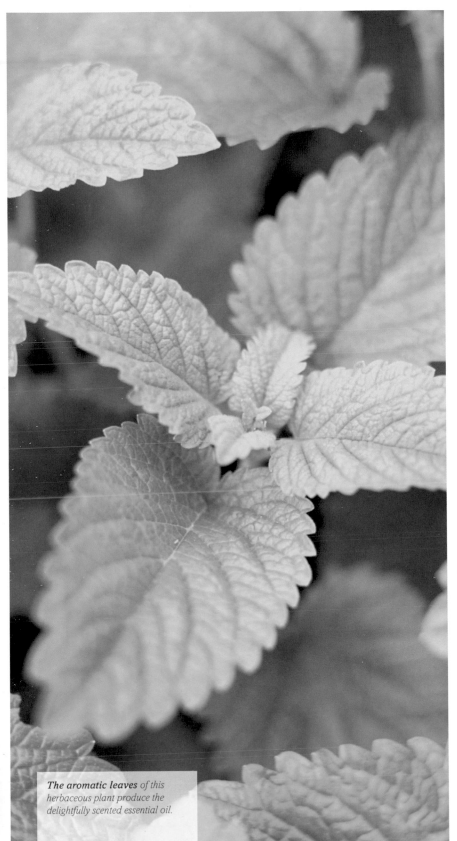

The aromatic leaves of this herbaceous plant produce the delightfully scented essential oil.

A calming oil, lemon balm is helpful for soothing insect bites or patches of irritated skin.

MASSAGE OIL   STEAM INHALATION

Peppermint

Mentha piperita

Applied to the skin, peppermint feels initially cooling and **refreshing**, then gently warming. Its **stimulating** and analgesic properties make it an effective remedy for neuralgia and muscular pains and headaches. It's also a high-quality **antiseptic**, and a popular addition to all types of beauty products.

A PERFECT BLEND

Try blending peppermint essential oil with eucalyptus, lavender, lemon, pine, or rosemary essential oils.

What is it **good for?**

Fights odor Peppermint is an effective body deodorant. Used in toothpaste, mouthwash, and other dental preparations, its antiseptic and deodorizing properties can also help combat bad breath.

Soothes skin Diluted peppermint oil has cooling and toning effects on the skin and can be particularly soothing for skin that is irritated after excessive exposure to the elements. It can also be used to relieve hives and other allergic skin reactions.

Acts as an antiseptic Its antiseptic and antiviral properties make this a useful oil for treating cold sores, even for resistant strains of the herpes virus that causes them, and for products such as lip balms and hand creams.

Eases digestive upsets A stomach massage with a peppermint blend can ease indigestion and flatulence, calm nausea and motion sickness, and improve a sluggish digestion.

Fights cold symptoms The oil acts as an expectorant to help alleviate coughs and clear sinuses.

Soothes bites and stings Peppermint essential oil makes an effective insect repellent, and it can also be used to help soothe mosquito bites and other skin irritations.

Relieves headaches Peppermint oil has long been recognized as a safe and effective treatment for tension headaches.

Best **uses**

In a massage oil Add 1–2 drops of peppermint essential oil to 1 tablespoon base oil and gently massage the abdomen in a clockwise motion to help bring relief to symptoms of indigestion, constipation, and nausea.

In an inhalation Add 3–4 drops of peppermint essential oil to a steam inhalation (not suitable for children or those suffering with asthma) or to a diffuser or vaporizer and use as a decongestant to help clear sinuses and congested lungs.

Safe usage Use well diluted (less than 2 percent). Avoid use in cardiac fibrillation and near the nose in children under seven years old.

The plant

This popular herb is actually a hybrid of Mentha aquatica (water mint) and Mentha spicata (spearmint). It has been used as a medicinal herb for thousands of years, particularly as an infusion for digestive disorders, though in modern times it is mostly used in the flavoring and toothpaste industries. The essential oil is extracted from the flowering herb.

The essential oil

Peppermint essential oil is steam-distilled from the flowering herb. The thin, almost watery oil has a fresh, sharp, strongly menthol aroma with a sweet-smelling undertone and it is a clear to pale yellow in color.

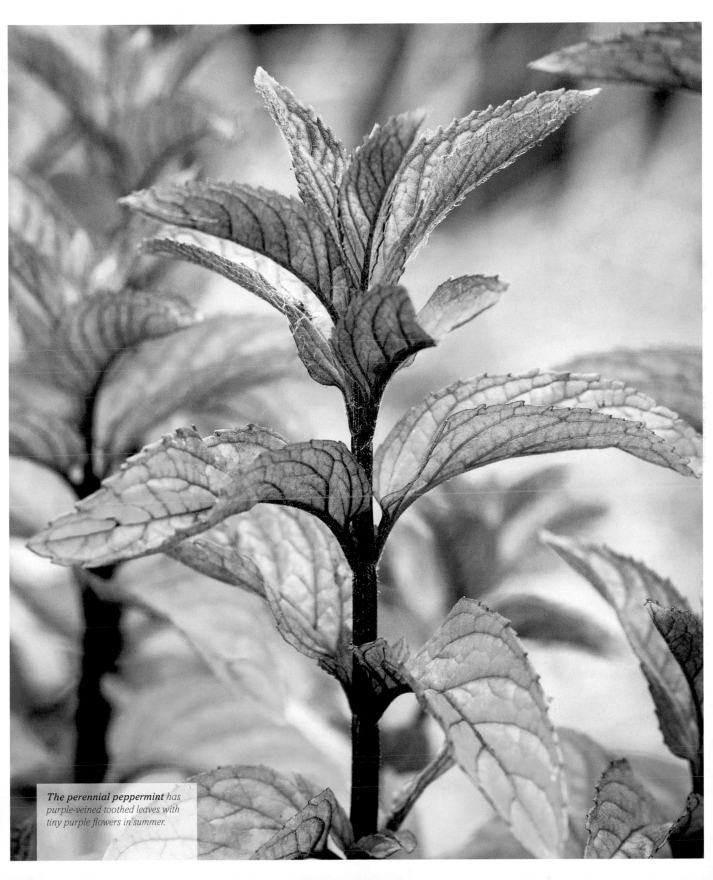

*The **perennial peppermint** has purple-veined toothed leaves with tiny purple flowers in summer.*

MOUTHWASH   BATH OIL

Nutmeg
Myristica fragrans

This **warming** oil with anti-inflammatory properties is useful for relieving muscle and joint pain. It helps **balance** the nervous system, **stimulating** or **calming** as needed, and also has a **detox** action that can improve digestion.

What is it **good for?**

Tooth and gum health Used well diluted as a mouthwash, nutmeg oil has an antiseptic and deodorant action that attacks the bacteria that cause bad breath and tooth decay.

Eases aches and pains A warming massage with a nutmeg oil blend can relieve inflammation and muscle pain, and boost circulation. Its mild analgesic action gives localized pain relief.

Aids sleep A well-known sedative, nutmeg helps relieve stress and can improve the quality of sleep.

Enhances well-being When suffering from anxiety or exhaustion, nutmeg can lift the spirits and help you regain focus.

Eases digestion Nutmeg stimulates appetite and digestion, reducing gas and soothing upsets.

Best **uses**

In a mouthwash Dilute 2—3 drops in 1 teaspoon glycerin or calendula tincture and add to half a glassful of lukewarm water. Do not swallow.

As a bath oil Add 5–6 drops to a base oil or 1 tablespoon of milk and disperse in a bath to relieve muscle aches and indigestion, and aid sleep.

Safe usage *Use well diluted (less than 1 percent).*

The plant

A native of the Banda Islands of Indonesia, the evergreen nutmeg tree produces a fruit similar to a peach. This fruit is the source of two spices: nutmeg and mace. Nutmeg (the spice and oil) comes from the seed itself, while mace comes from the covering of the seed.

The essential oil

Nutmeg essential oil is obtained by steam distilling the dried seeds of the nutmeg. This produces a clear oil with a sharp, spicy, musky aroma. West Indian nutmeg is milder and more suitable for aromatherapy than East Indian.

DIFFUSER

Myrtle

Myrtus communis

Myrtle oil gained its popularity because of its **antimicrobial,** astringent, antiseptic, anti-inflammatory, expectorant, decongestant, and **stimulant** properties. Today, the oil is commonly used for skin health and respiratory ailments.

What is it **good for?**

Tones skin Its astringent properties work on oily skin, open pores, and sagging skin, as well as on spider veins and hemorrhoids.

Relieves congestion A mild expectorant, myrtle can ease asthma, coughs, and bronchitis. Its anti-inflammatory properties also calm respiratory inflammation caused by allergic reactions.

Acts as an antiseptic The oil can be applied to wounds, pimples, and boils, and has been shown to inhibit the growth of several types of bacteria including *Escherichia coli, Staphylococcus aureus, Bacillus subtilis, Salmonella,* and *Listeria.*

Acts as a mild sedative Myrtle calms nerves and its sedative action can relieve depression and insomnia.

Supports the thyroid Myrtle's balancing action helps it to regulate over- and under-active thyroid glands.

Acts as an insect repellent Used in a room spray or diffuser, the oil can help to ward off insects.

Best **uses**

In a diffuser Add 4–5 drops to a diffuser, vaporizer, or oil burner (or add to a steam inhalation) to help clear sinus congestion.

Safe usage Use well diluted (less than 1.5 percent).

The plant

Myrtle is an evergreen shrub with fragrant white or pink flowers. Native to North Africa, it is commonly found in the southern Mediterranean region. It belongs to the same plant family as tea tree and eucalyptus, and has similar medicinal characteristics.

The essential oil

Myrtle oil is steam-distilled from the leaves. It is a pale yellow to green oil with a stimulating, slightly camphorous aroma somewhere between eucalyptus and frankincense.

The glossy evergreen myrtle produces delicate white flowers and sprays of purple berries.

COMPRESS   DIFFUSER

BATH OIL   MASSAGE OIL

Basil

Ocimum basilicum

The name basil comes from the Greek word **"basilikon phuton"** meaning "king." Basil is highly valued in traditional Ayurvedic medicine as a protector of both mental and physical **well-being.** Its crisp aroma clears and refreshes the mind and helps **calm** anxiety.

What is it **good for?**

Enhances well-being Basil balances, revives, and strengthens to combat exhaustion, anxiety, or depression.

Tones and balances skin The oil refreshes skin and helps to control acne.

Supports women's health Basil can help stimulate light or delayed periods caused by debility and stress.

Eases digestion Soothing basil can relieve indigestion. Its antiseptic action also helps treat intestinal infections.

Fights cold symptoms The oil helps clear sinuses and soothe coughs.

Eases aches and pains Basil can ease gout and rheumatic pain.

Acts as an insect repellent Its insecticidal properties repel insects. It also relieves the irritation of insect bites.

Best **uses**

In a compress Add a few drops to warm water and make a compress with a cloth to ease pain and congestion.

In a diffuser Add 3–4 drops to a diffuser, vaporizer, or oil burner to clear headaches and refresh the mind.

Safe usage Potentially toxic over time. Dilute extremely well (less than 0.5 percent) and do not use for prolonged periods. Avoid in pregnancy, when breast-feeding, and in children under 15 years old.

The plant

***Originally from tropical Asia** and the Pacific Islands, basil is now cultivated worldwide. The flowers range from white to pink in color, and are popular with bees and other garden pollinators.*

The essential oil

***The oil is steam-distilled** from the leaves and the flowering tops of the plant. It has a sweet, spicy, fresh and slightly balsamic scent, and is clear to pale yellow in color.*

Marjoram

Origanum majorana

This aromatic, **warming,** and **relaxing** oil is known for its ability to aid digestion and relieve stomach and menstrual cramping. It has a gently **sedative** effect that can lower blood pressure and heart rate, ease anxiety, and promote restful sleep.

What is it **good for?**

Relieves anxiety A gentle sedative, the oil can treat nervous tension, anxiety, panic attacks, and insomnia.

Improves circulation The oil has a toning effect on circulation that makes it useful for treating high blood pressure.

Eases cold and flu symptoms The oil's warming decongestant action can fight off chills and help clear sinus and lung congestion.

Acts as a pain reliever The oil's analgesic action can ease tension headaches and migraines. Massage into muscles, joints, and tender areas for local relief from muscle pains, sprains, strains, rheumatism, and arthritis.

Supports women's health Its warming action relieves menstrual pain and premenstrual symptoms such as anxiety, weariness, and irritability.

Eases digestion
Its stimulating effect supports healthy digestion. An antispasmodic action relieves gas and reflux.

Best **uses**

As a bath oil Add 15 drops to 1 tablespoon base oil or 1 tablespoon of milk for a reviving soak.

In a massage oil For abdominal pain, add 20 drops to 2 tablespoons of base oil and massage the abdomen in a clockwise direction.

Safe usage *Nontoxic, nonirritant in dilution.*

The plant

Mediterranean sweet marjoram *has a long history of use as a medicinal herb.*

Spanish marjoram (Thymus masticina) has some similar properties, but is a harsher oil that should be avioded in children under seven years old.

The essential oil

The essential oil*, steam-distilled from the dried flowering herb, is a pale yellow or pale amber hue with a warm, spicy, slightly camphorous smell.*

HAND WASH   DIFFUSER

Oregano

Origanum vulgare

Prized for centuries for its **healing** qualities, oregano has a powerful **antibacterial** action. The essential oil is traditionally used to treat complaints as diverse as indigestion and diarrhea, insect bites, earaches, rheumatism, and coughs.

What is it **good for?**

Has an antibacterial action
Oregano contains compounds that have been shown to inhibit the growth of bacteria such as *Pseudomonas aeruginosa* and *Staphylococcus aureus*. The oil can also help to relieve urinary tract infections.

Helps fight fungal infections
The essential oil has been shown to inhibit the growth of *Candida albicans*, the fungus that causes oral yeast, canker sores, skin rashes, and athlete's foot, and also inhibits the fungi that cause nail infections.

Relieves menstrual cramps Its analgesic action can ease menstrual cramps and other abdominal pains.

Clears sinuses A few drops of the oil on a tissue or in a steam inhalation can help to clear blocked sinuses and loosen phlegm.

Best **uses**

As an antibacterial wash Add 8–10 drops to an unscented liquid soap for an antibacterial hand wash.

In a diffuser Add 2–4 drops to a diffuser to ease congestion.

Safe usage *Dilute well before use (less than 1 percent). Avoid using in pregnancy, when breast-feeding, and in children under seven years old.*

The plant

A member of the mint family*, this aromatic, culinary herb, sometimes called wild marjoram, originates from hilly, Greek countryside, but is now grown around the world.*

The essential oil

The pale yellow oil *is produced by steam distillation of the fresh oregano leaves. It has a spicy, peppery aroma with a hint of camphor.*

BATH OIL   DIFFUSER

Geranium

Pelargonium graveolens

A **cheerful** oil, appreciated by both adults and children, geranium essential oil has a balancing, cooling, and **reviving** effect on skin, especially when it is weather-damaged or irritated. The oil is also a mild diuretic, making it a useful aid to **detox**, and it can help soothe urinary tract infections.

A PERFECT BLEND

Geranium essential oil blends well with bergamot, lavender, lemon, marjoram, neroli, orange, palmarosa, rose, and sandalwood oils.

What is it **good for?**

Aids detox The oil's gentle diuretic effect helps the body to eliminate excess water and reduce puffiness.

Balances emotions Both calming and uplifting, geranium makes a natural antidepressant. It can reduce restlessness and help treat anxiety in children and adults.

Acts as a pain reliever Geranium has mild analgesic properties that can relieve the pain of neuralgia and conditions such as shingles.

Tones the scalp Geranium oil helps to balance the secretion of sebum on the scalp, making it a useful treatment for flaky dandruff.

Tones skin This balancing oil is suitable for all skin types. Its antiseptic and anti-inflammatory properties help to control acne, and it is cooling for dry, inflamed skin. Its reviving effect helps to reduce the appearance of wrinkles, scars, and blemishes.

Supports women's health Geranium essential oil's cooling and balancing properties can help to relieve menopausal symptoms such as hot flashes and vaginal dryness. The oil can also soothe painful urinary-tract infections.

Best **uses**

As a bath oil To relieve cystitis or pruritus, add 5 drops of geranium and oil and disperse in a shallow bath.

In a diffuser To ease anxiety and lift the spirits, add 5 drops of geranium and 5 drops of orange to a diffuser, vaporizer, or oil burner.

Safe usage Nontoxic, nonirritant in dilution. Sensitization possible.

The plant

A native of South Africa originally, geranium is now grown mainly in Réunion, China, and Egypt. Of the 700 different varieties of the Pelargonium plant, only 10 can be used to make the essential oil. Plants are harvested shortly after flowering to capture the highest concentrations of the oil, which comes from the plant's leaves, and not from the flowers as many assume.

The essential oil

The green to amber-colored essential oil has a powerful, sweet, floral aroma with distinct minty undertones. Once the plant has been harvested, the oil is steam-distilled from the glands found in the leaves and from the green stems of the plant.

This balancing oil keeps emotions on an even keel.

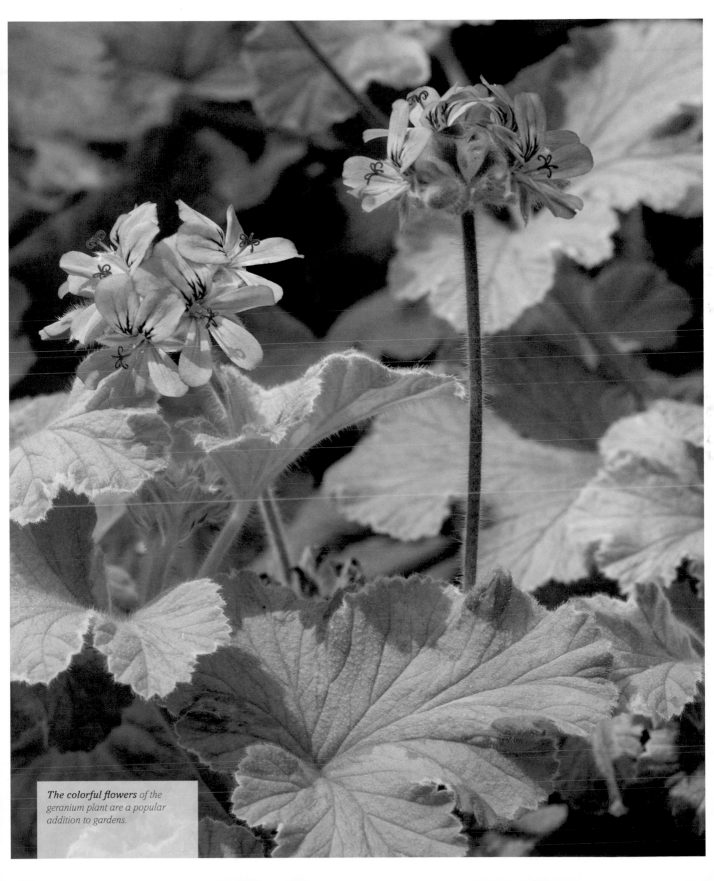

The colorful flowers of the geranium plant are a popular addition to gardens.

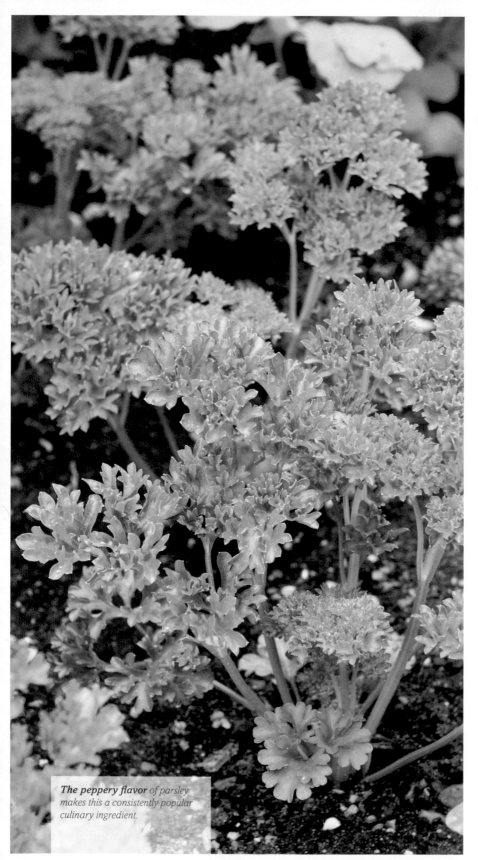

The peppery flavor of parsley makes this a consistently popular culinary ingredient.

This well-known herb has a multitude of therapeutic benefits that are present in its essential oil.

SKIN CARE   BATH OIL

Parsley seed

Petroselinum crispum

More than just a garnish on your plate, parsley produces an essential oil that is **antibacterial** and has valuable **detoxing** properties that can help to reduce water retention and strengthen digestion. Its **spicy** aroma is much prized as an ingredient in soaps and perfumes—in particular, men's colognes.

A PERFECT BLEND

Try blending parsley essential oil with clary sage, orange, rose, tea tree, or ylang-ylang essential oils.

What is it **good for?**

Boosts circulation The oil has a strengthening effect on blood vessels, making it useful for toning varicose veins and slowing down the spread of broken facial capillaries.

Tones skin Its antibacterial and antifungal properties help to treat pimples, acne, and skin infections, as well as disinfect pores.

Stimulates hair growth Diluted in a scalp massage, parsley essential oil encourages hair growth.

Has an antibacterial action Parsley oil helps to inhibit and kill microbes, protecting against various infections and diseases.

Acts as a pain reliever By helping to boost the circulation and in turn prevent the accumulation of uric acid in the muscles and joints, parsley can act as a mild analgesic for sufferers of arthritis and rheumatism.

Aids detox Parsley essential oil supports the healthy function of the kidneys and bladder. It has a diuretic action that can help to reduce fluid retention, and is also a mild laxative. It has an overall strengthening and tonic effect on the digestive system.

Aids digestion Like the fresh herb, the essential oil has carminative properties that can help relieve and treat indigestion, nausea, flatulence, vomiting, and stomach aches.

Calms the mind Parsley is a great de-stresser since it soothes the nerves and has a grounding and calming effect on the mind and emotions.

Enhances well-being The aromatherapeutic properties of parsley are purported to help strengthen confidence in overcoming difficulties and to enhance focus and provide a strong sense of purpose.

Best **uses**

As a facial elixir To help combat spider veins, mix 1 tablespoon base oil, 1 drop of parsley essential oil and 2 drops of rose essential oil. Massage very gently into the affected areas.

As a bath oil Add 6–9 drops of parsley essential oil to 1 tablespoon of base oil or 1 tablespoon milk, and add to a warm bath for a soothing soak.

Safe usage *Use well diluted (less than 1 percent). Avoid using during pregnancy and when breast-feeding.*

The plant

Parsley is native *to the Mediterranean region, but is now grown in gardens worldwide as a versatile culinary herb. The seeds contain most of the essential oil, although the entire plant can be used for making the oil.*

The essential oil

Parsley oil is *steam-distilled from the seeds of the plant. It is a colorless to pale yellow oil with a surprising sweet, warm, woody–spicy, herbaceous aroma.*

DIFFUSER   OINTMENT

Allspice
Pimenta dioica

A stimulating, potent, **spicy** oil that many associate more with cooking than spa days. Yet small amounts of allspice oil added to an aromatherapy blend help **relieve** muscle and menstrual cramps, and provide **warming** localized pain relief for sprains or strains.

What is it **good for?**

Acts as a pain reliever The oil has a local numbing effect that is useful for treating pain caused by neuralgia, muscular injuries, and joint strain, as well as pain from insect bites and stings.

Relieves muscle cramps Allspice has a warming, calming effect that soothes muscle cramps and spasms.

Acts as a mild sedative Its relaxing effect on the body and mind makes the oil useful for treating tension and anxiety. The oil's gently soothing action can help induce sleep.

Relieves indigestion Add to a massage oil blend to relieve indigestion, nausea, and trapped gas.

Eases cold symptoms Use in an inhalation to help relieve congestion.

Best **use**

In a diffuser Add 3–4 drops to a diffuser or vaporizer to ease anxiety.

As a rub A very small amount of the oil in a base oil or ointment can be used in a warming chest massage to help clear mucus, congested coughs, and bronchitis.

Safe usage *Nonirritant in dilution, sensitization possible. Potentially toxic with prolonged use. Dilute extremely well (less than 0.25 percent). Avoid in pregnancy, when breast-feeding, and in children under 15 years old.*

The plant

Native to the *Caribbean Islands and South America, the pimento tree produces small berrylike fruits, that are ground for use as a cooking spice. Both the leaves and berries are aromatic and are used to make the essential oil.*

The essential oil

Sometimes called pimento oil, *the light to pale brown oil is steam-distilled from the leaves and fruit. The oil's warm, spicy aroma is akin to that of clove and cinnamon essential oils.*

FRAGRANCE

Pine

Pinus sylvestris

Uplifting pine has a **warming** effect on sore joints and muscles, and its **clearing** action helps to unblock sinuses and **ease** breathing. The oil is valued by perfumers for the sweetness it adds to fragrance blends.

A PERFECT BLEND

Blends well with cedarwood, eucalyptus, lavender, lemon, rosemary, sage, and juniper.

What is it **good for?**

Eases breathing Decongesting and antiviral, pine oil protects against viruses, helps clear mucus, and eases hay-fever symptoms.

Acts as a pain reliever A warming oil, pine's analgesic and anti-inflammatory properties soothe muscle aches and painful joints. It can be applied locally to boost circulation to affected areas.

Acts as an antiseptic The oil can be used to treat infectious skin problems such as impetigo and boils.

Acts as an insect repellent Add a few drops to fabric or wood and put with clothes to protect from moths.

Supports urinary health The oil is effective for soothing cystitis, prostate problems, and urinary tract infections.

Enhances well-being A grounding oil, pine's aroma revitalizes mind and spirit, relieving exhaustion, tension, and other stress-related symptoms.

Freshens air Pine is ideal for clearing stale smells and eliminating odors.

Best **uses**

As an air freshener Add 20–30 drops to 2 fl oz (60 ml) each of vodka and water. Pour into a spray bottle and use to clear the air, avoiding furniture.

Safe usage Nontoxic, nonirritant in dilution. Make sure you use the variety Pinus sylvestris because other varieties may be toxic or irritant.

The plant

There are 90 species of pine tree. The essential oil comes from the Scots, or forest, pine, grown in Europe and Asia. Oil is distilled from the evergreen needles and twigs year-round.

The essential oil

The pale yellow oil is steam-distilled from the twigs and buds of the tree. It has the distinctive fresh, sweet, resinous aroma of a pine forest.

The distinctive blue–green needlelike leaves of the pine tree are unmistakable.

DIFFUSER   MASSAGE OIL

Black Pepper

Piper nigrum

A warming, spicy oil, black pepper has strong **antiseptic** properties. Its **stimulating** aroma has a clearing effect on the **mind,** making this a useful oil for improving **focus,** while its ability to boost circulation can **revive** tired muscles and joints and speed the healing of bruises.

A PERFECT BLEND

Black pepper blends well with bergamot, geranium, grapefruit, lemon, frankincense, sandalwood, ylang-ylang, rose, fennel, and lavender essential oils.

What is it **good for?**

Eases aches and pains Black pepper's main constituent, piperine, is an anti-inflammatory, which makes this essential oil a potent ingredient in ointments and salves for aching limbs and sore muscles. The oil also has a warming action that is effective for relieving sports injuries and improving muscle tone.

Stimulates circulation Black pepper essential oil helps to encourage circulation to the extremities, so use for cold hands and feet. Regular use may also help to improve the appearance of cellulite.

Aids detox The oil encourages perspiration and can be used in small doses to support the effective functioning of the lymphatic system. It also has a mild diuretic effect.

Boosts immunity If you are feeling run down, this essential oil is a good choice since it bolsters the body's defenses against infections.

Eases breathing A penetrating oil, black pepper can help loosen and clear congestion in the lungs.

Helps to quit smoking Studies have shown that inhaling black pepper vapors can help reduce cravings for cigarettes.

Enhances alertness The oil imbues a general feeling of warmth that can enhance the senses, and it also helps to clear the mind and bring a sense of clarity that can aid focus, motivation, and stamina, while combating mental fatigue.

Best **uses**

In a diffuser If your "can do" attitude is feeling a little worn out, add 3–4 drops of black pepper essential oil to a diffuser, vaporizer, or oil burner to improve motivation and help your levels of concentration.

In a massage oil For a general massage, black pepper essential oil is best used as part of an oil blend. To make a quick oil blend to reduce bruising and relieve sore muscles and joints, add 15 drops of black pepper oil to 1 tablespoon of base oil, and apply locally.

Safe usage Nontoxic, nonirritant in dilution.

The plant

Black peppercorns *are actually the dried fruits of a climbing vinelike shrub native to Indonesia, where the spice is still mainly cultivated today. Best known as a cooking spice, black pepper also has a long established history of use as a medicinal spice in India and China. Black pepper essential oil is valued by perfumers for adding a warming spicy note to perfume blends.*

The essential oil

The essential oil *of the black peppercorn is steam-distilled from the dried, crushed unripe fruit. The thinly textured oil is an amber to yellow–green color and has a distinctive pungent, spicy aroma that is both warming and fresh.*

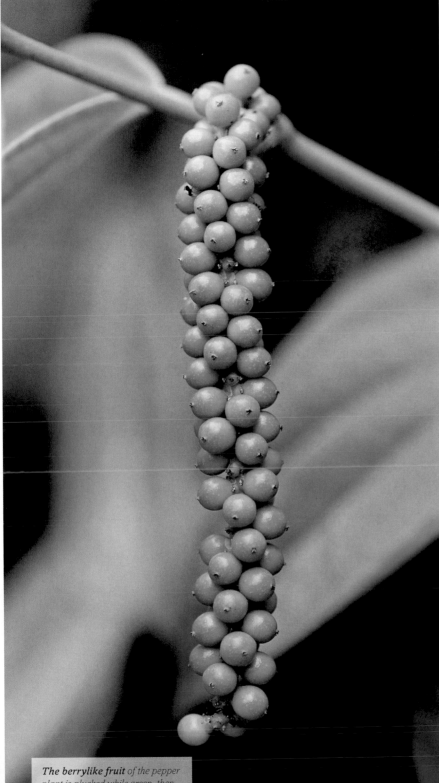

Soothing and warming, black pepper essential oil eases aches and pains and stimulates the circulation.

The berrylike fruit of the pepper plant is plucked while green, then dried to produce black peppercorns.

FRAGRANCE   MASSAGE OIL

The essential oil comes from the toothed leaves of the patchouli.

Patchouli
Pogostemon cablin

A tried and tested aromatherapy favorite, patchouli oil **soothes** and **heals** the skin, improving the appearance of scar tissue and stretch marks. It also **revitalizes** aging complexions, and its **antiseptic** properties help to treat pimple-prone skin.

What is it **good for?**

Repairs, tones, and cleanses skin Patchouli oil regenerates skin cells, helping scars and stretch marks to fade, and moisturizing dry skin. An astringent, the oil balances sebum secretions to normalize oily and acne-prone skin. It helps to control acne, and to treat sores and impetigo. Its antifungal action is useful for treating athlete's foot.

Repels insects The oil can ward off insects. Use undiluted on bites and stings.

Aids detox Patchouli oil has a diuretic effect, making it useful in anticellulite skin–care products and massage oils.

Enhances well-being The oil acts as an antidepressant, and is useful for treating exhaustion, stress, and anxiety. It's also used as an aphrodisiac.

Aids digestion Its balancing effect relieves diarrhea and constipation.

Best **uses**

As a perfume Patchouli and rose make a classic scent. Add 10 drops of patchouli and 20 drops of rose absolute to 2 tablespoons base oil or vodka.

In a massage oil Add patchouli oil to a base oil for an uplifting and relaxing massage that relieves tension and anxiety, and can also help to boost sluggish digestion.

Safe usage *Nontoxic, nonirritant in dilution.*

The plant

The patchouli bush, native to India and Malaysia, is called "puchaput." To produce the oil the leaves are lightly fermented or scalded to break the cell walls and release the aroma.

The essential oil

The leaves are steam-distilled to produce a pale yellow to pale green oil with a spicy, woody, musky scent prized by perfume makers. The smell is somewhat "love it or hate it," so it's best used in small amounts and in blends.

MASSAGE OIL   DIFFUSER

Tuberose

Polianthes tuberosa

Tuberose helps to **calm** the nervous system and is widely used to provide **relief** from depression, anger, nervous exhaustion, stress, and tension. The same calming and uplifting properties make it a natural **aphrodisiac** for both men and women.

What is it **good for?**

Acts as a mild sedative Calming on the nervous system, the oil acts like a sedative to help promote restful sleep.

Boosts circulation This warming oil can help to improve circulation and chase away winter chills.

Balances emotions Tuberose is a grounding oil. It increases emotional stamina, relieving stress, tension, anxiety, depression, and anger, and also inspires creativity and calm.

Acts as an aphrodisiac A relaxing oil, the heady, sensual aroma helps to release inhibitions and lift a low libido, especially when due to stress.

Combats body odor A strong, long-lasting, floral aroma combined with antibacterial properties helps to eliminate body odor.

Best **uses**

In a massage oil Make a warming massage oil by adding 5–10 drops of tuberose to 1 tablespoon base oil. Since it has a strong, heady aroma, a little goes far, so it's best to dilute well.

In a diffuser Spice up the atmosphere in a room by adding 3–4 drops of the oil to a diffuser, vaporizer, or oil burner.

Safe usage Use well diluted (less than 1 percent). Avoid use on hypersensitive skin and on children under seven years old.

The plant

The night-blooming tuberose is also known as the "Night Queen." It takes around 3000 lb (1550 kg) of handpicked flowers to extract 1 lb (0.5 kg) of the absolute oil. Tuberose is related to narcissus and jonquil and has distinctive tubular flowers.

The essential oil

The dark orange–brown viscous absolute is solvent-extracted from the flowers. It has a strong, spicy–sweet, creamy aroma.

The bright white blooms of the tuberose plant produce an intense, heady fragrance.

STEAM
INHALATION   OINTMENT

Ravensara, Ravintsara

Ravensara aromatica, Cinnamomum camphora

A warming, stimulating oil with **antiviral** and **antiseptic**
properties, this oil is a natural choice during the cold and flu season.
Confusion around the oil's source (see box, below), means the oil is now
commonly called ravintsara, though the name ravensara is still seen.

What is it **good for?**

Provides cold and flu relief
The oil's decongestant and antiviral
properties can ease cold and flu
symptoms such as coughs and
sinusitis, and cleanse air in sickrooms.

Combats viruses Its antiviral
properties are useful for treating cold
sores, shingles, and herpes.

Enhances well-being Stimulating
and reviving, the oil eases nervous
exhaustion and stress, and helps to lift
depression and negative thoughts.

Boosts immunity The essential
oil has immunostimulant properties,
which means it can help support
immunity, especially when defenses
are low due to stress and overwork.

Aids digestion Gently massaged
into the abdomen, the oil stimulates
digestion, while its antiseptic properties
make it a useful treatment for stomach
upsets and gastric viruses.

Relieves pain The oil has a relaxing
and analgesic action on aching
muscles and joints, and can be used
in a compress to soothe and treat
sprains and strains.

Best **uses**

In a steam inhalation To relieve
sinus or respiratory-tract infections,
add 3–4 drops to a bowl of hot water,
cover your head and the bowl with
a towel, and breathe deeply for 15
minutes. Blend with oils that have
similar decongestant properties,
such as eucalyptus, thyme, or pine.

As a cold-sore treatment The oil
can be used undiluted to treat cold sores.
Dab on with a cotton swab as needed.

Safe usage Nontoxic, nonirritant
in dilution.

The plant

There is confusion around this oil.
In the past, the name ravensara was
used for oil from the Agatophyllum
aromaticum tree. However, ravensara
is used in perfumery; the aromatherapy
oil ravintsara is from the leaf of a
variety of camphor tree in Madagascar.

The essential oil

The essential oil is steam-distilled
from the young, leafy twigs. It is a
thin, clear to yellow oil with
a camphorlike
aroma that is
somewhere
between lavender
and tea tree
essential oils.

*This immune-boosting oil offers
protection in the winter months.*

SKIN CARE   MASSAGE OIL

Rose

Rosa damascena, R. centifolia

Roses have been used as **medicinal** plants since antiquity, and are celebrated for their calming, **uplifting** aroma. The oil has a toning, **anti-inflammatory**, and **rejuvenating** effect, and its mild detoxifying and antiseptic properties can relieve pain and nausea.

A PERFECT BLEND

Try blending rose with bergamot, chamomile, clary sage, geranium, jasmine, lavender, or patchouli.

What is it **good for?**

Rejuvenates skin Rose oil supports cell and tissue regeneration, which helps maintain the skin's elasticity and reduce the appearance of fine lines. It makes an excellent choice for minimizing the appearance of broken capillaries on the skin.

Heals skin The oil helps to repair sun-damaged skin and damage from burns and scalds, as well as reduce the appearance of stretch marks. Its skin-calming and anti-inflammatory properties can soothe dry, hot, itchy skin.

Fights bacteria Rose oil has been shown to have antimicrobial properties. In one study, Damask rose demonstrated antibacterial activity against 15 strains of bacteria.

Enhances well-being The oil creates a sense of relaxed well-being and can help to increase feelings of vitality. This calming property makes it useful for taking the edge off stress-related conditions.

Supports women's health Rose oil has a toning effect on the uterus that can help to ease heavy, clotted, or painful periods. It is also used to limit the effects of, and provide relief from, premenstrual syndrome.

Relieves digestive discomfort A mild detoxifying and antiseptic effect, combined with nerve-soothing properties, help relieve stomach upsets, nausea, and constipation. The oil has a fortifying effect on the gallbladder and liver, supporting efficient digestion and absorption of nutrients.

Best **uses**

As a skin toner Make a toner by combining 2 tablespoons witch hazel and 4 tablespoons rose flower water with 4 drops of rose absolute. Put in a plain bottle or spray bottle and use as needed. Shake well before use.

As a massage oil Rose can relieve feelings of depression, anxiety, and grief. Try blending 4 drops of rose, 4 drops of geranium, and 6 drops of orange essential oils in 2 tablespoons base oil for an uplifting body massage.

Safe usage *Nonirritant. Absolute is nontoxic; use essential oil in dilutions of less than 1 percent due to its methyleugenol content.*

The plant

A popular garden shrub, roses are widely grown for their beauty and, with some species, for their fragrance.

The essential oil

When steam-distilled, the essential oil is known as rose otto, and is a clear or pale yellow oil with an intense floral aroma. Rose absolute is also available, which is somewhat less costly, and is an amber-colored, more viscous liquid.

The velvety, voluptuous rose has a soothing and uplifting aroma that is deeply relaxing.

SHOWER   MASSAGE OIL

Rosemary
Rosmarinus officinalis

Toning and **cleansing** rosemary oil helps to clear the mind. It contains potent **antibacterial** and antifungal substances that can fight infection, and has a warming **anti-inflammatory** action that helps relieve pain. Its **stimulating** effect on the lymphatic system aids detox and improves circulation.

A PERFECT BLEND

Try blending rosemary with essential oils such as basil, lavender, lemongrass, orange, lemon, peppermint, petitgrain, or pine.

What is it **good for?**

Helps fight germs Rosemary essential oil contains rosmarinic acid, which in addition to being anti-inflammatory, is also antiviral and antibacterial. This makes rosemary useful for fighting off respiratory infections and for using topically on skin infections. The oil can be dabbed undiluted on sores, bites, and scabies to reduce inflammation and aid healing.

Acts as a hair tonic The oil helps to stimulate the circulation, which in turn combats hair loss and dandruff.

Aids detox The oil stimulates both the circulatatory and lymphatic systems, aiding the removal of waste products and relieving water retention, which in turn helps fight cellulite.

Boosts circulation Rosemary is useful for treating low blood pressure and warming cold hands and feet. Its boost to circulation also brings some relief to sprains and strains, and soothes sore muscles after exercising.

Improves focus Rosemary essential oil stimulates the nervous system and increases circulation to the brain, which in turn helps to improve memory, concentration, and mental alertness. The oil has a reviving effect when you are feeling tired, debilitated, or lethargic, which also makes it an especially useful remedy for jet lag.

Relieves menstrual cramps The oil's warming and anti-inflammatory properties help to relieve painful period cramping.

Best **uses**

As a shower gel To revive both body and mind, try this postworkout scented shower gel. Add 55 drops rosemary, 30 drops of peppermint, and 40 drops of lemon essential oils to a 9 fl oz (250 ml) bottle of unscented shower gel, and enjoy a refreshing and stimulating shower.

In a massage oil Add 10 drops of the essential oil to 2 tablespoons of base oil to create a simple, warming, pain-relieving, and detoxifying massage oil.

Safe usage Nonirritant in dilution. Avoid use near the nose in children under seven years old.

The plant

Rosemary is a popular aromatic herb with silvery-green leaves and pale-blue flowers. The plant is a Mediterranean native and today is still produced mainly in France, Spain, Croatia, Tunisia, and Morocco. This ubiquitous herb has been used widely in food and medicine, and during religious ceremonies, for thousands of years.

The essential oil

The virtually colorless oil that is extracted from rosemary is steam-distilled from the fresh flowering tops of the herb. The essential oil has a pungent, fresh, and pleasant herbaceous aroma.

This refreshing and cleansing oil is a popular addition to hair treatments, adding shine to lackluster hair.

Rosemary has *highly fragrant, needle-shaped leaves with delicate lavender-blue to purple blooms.*

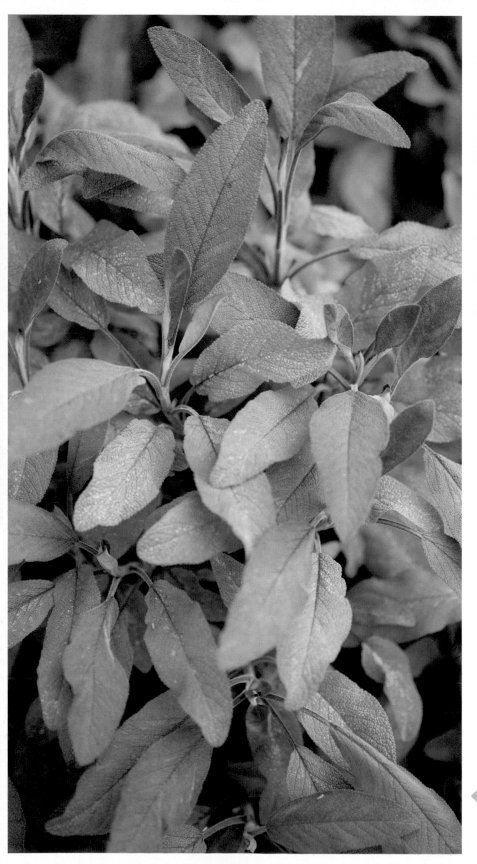

This warming, antibacterial oil has a potent effect and should be diluted well before use.

◀ **The finely veined, distinctive leaves** of this evergreen shrub are highly aromatic.

MOUTHWASH   FOOTBATH

Sage, Dalmatian

Salvia officinalis

An extremely stimulating oil, sage is primarily used as a warming oil that can help to relieve aching muscles. The oil also has an **astringent** quality that makes it a useful skin toner. Use it to **relieve** stress and improve mental **focus** when you are tired or under pressure.

What is it **good for?**

Acts as an antiseptic Sage essential oil has a particular affinity to the gums, and its antibacterial properties can help to eliminate the bacteria harbored in the mouth that cause bad breath and gum disease.

Brightens the complexion Sage has circulation-boosting properties that help to improve skin tone and minimize the appearance of open pores. Its antioxidant action reduces the harmful effects of free radicals, which can make skin look dull, so it can help brighten tired-looking complexions.

Acts as a hair and scalp tonic Sage has an effective antifungal action, and so is a useful oil to help control dandruff.

Calms nerves During periods of stress and exhaustion, sage can have a tonic effect on the nervous system. It revives and stimulates, bringing renewed vitality.

Acts as a deodorant Sage essential oil has a naturally deodorizing effect that can help to fight body and foot odor. It's useful for relieving excessive sweating, particularly during menopause.

Best **uses**

As a mouthwash Make an antiseptic mouthwash to treat inflamed gums or combat bad breath by adding 1 drop of sage essential oil to 1 teaspoon glycerine or calendula tincture, then dilute the mixture in half a glass of water. Rinse the mouthwash around the mouth and gums and then spit it out.

In a footbath To fight foot odor, add 4–5 drops of sage essential oil to a shallow basin of warm water. Soak the feet for 10–15 minutes, then dry the feet thoroughly.

Safe usage Use very well diluted (less than 0.5 percent). Avoid using during pregnancy and when breastfeeding, and avoid using on children under 15 years old. Toxic if ingested.

A PERFECT BLEND

Essential oil blending partners for sage include bergamot, lavender, lemon, and rosemary.

The plant

Another popular culinary herb, with an established history of medicinal use, the name "sage" is derived from the Latin word "salvare," which means "heal" or "save." The plant, which has silver-gray leaves and blue to purplish flowers, is a native of the Mediterranean region, but now grows throughout much of the world.

Spanish sage (Salvia lavandulifolia) is often preferable to use instead of Dalmatian sage since it is considerably less harsh, although it should still be avoided during pregnancy and when breastfeeding.

The essential oil

Steam-distillation of the dried leaves of the sage plant produces a thin, clear essential oil that has a sharp, slightly spicy, fresh, and herbaceous aroma.

BATH OIL MASSAGE OIL

Clary Sage
Salvia sclarea

Renowned for **uplifting** the mind and emotions, clary sage also has a **tonic** effect on many body systems, including the digestive and circulatory systems. It can **revive** tired muscles and relieve menstrual and labor pains, and is considered an **aphrodisiac**.

What is it **good for?**

Lifts mood Clary sage lifts depression and calms nerves, creating a sense of peace and, in some, euphoria. It is used to return vitality after an illness.

Relieves aches and pains A powerful muscle relaxant, clary sage can ease muscular aches and pains.

Aids digestion Massaged over the abdomen, the oil can aid digestion and relieve stomach upsets and gas.

Boosts circulation Its tonic effect is partly due to it boosting the circulation. It can help lower high blood pressure.

Supports women's health The oil can be used to treat symptoms of PMS, ease menstrual cramps, and relieve anxiety and hot flashes in menopause.

Acts as an aphrodisiac Clary sage can help restore libido and vitality.

Best **uses**

As a bath oil To relieve menstrual pain or stress, add 5–6 drops to a base oil or 1 tablespoon milk and disperse in a bath. Soak for at least 10 minutes.

In a massage oil Add 1–2 drops of clary sage and 2 drops of lavender oils to 1 tablespoon base oil for a massage to aid digestion and boost circulation.

Safe usage *Use very well diluted to avoid potential skin irritation (less than 0.5 percent). Avoid on hypersensitive skin and on children under seven years old.*

The plant

Related to sage, *but with tall, dramatic flower stems, clary sage is a native of southern Europe. The herb has long been prized as a medicinal plant and is also a popular ingredient in perfumes.*

The essential oil

The oil is a colorless *to pale green liquid with an herbaceous, sweet, slightly nutty aroma. It is steam-distilled from the flowering tops and leaves.*

The upright stems of clary sage carry a mass of delicate pink flowers.

DIFFUSER   FRAGRANCE

131

Sandalwood
Santalum album

Aromatic sandalwood has elegant, oval-shaped leaves.

Sandalwood has a long history in Ayurvedic and Chinese medicine. Its **anti-inflammatory** and antiseptic properties **revive** and **heal** dry and damaged skin. It has a **restorative** effect on mind and emotions, and calms respiratory conditions.

What is it **good for?**

Protects and balances skin The oil's anti-inflammatory and astringent effects help to balance skin. It treats oily skin effectively, while also soothing dry, itchy, or inflamed skin. It can reduce the appearance of scars and blemishes and soothe razor burn.

Restores vitality Sandalwood can dispel anxiety and lift depression, aiding sleep and helping to reignite a passion for life. The oil is considered an aphrodisiac, especially for men.

Acts as an antiseptic Its mild antiseptic action is used to ease the effects of genitourinary-tract infections.

Eases breathing Sandalwood has a cooling and anti-inflammatory effect on the mucous membranes and can help calm chronic coughs. A mild decongestant and antiseptic, it can help to treat bronchitis, laryngitis, and respiratory-tract infections.

Best **uses**

In a diffuser Add 3–4 drops to a diffuser or vaporizer to perfume air and promote a sense of calm.

As an aftershave balm For a reviving and calming aftershave balm, add 1 drop of sandalwood essential oil to 1 teaspoon almond base oil. Warm the oil between the palms and then use to soothe skin after shaving.

Safe usage Nontoxic, nonirritant in dilutions of less than 2 percent.

The plant

The sandalwood tree, a native of India, was for many years such a popular source of essential oil that it became seriously endangered. When buying the oil, it is important to check that it comes from a sustainable source.

The essential oil

The essential oil is steam-distilled from the heartwood of the tree. It is pale yellow to pale gold in color and has a subtle, sweet, and soothing woody aroma.

FIRST AID   MASSAGE OIL   STEAM
INHALATION

Summer Savory

Satureja hortensis

Because summer savory was once believed to be a powerful **aphrodisiac**, monks of the Benedictine order were banned from growing it in their gardens. Today it is recognized for its **calming** effect on the digestive system, helping to ease trapped gas. It is also helpful for **boosting strength and resolve** in times of stress.

What is it **good for?**

Helps fight infection Savory has antiseptic properties that help to combat the bacteria that can cause skin infections. This makes it a useful remedy for first-aid applications. Research has shown that savory essential oil can inhibit the growth of *Candida albicans*, the fungus responsible for athlete's foot and yeast.

Aids digestion The gentle aromatic, carminative, and digestive properties of savory essential oil make it a useful treatment for digestive problems such as flatulence, nausea, and diarrhea.

Relieves stress Savory essential oil has a bolstering effect when you are feeling stressed to the point of giving up. It also helps to motivate when you feel exhausted at the prospect of a difficult task.

Soothes sore throats Using the oil in a diffuser or steam inhalation helps ease coughs, colds, and sore throats.

Treats bites and stings Dab the diluted oil onto skin for instant relief from insect bites and stings.

Promotes hair growth Summer savory is a traditional remedy for encouraging hair growth. The diluted oil can be massaged into the scalp.

Best **uses**

For first aid Mix 3–4 drops of the essential oil in 1 tablespoon St. John's wort macerate or 2 tablespoons vodka and dab onto insect bites, or patches of athlete's foot or other fungal infections.

In a massage oil For a soothing massage after you've overindulged, mix 2–3 drops of the essential oil in 1 tablespoon base oil. Massage the abdominal area gently in a clockwise motion.

In an inhalation Add a few drops to a bowl of warm water and inhale to relieve congestion and cold symptoms.

Safe usage Use well diluted (less than 1.5 percent). Avoid using on hypersensitive skin and on children under seven years old.

The plant

The Saxons named savory after its spicy, pungent taste. A member of the mint family, summer savory is a Mediterranean native, with small leathery leaves and light purple flowers. It is widely used in cooking.

Winter savory (Satureja montana) is thought to have a stronger antiseptic action and aroma that makes it less popular in aromatherapy, but useful in small quantities to boost the medicinal properties of other oils.

The essential oil

Steam-distilled from the leaves and stems, the essential oil is pale yellow to pale orange with a spicy, herbaceous aroma.

With its tubular lilac flowers and elongated leaves, summer savory has a calming effect.

HAIR CARE

DIFFUSER

STEAM INHALATION

DIFFUSER   OINTMENT

Benzoin

Styrax benzoin

Benzoin, also known as gum benzoin, is a traditional ingredient in **incense**. Today the oil is added to skin creams for its antiseptic, **healing**, and **calming** properties. In scents, it is a popular fixative, slowing the evaporation of the perfume to help it last longer.

What is it **good for?**

Calms itchy skin Benzoin is an effective remedy for a range of dry, irritable, and itchy skin conditions, including sun- and wind-damaged skin and conditions such as eczema and psoriasis. The oil gives mature skin a boost by increasing elasticity.

Heals wounds The oil has useful antibacterial properties that help heal cuts and wounds. It can be used to treat acne and other skin eruptions.

Eases aches and pains Benzoin essential oil has a local stimulating effect that improves circulation. Used in a massage blend, it can help to loosen stiff muscles and relieve the soreness of arthritis and rheumatism.

Enhances well-being Soothing and warming, benzoin is known to have a calming effect on the mind and to help ease depression.

Best **uses**

For hair For an itchy scalp, add 5 drops to a mild, unscented shampoo.

In a diffuser Add to a diffuser, oil burner, or vaporizer to sweeten the air.

In an inhalation A steam inhalation helps clear congestion.

Safe usage Use well diluted (less than 2 percent). Avoid on hypersensitive skin; children under two.

The plant

This large tropical tree is native to Thailand and its adjacent islands. Benzoin resin is collected by making an incision in the trunk that allows the sap to escape. As it flows, the fresh gum is yellowish, but becomes a darker red–brown color as it dries.

The essential oil

Benzoin oil is golden brown with a sweet, vanillalike scent. Too thick and sticky to be used undiluted, it is sold as an oleoresin or tincture to be used like an essential oil.

Clove

Syzygium aromaticum
Eugenia caryophyllata

Clove yields a **warming** oil that can be used in small amounts to add **antiseptic** and **analgesic** properties. It is a useful mouthwash for oral infections, and its spicy aroma is comforting and relaxing.

What is it **good for?**

Cares for teeth and gums Widely used in both conventional and complementary dental health products, clove is both an antiseptic and anesthetic, helping fight the germs that cause bad breath and relieve swollen gums and toothaches.

Calms and treats skin Added to acne treatments, clove oil helps to reduce red, painful inflammation and kill the bacteria that causes acne. It can also be used to treat warts.

Clears congestion Expectorant properties make the oil useful for respiratory infections, such as coughs, colds, sinusitis, and asthma. As a room scent, it clears and disinfects the air.

Relieves anxiety Clove oil has a relaxing, comforting aroma that can reduce anxiety and enhance focus on the task at hand.

DIFFUSER   OINTMENT

Clove's tiny flower buds are picked before they open, then dried until they brown.

Soothes muscles Its warming effect loosens sore muscles and eases joints.

Best **uses**

In a diffuser Diffuse 2–3 drops to clear or disinfect air.

As a muscle rub Add 3 drops to 1 tablespoon base oil for a warm rub.

Safe usage Use very well diluted (less than 0.5 percent). Avoid on hypersensitive or damaged skin and on children under seven years old.

The plant

We tend to think of clove as a spice, but it is actually an herb derived from the dried flower buds of the tree.

The essential oil

The essential oil can be steam-distilled from the leaves, stems, and buds. This yields a clear to pale yellow liquid with a rich and appealing spicy aroma.

Tagetes

Tagetes erecta

Tagetes is traditionally used to treat infections and wounds, **repel** insects, and to clear congestion. The oil also has a **mild sedative** effect that **calms** anxiety and nerves. With its **uplifting** aroma, it is a popular perfumery ingredient, especially in men's fragrances.

What is it **good for?**

Heals wounds The oil has an antiseptic action that can help to treat infection in wounds, cuts, and abscesses, as well as fungal infections.

Relieves cramping Tagetes calms digestive irritation and inflammation and its antispasmodic action relieves menstrual and muscle cramps.

Clears congestion The oil helps to open up the bronchial passages and encourage the removal of phlegm from the sinuses and lungs.

Calms nerves With its mild sedative effect, tagetes eases anxiety, panic, and stress, lifts depression, dispels anger, and can induce relaxation.

Acts as an insect repellent The oil's insecticidal properties can help to repel flies and mosquitoes. Pop some in your bag for vacations.

This popular shrub is festooned with bright yellow and orange blooms in summer and fall.

Best **uses**

In a diffuser Add 3–4 drops to a diffuser, vaporizer, or oil burner to ease coughs, bronchitis, and chest infections, or to use as an insect repellent.

In an ointment To treat fungal infections, add 10–15 drops to an ointment base. Apply as needed.

Safe usage Use well diluted (less than 2 percent). Highly phototoxic even in low dilutions, so avoid on the skin for 24 hours before exposure to the sun.

The plant

Also called Southern marigold, this member of the marigold family, a popular border shrub, has bright yellow-orange flowers.

The essential oil

The essential oil is steam-distilled from the flowers. It has a golden color and an aromatic, earthy, floral aroma with hints of citrus.

BATH OIL   SKIN CARE

Thyme
Thymus vulgaris

A popular oil for baths and ointments, thyme **boosts** circulation and **relieves** tired and sore muscles and joints. The oil is an effective **antiseptic**, helping to clear up fungal infections, as well as fight colds and loosen stubborn phlegm. Its **stimulating** aroma can help clear and **refresh** the mind.

A PERFECT BLEND

Try blending thyme essential oil with bergamot, clove, eucalyptus, lavender, tangerine, lemon, or pine essential oils.

What is it **good for?**

Soothes coughs The antiseptic and antispasmodic properties of thyme essential oil make it a great remedy for easing the symptoms of colds, such as coughs and sore throats, and for soothing the symptoms of chronic bronchitis.

Fights fungal infections Try adding thyme essential oil to hair rinses, or massaging the diluted oil into the scalp, nails, or feet to help clear conditions such as dandruff and seborrheic dermatitis, athlete's foot, and fungal nail infections.

Eases aches and pains The oil has a warming effect that helps to loosen tight muscles and ease aching joints.

Helps clear acne Studies show that constituents in thyme can be more effective than benzoyl peroxide, the active ingredient in most acne creams or washes, at killing propionibacterium—the bacterium that causes acne.

Enhances well-being Thyme essential oil brings relief when you are feeling anxious, stressed, or low.

Treats urinary-tract infections Thyme essential oil's antiseptic and antifungal properties make this oil an ideal choice to help deal with uncomfortable urinary-tract infections, such as cystitis.

Improves circulation Thyme essential oil has a stimulating and general toning effect on the circulatory system, which makes it a useful treatment for low blood pressure, weakness, and anemia.

Best **uses**

As a bath oil Add 5–6 drops of thyme essential oil to 1 tablespoon base oil or 1 tablespoon of milk and disperse in a warm bath to help treat urinary-tract infections.

As a skin toner Try blending 2 drops each of thyme and mandarin essential oils in a base of 2 teaspoons aloe vera juice to 3 fl oz (90 ml) witch hazel. Shake the blend well and apply with a cotton ball, or pour the blend into a spray bottle and use as a refreshing facial spritzer.

Safe usage Use well diluted (less than 2 percent).

The plant

This is a low, creeping aromatic herb that is a member of the mint family. Thyme is native to the Mediterranean region, where it thrives in the hot, sunny locations and the well-drained soil. Thyme is widely used as both a culinary and medicinal herb.

The essential oil

The flowering tops and leaves of the popular herb, thyme, can be steam-distilled to create the essential oil. Several different chemotypes are used in the aromatherapy essential oil. Thyme linalol (Thymus vulgaris ct linalol) is more gentle and the most suitable essential oil for general aromatherapy use.

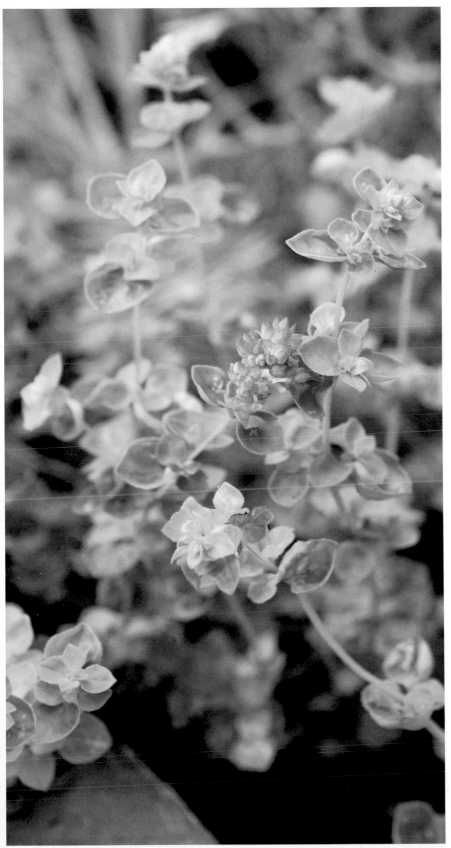

With its antiseptic properties, thyme essential oil is a useful oil for fighting winter colds.

◀ **This evergreen shrub** has tiny oval-shaped leaves with white or pink flowers in early summer.

SKIN CARE   MASSAGE OIL

Fenugreek

Trigonella foenumgraecum

Each fine stem *has a trio of oblong leaves.*

A well-known **digestive aid** and laxative, fenugreek also has a **relaxing** effect on the nerves and an **antiseptic** and expectorant action on respiratory infections. It **stimulates** the circulation and can treat bruises and swelling when applied to the skin.

What is it **good for?**

Clears and soothes skin The oil's antibacterial and antifungal properties help treat skin infections such as boils. It also has an anti-inflammatory quality that relieves itchy, dry skin conditions.

Aids relaxation The oil has a relaxing effect on the nerves that can soothe anxiety and help lower blood pressure.

Eases congestion Fenugreek acts as an expectorant and soothes and relaxes inflamed respiratory tissues.

Aids detox Its tonic and antioxidant properties encourage perspiration and boost the metabolism. A mild laxative, it helps the body to remove waste.

Aids digestion Fenugreek soothes digestive upsets and aids digestion.

Supports women's health The oil can help to ease menstrual pain, regulate cycles, and calm hot flashes.

Best **uses**

As a facial oil Add 4–6 drops of the oil to 1 tablespoon of a light base oil for use on inflamed or acne-prone skin.

In a massage oil Make a relaxing and skin-soothing massage blend by adding 15 drops of fenugreek essential oil to 1 tablespoon base oil. You can also use this to ease indigestion, gently massaging the oil into the abdomen in a clockwise motion.

Safe usage Nonirritant in dilution.

The plant

Native to the Middle and Near East, the spice is also known as methi. Fenugreek produces distinctive, triangular, oil-rich seeds. Its round leaves can be dried and used as herbs.

The essential oil

The essential oil is actually an absolute extracted from the seeds. This produces a yellow–brown waxy liquid with a potent, sweet–spicy, earthy scent.

BATH OIL   MASSAGE OIL

Valerian

Valeriana officinalis

The most widely used herbal **sedative**, valerian is a recognized treatment for **insomnia** and tension. Its other psychological benefits include **lifting depression** and anxiety. It can help regulate blood pressure, slow palpitations, and settle digestion.

139

What is it **good for?**

Promotes restful sleep A powerful sedative, valerian can treat insomnia and improve sleep quality.

Balances emotions The oil can help to soothe nerves, and calm anxiety, depression, and restlessness. A good treatment for stress and tension.

Lowers blood pressure Valerian can help to regulate blood pressure and calm a rapid heartbeat.

Aids detox The oil's mild laxative effect encourages healthy bowel movements, and its diuretic action promotes urination. It can also calm an upset stomach, especially when this is linked to stress, and aid the effective metabolism of nutrients.

Supports women's health Valerian soothes stomach cramps and can ease premenstrual tension.

Best **uses**

In a bath oil Add 2 drops each of rose, valerian, and sandalwood essential oils to 1 tablespoon base oil or 1 tablespoon milk and disperse in a bath.

In a massage oil Added to an oil blend, valerian essential oil can be used to help encourage a state of deep relaxation. Try blending 4 drops each of valerian, lavender, and cedarwood essential oils to 2 tablespoons base oil.

Safe usage *Nontoxic, nonirritant in dilution.*

The plant

Native to parts of Europe and Asia, *the plant has distinctive leathery leaves and clusters of pink or white flowers. The name valerian is derived from the Latin "valere," which means "to be well" or "to feel good."*

The essential oil

Steam-distilled from the root, *the yellow to yellow–green oil has an earthy, musky, woody aroma that can be overpowering. For the best effect, blend with softer, sweeter oils.*

In the summer, valerian has an abundance of sweetly scented delicate flower heads.

HAIR CARE   DIFFUSER

Vanilla

Vanilla planifolia

A relative newcomer to aromatherapy, vanilla is familiar to most as a flavoring for desserts and baked goods. Its **soothing** and softening properties can help **repair** rough or **damaged** skin. It is a mild **pain reliever** and has antiseptic properties.

The green vanilla pods are dried prior to use.

What is it **good for?**

Soothes dry skin Vanilla essential oil has skin- and hair-softening and soothing properties. It is also rich in antioxidants that can help protect the skin from the damage caused by environmental pollutants and toxins.

Acts as a pain reliever The main aromatic chemical in vanilla is vanillin, which has similar pain-relieving properties to the capsaicin found in chilli peppers. When vanilla oil is diluted, it can be used on the skin to provide temporary, localized relief from general aches and pains and from toothaches.

Helps relieve stress Vanilla can be used to help dispel general feelings of negativity as well as feelings of anxiety. This uplifting property is also thought to contribute to its aphrodisiac effect.

Helps to treat acne A mild antibacterial action enables vanilla essential oil to help fight the bacteria that cause acne and to reduce the occurrence of more minor pimples and blackheads.

Best **uses**

As a hair conditioner Add 10 drops of vanilla essential oil to 1 tablespoon coconut oil to make a hair mask that will condition and add shine to hair. Coat hair thoroughly and wrap in a towel for 10—15 minutes before shampooing and rinsing.

In a diffuser To help relieve stress and ease anxiety, add 1—2 drops of vanilla absolute to a diffuser, vaporizer, or oil burner.

Safe usage *Nontoxic and nonirritant..*

The plant

The vanilla bean is actually the fruit pod from a type of orchid. The green pods are dried slowly until they turn black. Once they start to curl, the pods are ready to use either as a culinary flavoring or to produce an essential oil absolute.

The essential oil

A thick, dark brown oil, vanilla absolute is solvent-extracted from the cured seedpods. Its familiar, sometimes overwhelming, scent, should be used sparingly in any blend.

With its strong scent, just small amounts of vanilla are needed.

BATH OIL DIFFUSER

Vetiver

Vetiveria zizanioides

Working mostly on an emotional level, vetiver has a profoundly **grounding** effect for those who are distressed or panicky. The essential oil can help to improve circulation and is a useful **antiseptic** and **astringent** in the treatment of oily and combination skin.

A PERFECT BLEND

Vetiver blends well with clary sage, cedarwood, jasmine, lavender, patchouli, rose, ginger, ylang-ylang, and citrus oils.

What is it **good for?**

Soothes sore muscles Vetiver oil makes a warming and pain-relieving remedy for muscular aches and pains, sprains, general stiffness, and for rheumatism and arthritis.

Helps heal wounds Its antiseptic and slightly astringent properties make this oil a good treatment for cuts, scrapes, wounds, and sores.

Helps fade scars and marks By promoting skin healing and the growth of new tissue, vetiver is ideal for reducing the appearance of stretch marks, scars, and burns.

Has a cooling action Add vetiver to a cold compress to cool fever and sunstroke, and soothe headaches.

Promotes emotional balance Vetiver is grounding and calming when you are feeling emotionally overwhelmed, weepy, under pressure, and uncertain which direction to take. It can help relieve distress, anger, and hysteria in both adults and children.

Acts as an aphrodisiac Vetiver is thought to enhance libido and is often used to awaken sexual desire in men and women, especially when libido has been dampened by overwork and mental fatigue.

Promotes restful sleep A natural sedative, the oil is often used to promote relaxation and restful sleep.

Best **uses**

As a bath oil Make a relaxing bath oil by mixing 4–6 drops in 1 tablespoon base oil or 1 tablespoon of milk. Disperse in a warm bath and have a quiet soak for at least 15 minutes.

In a diffuser Promote a peaceful, grounding atmosphere in your home or office by adding 3–4 drops of the essential oil to a diffuser, vaporizer, or oil burner.

Safe usage *Nontoxic, nonirritant in dilution.*

The plant

A tall perennial grass *native to India, vetiver is a relative of other fragrant grasses such as citronella, lemongrass, and palmarosa. Roots over 24 months old have the highest oil content, but take longer to distill, making this an expensive oil.*

The essential oil

The oil is steam-distilled *from the chopped up rootlets, which are soaked in water prior to distillation. The resulting oil is a thick, dark-amber liquid with a spicy, earthy fragrance that has a hint of lemon.*

STEAM
INHALATION

SKIN CARE

Violet

Viola odorata

Violet is renowned for its **relaxing,** soothing, and inspiring properties. It is a traditional remedy for calming irritations to the respiratory tract, **rejuvenating** mature or weather-damaged skin, and **soothing** sensitive skin conditions. Its elegant floral aroma is **calming** on the mind and emotions.

A
PERFECT
BLEND

Ideal blending partners for violet essential oil include tuberose, clary sage, lavender, benzoin, cumin, basil, sandalwood, geranium, and citrus essential oils.

What is it **good for?**

Soothes dry skin Violet essential oil has a gentle and reviving effect on the skin and is well known for its ability to help hydrate and soothe dry and sun- or wind-damaged skin. It is used to help minimize the appearance of spider veins and enlarged pores.

Acts as a pain reliever The oil contains anti-inflammatory compounds that can relieve pain and inflammation in muscles and joints; applied locally, it can encourage circulation to an affected area. It can also provide relief for headaches and migraines.

Helps treat anxiety The oil is comforting and calming when you are feeling nervous, anxious, or exhausted. This grounding effect can also help to ease feelings of dizziness brought on by anxiety and stress.

Eases congestion Violet has expectorant properties that help shift phlegm and relieve the pressure caused by blocked sinuses.

Best **uses**

As an inhalation Make a steam inhalation by adding 5—6 drops of violet essential oil to a bowl of hot water. Place a towel over your head and inhale deeply to loosen mucus or relieve anxiety. This is also an effective way to condition and cleanse the skin.

As a facial elixir Make a quick, but luxurious, facial oil by adding 2 drops of violet absolute and carrot seed oil absolute to 1 tablespoon rosehip seed oil.

Safe usage Nontoxic, nonirritant in dilution.

The plant

The essential oil of violet is an absolute, concentrated in the downy, heart-shaped leaves rather than in the purple flowers. It takes around 2,200 lb (1,000 kg) of violet leaves to produce just 2¼ lb (1 kg) of the absolute, which is why true violet absolute is so expensive, and mostly used in high-end perfume products.

The essential oil

The absolute essential oil of violet is solvent-extracted from the crushed leaves of the plant. This process produces a thick oil that is a green to brown color. It has an earthy aroma with intense, elegant floral notes that make it a valuable ingredient in perfumes.

The heart-shaped or oval petals of the violet are a welcome sign that spring is on its way.

COMPRESS

DIFFUSER

Plai

Zingiber cassumunar, Z. montanum

Although plai is related to ginger, it is a **cooling,** rather than a warming, oil, making it ideal for feverish conditions and inflammation. It has a general **tonic** effect on the body and is highly valued for its ability to **relieve** the pain of arthritis and rheumatism and even postoperative pain. Plai is also a traditional Thai treatment for stretch marks.

A PERFECT BLEND

Plai essential oil blends well with marjoram, black pepper, helichrysum, rosemary, cypress, lavender, and neroli essential oils.

What is it **good for?**

Acts as an antihistamine With its cooling, anti-inflammatory action, plai makes a natural antihistamine that can be helpful for managing conditions such as hay fever. Its soothing action has the potential to reduce the severity of asthma attacks in some individuals, where it can be used as a complementary treatment alongside prescribed medication.

Acts as a pain reliever Plai essential oil is a popular analgesic that helps to ease many types of pain, including pain caused by injury, strained muscles, arthritis, and rheumatism. Some evidence suggests it may help relieve postoperative pain and inflammation.

Fades scars and stretch marks In Thailand, plai is a traditional remedy used to reduce the appearance of stretch marks and scars.

Relieves abdominal cramps Plai essential oil has antispasmodic and analgesic properties that can help to relieve menstrual cramping as well as the pain that is caused by irritable bowel syndrome.

Best **uses**

As a compress To help soothe and relieve sprains and strains, add 4–5 drops of plai essential oil to a shallow bowl of cool water, then soak a small, clean cloth in the mixture, wring it out well, and apply the cloth to the affected area.

In a diffuser To relieve the misery of hay fever and help reduce the severity of asthma attacks, try adding 3–4 drops of plai essential oil to a diffuser, vaporizer, or oil burner to disperse in a room.

Safe usage Nontoxic, nonirritant in dilution.

The plant

The therapeutic properties of the plai plant are concentrated in its distinctive root. It is also an ornamental plant with its distinctive blade-shaped leaves and brightly colored "pseudostem" that resembles a pinecone.

The essential oil

Steam-distilled from the fresh roots of the plai plant, the colorless to pale yellow oil has an uplifting herbaceous, spicy aroma with hints of eucalyptus.

MOUTHWASH   MASSAGE OIL

Ginger

Zingiber officinale

Ginger has a *distinctive knobby appearance.*

Most of us know ginger as the remedy of choice for reviving and **relieving** the nausea that often accompanies pregnancy or motion sickness. In addition, it is also a useful **antiseptic** in cases of cold or flu, and it has an **analgesic** property that can help to ease tension headaches and muscular pain.

What is it **good for?**

Eases digestion Ginger has a wonderfully calming effect on the digestive system, helping to soothe unsettled digestion caused by stress or overindulgence. It also relieves pregnancy-related nausea and nausea caused by motion sickness or the side effects of medication.

Revives a tired mind Comforting and warming, ginger essential oil helps to lift feelings of general fatigue and is also reviving when you are suffering from nervous fatigue or mental confusion.

Helps to combat colds Antiseptic and pain relieving, ginger essential oil can help to ward off cold viruses, and once a cold has set in, it can soothe the pain and discomfort of sore throats, and ease congestion.

Relieves muscle pain Applied locally, ginger oil boosts circulation and provides warmth that revives and eases the pain of sore, tired muscles.

Relieves headaches Its anti-inflammatory and analgesic properties make ginger a natural choice for relieving headaches and migraines.

Best **uses**

For a gargle Add 2 drops of ginger essential oil to 1 teaspoon vodka and dilute in a small glassful of hot water. When sufficiently cooled, use as a gargle to treat sore throats.

In a massage oil For quick relief from headaches, migraines, and/or nausea, blend 2 drops of ginger essential oil with 1 teaspoon base oil. Massage gently into the temples and pulse points as needed.

Safe usage *Nontoxic, nonirritant in dilution.*

The plant

The ginger plant *produces a distinctive, knobby root that has been used as a culinary and medicinal ingredient for thousands of years, especially by the Chinese. Its enduring popularity is testament to the plant's therapeutic healing properties and its widespread culinary appeal.*

The essential oil

Ginger essential oil *is steam-distilled from the fleshy root of the ginger plant. The oil can vary in color from pale yellow to dark amber and has a warm, spicy, woody scent with a hint of lemon and pepper.*

Naturally soothing, ginger is the go-to remedy for digestive upsets.

Base Oils

Base, or carrier, oils provide a medium for **diluting and dispersing** concentrated essential oils, which can otherwise irritate skin. Derived from **vegetable, nut, or seed sources**, or made by macerating an **herb in a plant** oil, base oils have their own benefits.

Argan
Argania spinosa

Argan oil comes from a tree found growing only in Morocco. High levels of antioxidant **vitamin E** and essential fatty acids make it a soothing oil for all skin types, and good for hair and nails. It is **moisturizing** and protective against environmental factors, such as weather and pollutants.

The kernels *of Moroccan argan fruit produce the rich, skin-nourishing, golden-yellow oil.*

Argan oil *has a characteristic nutty aroma.*

What is it **good for?**

Makes a useful moisturizer A nongreasy, dry oil that can be used under makeup during the day and for skin repair at night, argan can minimize the appearance of scars and stretch marks and help to soften sun- or wind-damaged skin. Apply sparingly to lips before bedtime to aid healing and repair skin overnight.

Acts as a hand conditioner Warm a few drops of the oil in the palms, then massage well into the hands, taking extra time to work into the nails and cuticles.

Conditions hair For damaged or dry hair, argan oil conditions and restores shine. Use as a prewash deep treatment, or rub a few drops into newly washed hair for light control of frizziness.

Tones skin With regular use, the oil helps to balance oily skin and reduce inflammation around pimples and acne.

Borage
Borago officinalis

Pressed from the seeds of the borage, or starflower, plant, adding this oil to your base oil blend will have a **beneficial effect** on mature, damaged, **sensitive skin** or skin prone to breakouts due to hormonal fluctuations.

Borage seeds *are mainly grown commercially for their oil.*

This pale yellow, *almost odorless, oil has strong anti-inflammatory properties.*

What is it **good for?**

Rejuvenates skin Borage is a great choice for mature or damaged skin. It contains the fatty acid gamma linolenic acid (GLA), which helps to tone and rejuvenate skin. It has a hydrating effect and is regenerating, increasing skin-cell strength and improving elasticity.

Reduces inflammation Its anti-inflammatory properties make borage a good choice for skin prone to eczema, psoriasis, seborrheic dermatitis, and breakouts due to hormonal fluctuations.

Keeps nails healthy Use the oil regularly on nails to maintain strength and keep cuticles healthy.

Enriches skin Just a small amount of this oil enriches a base oil blend. In blends and serums, borage is used at 2–10 percent of the total base oil mix.

The borage herb *is native to the Mediterranean region.*

Canola

Brassica napus

Also known as rapeseed oil, canola has the benefits of being **widely available**, relatively **inexpensive**, and effective on dry, sensitive, or mature skin. However, it's often genetically modified and highly processed, so choose organic brands.

After harvesting, the seeds are crushed for the oil.

This golden oil is virtually odorless so works well in aromatherapy blends.

What is it **good for?**

Moisturizes skin Light and easily absorbed, canola helps maintain the moisture balance of dry skin.

It is a widely available base oil You don't need to go to a special store to find canola. Good, food-quality canola is available in the supermarket. Canola is also very stable so keeps for a long time.

Provides a neutral base The oil is largely odorless, so works well with

From the brassica family, canola has delicate yellow blooms.

most blends. Enrich it by adding avocado, borage, or rosehip seed oil, or enhance its skin-soothing properties by adding a healing macerate such as calendula or St. John's wort.

Safe usage *Ideally, choose organic oil to avoid possible pesticide residues that can be present in some genetically modified organisms (GMOs).*

Shea Butter

Butyrospermum parkii

Extracted from the nuts of African karite trees, shea butter has a long history in cooking, but has more recently found its way into cosmetic formulations where its thick, **waxy texture** acts like an **emulsifier** and provides **skin-enriching** properties.

Shea butter ranges from bright yellow in its raw state to white.

The oil has a nutty, sweet aroma. The less odor and color, the more refined it is.

What is it **good for?**

Repairs damaged skin Rich in fatty acids, antioxidant carotenoids, and vitamin E, shea butter helps to improve the condition of dry and mature skin and soothes eczema, psoriasis, skin allergies, and blemishes. It can also be used to treat dry, itchy scalp conditions.

Hydrates skin The fatty acids in shea butter are a good match for those in human skin. By helping to form a thin protective layer on the

skin, the oil helps prevent moisture loss and encourages healing of chapped lips. It also helps to soften cracked, dry skin on heels, elbows, and knees.

Can be used as a shaving balm Adding shea butter to shaving cream formulations helps to achieve a smoother shave.

Calendula Macerated Oil

Calendula officinalis

Calendula macerated oil is made by infusing calendula flowers into an oil such as sunflower. The result is a **rich** herbal oil with recognized **healing** properties. Calendula is especially popular for sensitive and dry skin due to its ability to **soothe** irritated skin quickly and **repair** skin tissue.

The dried flowers can be be used in infusions.

This macerated oil, made from the fresh flowers, is a rich golden color.

What is it **good for?**

Repairs skin Calendula is mildly antiseptic, so it can help ulcers, skin eruptions, cuts, and dermatitis to heal more quickly.

Can be used as after-sun skin care Calendula oil helps to condition and restore skin, and reduces inflammation after sun exposure.

Acts as a healing massage oil Calendula makes a good choice when a large area of skin requires attention since the oil spreads more easily over a large surface area than a cream-based product does.

Can be used for first aid Hypercal cream, which is a mainstay of most natural first-aid kits, is a mixture of hypericum (St. John's wort) and calendula. If you are making a skin salve or ointment, add calendula macerate to help speed healing time.

Coconut

Cocos nucifera

This is a light, **moisturizing**, and **nourishing** semisolid that quickly melts at body temperature. Coconut oil is suitable for all skin and hair types, but is especially beneficial for dry skin and hair. Raw, unrefined, unbleached organic coconut oil is best and adds a **pleasant aroma** to blends.

White coconut oil is a good base for essential oils

Coconut oil is a semisolid that melts at body temerpature to produce a liquid that can be used in aromatherapy blends.

What is it **good for?**

Conditions hair Coconut oil helps combat dandruff and can restore luster and shine to dry or damaged hair. Use the oil as a preshampoo conditioner or, for deeper conditioning, leave in overnight and wash the oil out in the morning.

Acts as a makeup remover Warm a little bit of coconut oil between the palms, then gently massage over the face and use a tissue or a damp washcloth to remove makeup.

Heals rough, irritated skin The oil has an anti-inflammatory effect that can help to heal wounds, blisters, and rashes and to soothe razor burn after shaving. Use in place of mineral oil for chapped lips and for eczema and dermatitis.

Cares for teeth and gums The practice of "oil pulling"—swishing 1 tablespoon coconut oil around the mouth for 20 minutes—helps to reduce bacteria, control plaque, and fight tooth decay and gum infection. Don't swallow; there's also no need to rinse afterward.

Hazelnut

Corylus avellana

A light oil with a fine texture and mild, nutty aroma, hazelnut is **rich in nutrients**, including vitamin E and linoleic acid, an essential fatty acid that protects the outer layer of skin. A **nourishing** oil, it is ideal for **reviving** dull, damaged, or dry skin. Its gentle **astringent** action improves skin tone.

Hazelnuts are high in protein and full of skin-nourishing healthy fats.

This pale yellow oil is rich in vitamins and minerals.

What is it **good for?**

Balances skin Hazelnut oil is an excellent choice for a facial massage oil, especially for oily or acne-prone skin types. Its astringent action helps to tone and balance skin, while its emollient properties provide moisture and protection for skin. The oil can also be used to balance and condition oily hair.

Protects skin Its light texture makes this oil a good choice for wind- and sun-damaged skin. It can be added to skin creams to take advantage of its mild SPF factor, and to after-sun treatments to help repair and condition skin.

Works in a blend Hazelnut can be used on its own or as an enriching oil for a base oil blend. For example, if skin is very dry but still needs toning, try blending this oil with a deeply moisturizing oil such as rosehip seed or avocado oil to create the combination that's right for your skin.

Sunflower

Helianthus annuus

A popular and affordable all-purpose oil, sunflower blends easily with other bases and essential oils. It is very high in **vitamin E**, which repairs and protects skin, and is easily absorbed into the skin.

Sunflower seeds are pressed to produce an oil rich in vitamin E.

A pale golden color, sunflower oil has a delicate, nutty aroma and is a natural emulsifier.

The cheery sunflower produces edible seeds.

What is it **good for?**

Hydrates skin There is evidence that sunflower oil can help to improve the barrier function of the skin, helping skin to retain moisture and fight off infection. This effect is due to the presence of light waxes, which help form a protective emollient barrier on the skin.

Heals skin The oil is protective and helps to repair sun-damaged skin. Healing vitamin E and carotenoids (a vegetable form of vitamin A) can reduce scarring and smooth the appearance of existing wrinkles and fine lines. In addition, the oil contains omega-6 linoleic acid, which helps decrease skin inflammation in acne, eczema, and sunburn, and helps to generate new skin cells.

Treats acne The carotenoids in the oil are excellent for cleansing and moisturizing acne-prone skin.

St. John's Wort macerated oil

Hypericum perforatum

The well-known **sedative** effects of St. John's wort herb also exist in the macerated oil, which is made by infusing a base oil with the fresh or dried herb. It has a **pain-relieving** effect, and its **anti-inflammatory** properties have a calming action on red, sore, or inflamed skin conditions.

St. John's wort herb is a popular remedy for depression.

The beautiful red macerated oil is made by infusing the fresh herb, traditionally in olive oil.

What is it **good for?**

Calms inflammation Try using this oil to treat dry, painful inflamed skin conditions, such as eczema, psoriasis, and some types of lupus. It can also be used at the first sign of a tingle to treat cold sores and viral skin lesions.

Acts as a pain reliever The oil can help calm nerve pain and soothe inflamed joints and tendonitis, as well as reduce inflammation in sunburn, minor scalds, cuts, and scrapes. It can also relieve muscle and nerve pain.

Is a good massage base St. John's wort adds a grounding, earthy aroma to a massage. It can be used on its own or added to massage oil blends to boost the effects of a relaxing massage. It also works well added to blends intended to treat nervousness, depression, and premenstrual or menopausal symptoms.

Safe usage Do not apply before sun exposure since the oil may increase the photosensitivity of the skin.

Flaxseed Oil

Linum usitatissimum

Pressed from the tiny seeds of the plant, flaxseed oil is **rich in omega-3 fatty acids** and vitamin E, making it a **rejuvenating** oil for tired, dry, or mature skin. Also known as linseed oil, it has **antioxidant** and **anti-inflammatory** qualities that can benefit acne-prone skin.

The tiny flaxseeds have antioxidant properties.

For the best-quality oil, look for cold-pressed and unfiltered products.

What is it **good for?**

Fades scars and stretch marks The high vitamin E content of flaxseed oil helps to reduce the appearance of scarring and stretch marks.

Hydrates skin Flaxseed oil seals in moisture, making a reviving remedy for dry skin conditions. Its anti-inflammatory action calms eczema and psoriasis.

Has antiaging effects The omega-3 fatty acids in flaxseed oil help protect and rejuvenate skin cells, brightening dull-looking skin and smoothing the appearance of lines.

Treats acne Use the oil to cleanse and condition oily or acne-prone skin and rosacea. It contains omega-3 alpha-linolenic acid (ALA), a powerful anti-inflammatory that reduces the soreness and redness around acne.

Enriches base oil blends Flaxseed generally isn't used on its own, but is added to other base oils, creams, and lotions to add skin-strengthening properties.

Macadamia
Macadamia ternifolia

This **protective, silky oil** is pressed from the native Australian nut. It has a sweet, nutty aroma and contains naturally high amounts of **palmitoleic acid**, also found in human sebum. This acid helps to protect skin from premature aging and weather damage.

Macadamia nuts are a good source of selenium.

The pale yellow oil produced from the macadamia has a nutty aroma and a similar texture to human sebum.

What is it **good for?**

Protects skin Macadamia oil contains nourishing fatty acids and sterols, or plant hormones, that help to moisturize and repair skin. It is a great choice for healing skin after too much exposure to the sun, wind, or cold weather conditions. The oil is also great for conditioning hair.

Has antiaging effects Macadamia is rich in omega-7 palmitoleic acid, which has been shown to help delay skin aging.

The oil has a particularly regenerating, moisturizing, and hydrating effect on mature skin. It is also nonirritating to the skin around the eyes—try patting the tiniest amount around the eyes to fight bags and sagging skin.

It is long lasting Macadamia will keep longer than most nut and seed oils (up to 12 months), but it needs to be stored in a cool, dark place to keep it at its best.

Neem
Melia azadirachta

Pressed from the fruit and seeds of the tree, neem oil is highly **antiseptic**—a little goes a long way. It has a strong, pungent odor so is best used to **enrich** other oils. It is particularly good at helping to **heal** infections and for dry skin conditions, and makes an effective **insect repellent**.

Neem seeds are not edible, but their oil has medicinal value.

The distinctive-looking oil has a strong aroma and should be used in small quantites only.

What is it **good for?**

Treats dandruff Neem is a useful dandruff remedy. Try blending with coconut oil for a prewash hair mask. Leave in for 10 minutes, then rinse off.

Works well in blends Neem is effective even in small amounts, and blending it helps to counter its strong aroma. To find what works for you, start with just a few drops diluted in a neutral base oil, such as sunflower or almond, and gradually increase the amount to no more than 5 percent of the blend.

Acts as an insect repellent Neem is a powerful insecticide that has become a staple of many natural head-lice treatments and mosquito repellents. For head lice, apply undiluted from root to tip and comb through with a nit comb, then wash out.

Heals skin The oil can be dabbed neat onto cold sores. Contains anti-inflammatory compounds that ease eczema and psoriasis. Its properties can improve dry skin.

Moringa
Moringa oleifera

Also known as ben oil, moringa is pressed from the seeds of the plant. It contains high levels of the fatty **oleic acid** and is a deeply penetrating oil with skin-softening properties. It is rich in **antioxidants**, which help to protect skin from premature aging due to free radicals.

The seeds of the moringa are dried to resemble beans.

This pale yellow, odorless oil is rich in fatty acids that soften and moisturize skin.

What is it **good for?**

It makes a good massage base Highly lubricating and similar in composition to olive oil, but much lighter and odorless, moringa oil makes an ideal oil base for aromatherapy massage blends. Its light texture in particular helps to make a pleasant facial massage or elixir.

Conditions skin Moringa can help to reduce the appearance of large pores, as well as fine lines, wrinkles, stretch marks, and scars.

Moisturizes skin Its high fatty-acid content nourishes skin and helps prevent moisture loss. The oil provides instant hydration for dry, damaged, or mature skin. Blend with coconut oil to make a hair and scalp treatment that restores shine and fights dandruff.

Helps controls acne With antibacterial and anti-inflammatory properties, the oil is useful for acne-prone skin. Studies show that moringa can help to kill off the germs that can cause skin infections.

Evening Primrose
Oenothera biennis

Cold pressed from the oil-rich seeds, evening primrose is an **enriching** oil that contains **skin-loving fatty acids**, such as omega-6 linoleic acid, which strengthens membranes around the skin, and **antiaging** gamma linolenic acid (GLA).

What is it **good for?**

The fragrant flowers of the evening primrose are edible.

The tiny seeds are rich in essential fatty acids.

Golden evening primrose oil is pressed from the seeds of the plant, but has a short shelf life.

Has antiaging effects Light and easily absorbed, the oil has anti-inflammatory and skin-rejuvenating properties that can improve tone and elasticity in mature skin.

Conditions skin Evening primrose helps skin retain moisture and increases skin cells' ability to absorb oxygen and fight off infection. The oil penetrates deep into the skin, helping to heal conditions such as eczema and acne. To help soften brittle and easily

breakable nails, rub in 1–2 drops daily.

Can be added to cosmetics If you are adding evening primrose oil to homemade cosmetics, it should make up 5–10 percent of the blend. The oil has a short shelf life, so once opened, it should be stored in the fridge and used within 6–9 months. If you need just a small amount for a massage blend or cream, add from capsules, rather than open a bottle.

Olive

Olea europea

Rich in skin-nourishing **fatty acids**, **antioxidants**, and **vitamin E**, over the years olive oil has earned its reputation as an affordable, but also superior, **moisturizing** and healing treatment. Use it undiluted or in a multitude of cosmetic formulations for skin and hair.

The bitter-tasting fruit is a native of the Mediterranean.

This heavy, viscous green oil is widely used for both culinary and cosmetic purposes.

What is it **good for?**

Conditions skin This deeply penetrating oil helps to keep skin soft and well conditioned. A naturally occurring compound, squalene, provides a barrier against water loss. Rub a few drops into the nails and cuticles to protect and condition them.

Has antiaging effects Its antioxidant properties help maintain the integrity of skin cells and fight off the effects of free radicals, which cause premature skin aging.

Can be used as a hair tonic
Olive oil can be used as a pretreatment before shampooing, or as an overnight hair mask to treat dry and damaged hair and irritated, sensitive scalps.

Acts as a makeup remover
Olive oil makes an effective and simple makeup remover, helping to lift all traces of grime and dirt and leave skin well moisturized and conditioned.

Avocado

Persea gratissima

Avocado is one of the best oils for **soothing** dry skin and softening rough skin patches, such as those on the elbows and heels. Naturally high in vitamins, minerals, and **antioxidants**, the rich oil is cold-pressed from the fruit and used in small amounts to **enrich** lighter oil bases.

The fruit is packed with nutrients.

Avocado oil is pressed from the fruit (not the skin) and is a distinctive dark green color.

What is it **good for?**

Conditions and soothes skin
Avocado helps to hydrate parched skin and aid the regeneration of skin cells. A high fatty-acid content means this is a great oil for conditioning rough skin on the feet, knees, or elbows, and also for reviving hair damaged by styling or the sun.

Repairs and protects skin
If used regularly, the oil can help to prevent or minimize the appearance of stretch marks.

Acts as an antiaging oil
Avocado oil gives luster and shine to tired or dull complexions. It contains fatty acids and phytosterols (plant hormones), which help to replenish and revitalize mature skin.

Acts as a natural SPF While it can't be used as a sunscreen on its own, avocado oil does contain a natural SPF factor at a low level that can help to protect skin and hair from sun exposure. The oil also relieves the pain of sunburn.

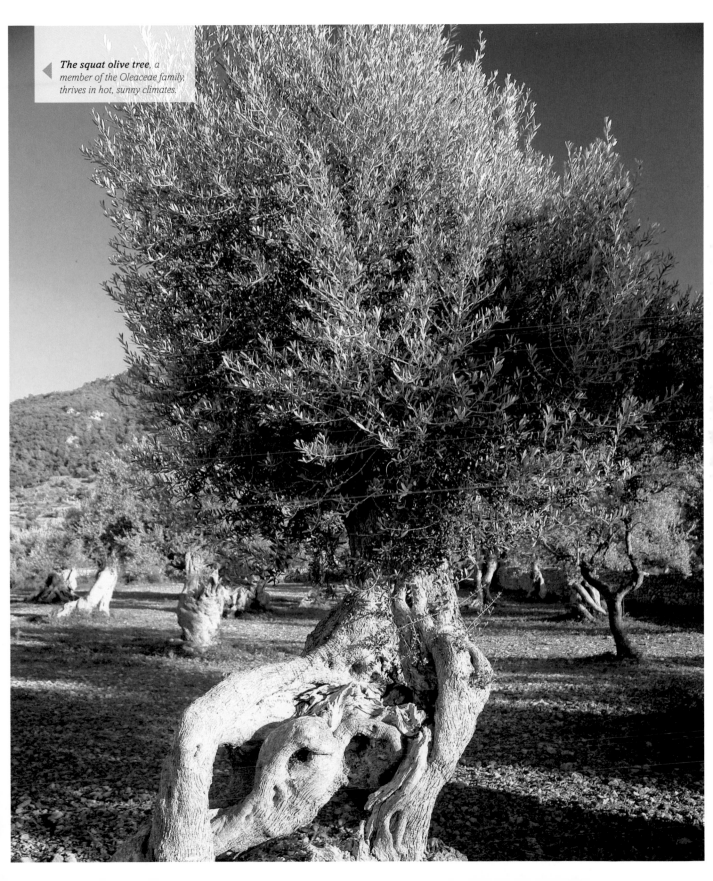

The squat olive tree, a member of the Oleaceae family, thrives in hot, sunny climates.

Almond

Prunus amygdalus dulcis

This light general-purpose oil is cold-pressed from the seeds of the sweet almond tree. Vitamin rich, the oil is suitable for **all skin types**, but especially for **sensitive skins**, and it is gentle enough to be used on children. It helps **soothe** dry, irritated skin and prevent moisture loss.

Almond nuts are high in vitamin E and other important nutrients.

Almond oil, pressed from the seeds of the tree, is a light oil with a subtle aroma.

What is it **good for?**

Acts as a natural moisturizer
Almond oil provides a long-lasting barrier against the elements that helps prevent moisture loss, soothes and encourages the healing of dry, irritated skin, and relieves inflamed skin conditions, such as eczema.

It is suitable for babies and young children
Almond oil is gentle enough to be used on babies and young children, for example to treat diaper rash or cradle cap. Other gentle oils, such as olive and sunflower, are also recommended for babies.

Helps lubricate massage blends
The oil is absorbed slowly, which makes it a popular choice as a massage oil base. It also has a delicate aroma that will not compete with the essential oils in a blend.

Acts as a makeup remover
Almond oil effectively removes dirt and makeup, leaving the skin feeling soft and supple.

Apricot Kernel

Prunus armeniaca

Apricot kernel oil is a **light, cold-pressed oil**, rich in the fatty acid known as gamma linoleic acid, or GLA, which helps skin maintain its moisture balance. Light enough to leave no oily residue, the oil is particularly suitable as a base for facial serums and light **moisturizing** lotions.

Apricot seeds have moisturizing properties.

Apricot kernel oil is an emollient oil that helps to soften skin. A pale to dark yellow, it has a nutty aroma.

What is it **good for?**

Helps restore moisture
If skin feels dry, itchy, or tight after bathing or cleansing, this is the perfect oil to apply lightly to damp skin before toweling off. For mature skin, it is softening and improves skin elasticity, helping to smooth out fine lines.

It is suitable for sensitive skin
Apricot oil soothes sensitive skin and provides a thin barrier against irritants. It makes an ideal substitute for petroleum-based baby oils.

Acts as a massage base
Apricot kernel absorbs more slowly than some oils, which makes it a great base for massage blends and nighttime skin treatments. A little goes a long way, so buy the best you can afford.

Conditions hair
The oil makes an effective treatment for flyaway hair and also minimizes the appearance of split ends. Work a few drops into damp hair and allow it to dry naturally to seal in moisture all day long.

Rosehip Seed
Rosa cannina

The oil from the seeds of the rose plant is a luxurious source of **skin-nourishing** fatty acids. Renowned for its **soothing** anti-inflammatory effect, it is suited to dry, mature, and weather-damaged skin.

Rosehip seeds are rich in rejuvenating fatty acids.

The golden oil can be used undiluted on small areas of skin, or added to blends to enrich other oils.

The rose plant produces clusters of bright red seeds.

What is it **good for?**

Has antiaging effects Rosehip contains the essential fatty acids omegas 3 and 6 that support cell and tissue regeneration, helping to keep skin supple and reduce the appearance of fine lines around the eyes. It is great for treating spider veins.

Prevents scarring The oil can be added to body lotions and creams to minimize the appearance of stretch marks. It can also reduce scarring from wounds and burns, and after surgery.

Treats acne The oil is a source of trans-retinoic acid, a form of vitamin A, which is a recognized treatment for acne-prone skin. Rosehip helps balance the skin's oils, and its toning action minimizes pores. It is also good for calming pimples and boils.

Eases itching Soothing and easily absorbed, when the skin is dry and itchy rosehip seed's cooling, anti-inflammatory action brings quick relief.

Sesame
Sesamum Indicum

Pressed from the familiar sesame seed, this oil is **packed with nutrients**, including vitamin E and potassium, both of which help to **rejuvenate** and **protect** the skin. The oil also has inherent **anti-inflammatory** properties, making it especially suited to healing dry skin conditions.

Sesame seeds are a rich source of vitamins and minerals.

The slightly thick, pale yellow oil was used traditionally as a healing salve and is a popular cooking oil.

What is it **good for?**

Tones skin This deeply penetrating oil helps to repair damaged cells and improve circulation, which in turn gives tired or weather-damaged skin a healthy glow.

Useful for head and face massage Ayurvedic practitioners believe that even without the addition of essential oils, sesame oil produces a calming and warming effect that boosts circulation and aids detox, while relieving stress and promoting sleep.

Moisturizes skin Sesame helps to keep skin hydrated, and is particularly well suited to those with dry to normal skin. The oil also relieves itchy, burning, and inflamed skin conditions.

Acts as a sunscreen While sesame oil can't be used by itself to protect the skin against the sun's damaging rays, adding some of the oil to facial and body preparations will boost their SPF factor, while also helping to protect skin from the harmful effects of free radicals that are generated by the sun's rays.

Jojoba

Simmondsia chinensis

Jojoba is actually a **liquid wax** rather than an oil, and because it is so similar to human sebum, it is considered one of the main treatments for dry and mature skin. Its waxy nature adds a **protective** layer that helps skin retain moisture. Readily absorbed, it can be used on all skin types.

The oil from the seeds has long been used in skin care.

Jojoba oil is a long-lasting oil which is actually a liquid wax that has a bright golden appearance.

What is it **good for?**

Conditions skin and hair Jojoba can be used to soften hard, dry, or rough skin and to relieve the symptoms of skin conditions such as eczema and psoriasis. Just a little added to hair gives instant shine, and it can also be used to treat dry scalp conditions and dandruff.

Has antiaging effects Jojoba is a good oil for dry, chapped, weather-damaged, and mature skins. It helps to reduce water loss and improves suppleness and elasticity, helping to reduce the appearance of fine lines, wrinkles, and scars.

Acts as a makeup remover Jojoba oil is suitable for all skin types, and can be used to lift and dissolve the dirt and oil that clog pores, leaving skin instantly moisturized. Its thick texture makes it a great substitute for soap when shaving: a little applied to the legs or face helps to lubricate the skin, enabling an extra-close shave that also helps to prevent razor irritation.

Cocoa Butter

Theobroma cacao

A natural and effective **emollient** with a distinctive chocolate–vanilla aroma, cocoa butter can be added to body and face creams and balms to **provide a barrier** against moisture loss and environmental damage. Good for dry, damaged, or mature skin, and effective on stretch marks.

The waxy butter is melted down to make a liquid used in skin- and hair-care products.

When melted down, the oil can be used as an emulsifier to hold oil- and water-based products together.

What is it **good for?**

Prevents moisture loss Cocoa butter acts as a barrier to prevent water loss and keep skin hydrated. The oil aids skin elasticity and tone by supporting collagen production, helping to prevent premature wrinkles and reduce stretch marks. It also helps soften and hydrate the hair.

Thickens creams and acts as an emulsifier Solid and pale yellow at room temperature, cocoa butter can be gently melted into face- and body-care formulations to thicken them and add benefits. Cocoa butter is a natural emulsifier, helping oil- and water-based lotions hold together.

Best for clear skin and dry complexions Cocoa butter can be occlusive, which means it can clog pores. For this reason it may not be suitable for skin that is prone to acne or pimples.

Wheat Germ

Triticum vulgare

A **nurturing** and **skin-protecting** oil, wheat-germ oil has the highest vitamin E content of any vegetable oil and is also rich in betacarotene. While too sticky and thick to use on its own, the oil adds multiple **skin-conditioning** benefits to base oil blends and lotions and creams.

The tiny wheat seeds contain the nutritious germ at their very center.

This golden-colored oil has a dense texture and a distinctive aroma.

What is it **good for?**

Repairs skin Wheat-germ oil moisturizes and heals dry or cracked skin, and also helps to fade scarring and stretch marks. It is an especially rich source of vitamin E, which helps to protect skin from the effects of the weather, to moisturize and heal dry or cracked skin, and to maintain an even skin tone.

Has antiaging effects Vitamin E helps fight the effects on the skin of damaging free radicals and supports cellular regeneration and collagen formation. As a result, wheat germ has a revitalizing effect on mature or weather-damaged skin, helping to rejuvenate and prevent the development of premature fine lines around the eyes and mouth.

Works well in a blend With its thick, sticky consistency and distinctive grassy-nutty aroma, wheat-germ oil is best used to enrich the powers of other lighter base oils. It should make up 5–10 percent of a base oil blend.

Grape Seed

Vitis vinifera

This light, odorless, and inexpensive all-purpose oil can be used in a wide array of applications from massage to skin care. High in **antioxidants**, it is mild, but very nourishing. It has good **emollient** properties and a gentle **toning** effect that benefits both mature and acne-prone skin.

Pressed grape seeds are used in cosmetics and food.

This smooth, pale oil has a short shelf life of around six months and keeps best in a cool, dark place.

What is it **good for?**

Has antiaging effects Rich in the emollient linoleic acid (omega-6), grape-seed oil leaves the skin with a satiny finish. The oil is easily absorbed and has a mildly astringent effect that helps to tone and condition tired or dull-looking skin.

Is suitable for allergenic and sensitive skin This nonallergenic oil is suitable for those who cannot use nut oils. It is mild enough to use on infants and on sensitive skin.

Treats acne Grape seed's astringent properties help to balance oily and acne-prone skin, refreshing the complexion and reducing redness and irritation.

Is a good massage base Grape-seed oil makes a great nongreasy base oil for massage blends. It also has the added benefit of dispersing in water, making it an ideal choice for bath-oil blends.

Essential Oil
Recipes

Create your very own **home spa**. With these simple recipes and all-natural ingredients you can make a **range of luxurious products** to revive body and mind, from aromatic blends to fragranced candles and **pampering bath and beauty** products.

Blending Essential Oils

The **art of blending** oils successfully to create **pleasing** and uplifting scents comes with practice. The fragrance families on pages 166–67 will help you understand which scents work especially well together. Below are a few practical **guidelines** to help you get started. Enjoy **experimenting** with scent combinations and discovering which aromas appeal to you. Over time, your confidence will grow and you will develop an **instinct** for blending.

How Oils Work **Together**

Each essential oil is made up of multiple components, all of which are responsible for the different attributes and properties of the oil. The beauty of essential oils is that a fragrance is not just one individual note, but is composed of a complex harmony of notes (see box, right). You can work with these different notes to create favorite blends, adding citrus notes by blending with lemon, grapefruit, or lime, for example; or enhancing a blend with spicy notes by adding cardamom or black pepper.

The art of creating a beautiful blend of oils often comes down to practice, but there are some tips to make life easier. And while you won't want to waste oils, a little trial and error can help you to understand how they work together and to gain confidence blending, so don't be afraid to make a few mistakes.

Blending guidelines Start off by creating very simple blends. As you work with the essential oils and become more familiar with them, you will notice that some are stronger smelling and more pervasive than others. These oils will dominate the ones that have a more subtle smell, so keep this in mind and blend carefully, drop by drop, while you are practicing and gaining confidence.

● **Always dilute essential oils** before applying to the skin (see the blending table on page 37 for guidelines of quantities of essential oil to base oil).

Aromatherapists use the following guidelines: 1 percent dilution in a base oil for a product for sensitive skin, for a facial oil, for children, for the elderly, or for those with a weak immune system; 2.5 percent dilution in a base oil for a product for the body of a healthy adult; and 5 percent dilution for a local or topical application, for example for a compress.

● **Try to use four to seven oils** per blend and avoid adding more than seven oils. When you start blending, you might prefer to blend just two or three oils at once, and these simple blends can be effective. As you gain confidence and discover scent combinations you like, you can begin to add a few more oils.

● **If you make a mistake** while blending oils, maybe adding an oil whose smell you don't like, it is hard to rectify the mistake. In this case, it's best to abandon the blend and start again.

● **Blend oils** in a small cup or bowl. If you need to store a blend, transfer it to a sterilized dark-glass bottle and label the bottle with the date and the ingredients of the blend.

Top, Middle, and Base Notes

Fragrances are built using "accords," which means that individual scents, or notes, are blended to create a new, unified aroma. Each fragrance is made up of top, middle, and base notes, which are combined to give structure to the blend and to create appealing, balanced, long-lasting fragrances.

● *Top notes* are light and refreshing, and give the first impression.

● *Middle notes* are the heart of the fragrance and include most of the herbaceous scents such as geranium.

● *Base notes* are rich aromas, such as sandalwood and ylang-ylang, which give a scent body and longevity.

Mix small quantities of oil to start with as you learn the art of blending.

Perfect Blends

Essential oils can be categorized into **fragrance "families,"** which can guide your blending choices. Typically, the **aromas** each of us most enjoy belong to just one or two families. Here, families are arranged in a circle. While there are no rules, scents tend to marry well with those in their own family, and also with **neighboring families**.

Floral Oils

Florals are full-bodied scents such as rose that form the heart of an aroma. They can be used alone, or blended for more complex scents. Add citrus oils to lighten heady florals; spicy oils for a warm scent; or herbaceous oils for a cool aroma.

Essential oils
- Rosewood • Violet • Geranium
- Neroli • Rose • Ylang-ylang
- Jasmine • Lavender
- Tagetes • Helichrysum
- Palmarosa • Mimosa

Floral lavender

Herbaceous Oils

Herbaceous oils, such as basil, parsley, and chamomile, have a natural, elegant "green" scent and often form the "middle" note (see p164) of an aroma. Their clear scent can temper sweeter floral oils, and they can soften sharper citrus ones.

Essential oils
- Basil • Clary sage • Oregano • Parsley • Tarragon • Thyme • Yarrow • Dill
- Mugwort • Caraway • Carrot seed
- Chamomile • Fennel • Marjoram
- Myrtle • Summer savory • Manuka

Herbaceous chamomile

*Essential oil **families** can be blended to create more complex aromas.*

THE FRAGRANCE **WHEEL**

In 1983, Michael Edwards, a fragrance industry consultant, devised a fragrance "wheel." He divided scents into floral, oriental, woody, and fresh, and most groupings are based on these classifications.

Citrus Oils

Zingy and vibrant, the citrus family includes citrus oils, as well as oils such as fragonia that have scents reminiscent of citrus. These oils add tartness to floral and herbaceous oils, and make a crisp scent when blended with medicinal oils.

Essential oils
- Bergamot • Lemon • Grapefruit
- Mandarin • Orange • Lemon verbena • Lemongrass • Lemon balm • Lime • Buchu • Fragonia
- Petitgrain • Citronella • Litsea

Citrus orange

Oriental cinnamon

Woody pine

Medicinal sage

Spicy Oils

This exotic family of scents is made up of warm, sensual, spicy, and velvety aromas. Oils such as cinnamon can form the central note in a scent, and rich oils such as vanilla create a "base" note (see p164), giving longevity to a scent. Try marrying spicy oriental oils with woody ones, such as sandalwood, to create blends that are earthy and deep. Oriental oils also blend naturally with many floral scents, such as ylang-ylang, jasmine, and lavender, where the floral note tempers the oriental one to prevent it from being overpowering.

Essential oils
- Vanilla • Cinnamon • Nutmeg • Cardamom • Clove • Juniper • Coriander • Black pepper • Cumin • Galangal • Litsea • Fenugreek • Ginger • Star anise • Tuberose • Allspice • Cistus

Woody Oils

Earthy, mossy, musky, and dense, these complex scents contain many dominant aromas. Woody scents tend to be deeply grounding and are often sensual, as with sandalwood; and oils such as cedarwood and myrrh accentuate oriental aromas. Adding zesty citrus notes to woody oils creates a lively, fresher scent, while mixing woody oils with medicinal ones, such as eucalyptus, creates cool, resinous, minty aromas that offset the deep, woody tones.

Essential oils
- Frankincense • Cypress • Pine • Myrrh • Patchouli • Sandalwood • Cedarwood • Angelica • Elemi • Benzoin • Valerian • Vetiver

Medicinal Oils

Crisp and clean, these often lighter scents produce a refreshing "top" note (see p164) to complement heavier woody aromas. Try also blending with woody or herbaceous oils to create a layered scent.

Essential oils
- Camphor • Sage • Wintergreen • Birch • Tea tree • Cajeput • Niaouli • Ravintsara • Rosemary • Bay laurel • Peppermint • Eucalyptus • Plai

Additional Ingredients

Essential oils can be combined with various ingredients to make a **range** of bath and body products and treatments. For **basic blends**, the oils on pages 148–61 make the ideal base for essential oils. In the following recipes, additional ingredients are used, such as **waxes**, floral waters, mineral salts, and citric acid to create **creams**, lotions, balms, scents, and infusions.

Castor oil is an excellent skin emollient because it creates a barrier. It's also an effective cleanser.

Aloe vera juice provides a hydrating base for essential oils. Calming and cooling, it has healing properties and can repair damaged skin, making it a useful ingredient in skincare products.

Beeswax is used in skincare products to form a protective film on the skin that helps reduce water loss. A rich moisturizer, this is a good base for creams and ointments. You can buy beeswax in a block or in pellets that are easier to melt down.

Emulsifying waxes help essential oils and water to combine in creams and lotions and remain stable over a period of time.

Rose floral water is a by-product of the steam distillation of the essential oil. Beautifully fragrant, it can be used on its own as a toner or added to recipes. Floral waters share some of the oil's properties, but are less concentrated.

Kaolin powder can be added to skin products to work as an exfoliator, helping to remove dead skin cells and cleanse skin.

Baking soda helps reduce inflammation and is cleansing. It soothes and softens the skin and promotes the release of toxins.

Candle wax can be made from beeswax, vegetable wax, or paraffin wax.

Glycerin is a colorless and odorless humectant, or moisturizer, that hydrates skin. It is a useful ingredient in cosmetics, and especially helpful in dry-skin treatments.

Citric acid is a naturally occurring fruit acid that cleanses the skin and helps to even skin tone.

Mineral salts are rich in detoxifying minerals that help to stimulate the lymphatic system, and magnesium, which helps reduce fatigue and soothes muscles after exercising.

Aromatherapy Blends

Using fragrant blends of essential oils in the way that best suits your lifestyle is a great way to enhance general well-being and health. Essential oils have wonderful properties that are calming, balancing, anxiety reducing, uplifting, cleansing, and stimulating, all of which will help you to relax, unwind, and release stress, as well as provide an overall boost to your body.

MASSAGE OIL   BATH OIL   DIFFUSER

Blend for Relaxation

Allowing ourselves time to relax is key to well-being. Lavender essential oil is well-known for **aiding relaxation** and blends well with **calming** rose oil. Vetiver oil has a woody, earthy, slightly bitter fragrance with relaxing and **sedative properties**, making it ideal for use before bedtime.

Ingredients

Makes 1 fl oz (30 ml)
Almond oil 2 tbsp
Lavender essential oil 5 drops
Rose essential oil 3 drops
Vetiver essential oil 2 drops

How to **make**

For a massage oil, combine all the ingredients in a bowl, then transfer the blend to a sterilized dark-glass bottle and seal with a cap or dropper, ready for use. Store the blend in a cool, dark place. It will keep for up to 3 months.

Best **uses**

As a massage oil Massage into the skin on the body (avoiding your face). Allow the oil to absorb into the skin before you get dressed.

In the bath For a relaxing bedtime wind-down soak, mix the essential oils with just 1 tablespoon of the almond oil, or alternatively mix the essential oils with 1 tablespoon of whole milk, then add to a warm bath.

In a diffuser Add the essential oils on their own to a diffuser, vaporizer or oil burner and gently fragrance your chosen environment as you relax and unwind.

Safe usage Take care not to slip when getting in and out of the bath.

Unwind and relax with a soothing aromatic blend.

BLEND
VARIATION
For other relaxing blends with an almond base oil try chamomile, mandarin, and bergamot, or marjoram, lavender, and orange.

Once your blend is made up, you can add it to a bath or use for a massage as you wish.

SHOWER

Uplifting Blend

This trio of **reviving** oils can lift spirits and boost flagging energy. Zesty, **energizing** grapefruit stimulates body and mind, and geranium helps to balance emotions by being both **calming** and **uplifting.** Jasmine completes the blend perfectly, its heady aroma increasing feelings of well-being.

Ingredients

Makes 1 fl oz (30 ml)
Unscented shower gel 2 tbsp
Grapefruit essential oil 4 drops
Jasmine absolute or essential oil 4 drops
Geranium essential oil 1 drop

How to **make**

Mix the essential oil drops with the unscented shower gel.

Best **uses**

In the shower Use this uplifting blend first thing in the morning for an energizing shower that will help you start the day on a positive note.

MASSAGE OIL   DIFFUSER

Soothing Blend

Calming aromatherapy provides a natural and easy way to deal with the symptoms of stress and feelings of anxiety. **Uplifting** floral essential oils, such as neroli, can be blended with other mood-boosting oils, such as frankincense, to create a wonderfully **soothing** massage- or body- oil blend.

Ingredients

Makes 1 fl oz (30 ml)
Almond oil 2 tbsp
Frankincense essential oil 3 drops
Neroli essential oil 3 drops
Orange essential oil 2 drops

How to **make**

For a massage oil, combine all the ingredients in a bowl, then transfer the blend to a sterilized dark-glass bottle and seal with a cap or dropper, ready for use. Store in a cool, dark place. It will keep for up to 3 months.

Best **uses**

As a massage oil Massage into the skin on the body (avoiding your face). Allow the oil to absorb into the skin before you get dressed.

In a diffuser Add the essential oils on their own to a diffuser, vaporizer or oil burner to create a calming and tranquil environment.

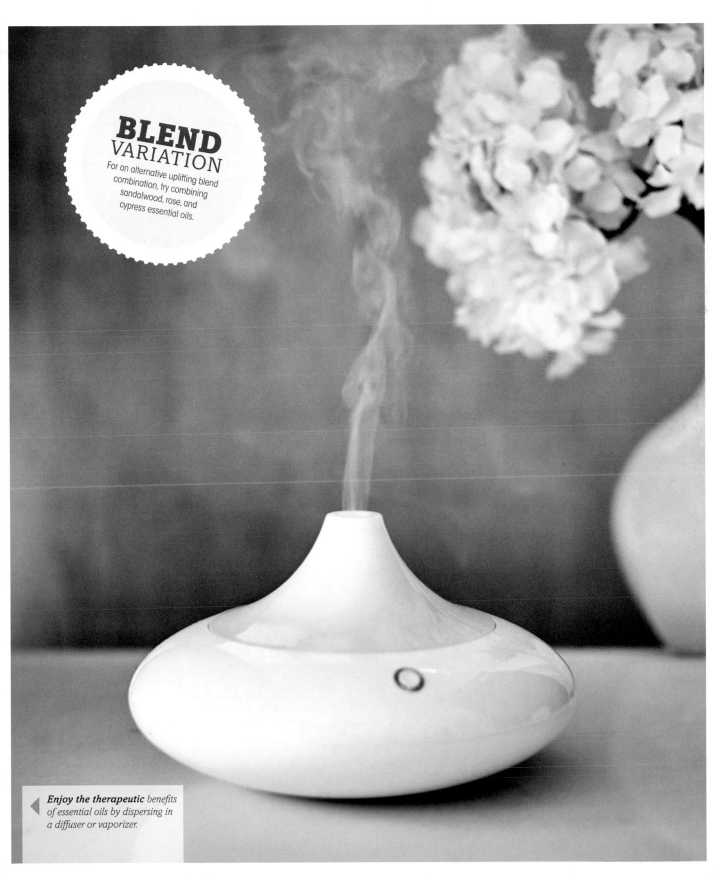

BLEND
VARIATION

For an alternative uplifting blend combination, try combining sandalwood, rose, and cypress essential oils.

Enjoy the therapeutic benefits *of essential oils by dispersing in a diffuser or vaporizer.*

MASSAGE OIL   DIFFUSER   BATH OIL

Calming Blend

The aromatherapeutic properties of certain oils work on both mind and body, helping to **calm** and **balance** the emotions and soothe skin. Rose essential oil helps to calm skin, reducing redness and inflammation, while geranium oil can balance oily skin and calm unsettled **emotions**. Light, versatile, and gentle on the skin, almond base oil makes an ideal carrier for this blend.

Ingredients

Makes 1 fl oz (30 ml)
Almond oil 2 tbsp
Rose absolute or essential oil 7 drops
Geranium essential oil 7 drops

How to **make**

For a massage oil, combine all the ingredients in a bowl, then transfer the blend to a sterilized dark-glass bottle and seal with a cap or dropper, ready for use. Store in a cool, dark place. It will keep for up to 3 months.

Best **uses**

As a massage oil Massage into the skin on the body (avoiding your face). Allow the oil to absorb into the skin before you get dressed. For a calming facial oil, blend 2 tablespoons almond or calendula oil with 1 drop each of rose and lavender essential oils.

In a diffuser Add the essentials oils on their own to a diffuser, vaporizer or oil burner and gently fragrance your environment with this soothing blend.

In the bath Mix the essential oils with just 1 tablespoon of the almond oil, or alternatively mix the oils with 1 tablespoon of whole milk or a bath-oil base, then add to a warm bath.

Safe usage *If using the oils in a bath, be careful not to slip when getting into and out of the bath.*

Rose essential oil has a soothing aroma.

BLEND VARIATION

Mandarin, German chamomile, and lavender essential oils, combined with an almond base oil, makes a soothing blend for frayed nerves.

FRAGRANCE

Blend for Focus

Essential oils have long been used to facilitate meditation since they help to deepen and slow breathing, as well as **balance** and **center energy**. Rosemary essential oil has a **stimulating** effect on the central nervous system so is useful for improving poor concentration. Clove and peppermint essential oils help to keep sleepiness at bay, so they are an ideal combination for maintaining focus.

Ingredients

Makes 1 fl oz (30 ml)
Sunflower oil 2 tbsp
Rosemary essential oil 6 drops
Clove essential oil 2 drops
Peppermint essential oil 2 drops

How to **make**

Combine the ingredients in a bowl, then transfer to a sterilized dark-glass bottle and seal with a cap or dropper, ready for use. Store in a cool, dark place. It will keep for up to 3 months.

Best **uses**

On the skin Dab the fragranced blend onto the pulse points on the wrists and temples. To apply it easily, use a bottle with a roller ball.

This centering group of oils helps to enhance concentration.

Reviving and stimulating, aromatic rosemary promotes mental alertness.

MASSAGE OIL   STEAM INHALATION   DIFFUSER

Purifying and cleansing blend

Enjoy a **detox** massage or **cleanse** your environment by using essential oils with key **purifying** properties. You can also deep cleanse skin by adding the oils to an unscented facial wash or oil blend, or to a steam inhalation to open pores. Juniper has stimulating and astringent properties, frankincense tones skin and helps to close pores, and lemon's citrusy scent refreshes, eliminating unwelcome odors.

Ingredients

Makes 1 fl oz (30 ml)

Jojoba oil 2 tbsp

Juniper essential oil 8 drops

Frankincense essential oil 4 drops

Lemon essential oil 2 drops

How to **make**

For a massage oil, mix the ingredients in a bowl, transfer to a sterilized dark-glass bottle, and seal with a cap or dropper. Store the blend in a cool, dark place. It will keep for up to 3 months.

Best **uses**

As a massage oil Massage into the skin on the body (avoiding your face). Allow the oil to absorb into the skin before you get dressed.

As an inhalation Add the essential oils on their own to hot water, cover your head with a towel, and allow the steam to act on your skin for 5 minutes. Wash skin with cool water and pat it dry with a clean towel.

In a diffuser Add the essential oils on their own to a diffuser, vaporizer, or oil burner and diffuse to cleanse and freshen the air.

Gently astringent and toning, this blend of essential oils has a potent cleansing action.

BLEND
VARIATION
For another blend that
works well as a cleansing facial
oil, try mixing palmarosa,
grapefruit, and lavender with
1 tbsp grapeseed oil.

Adding therapeutic oils to a
steam inhalation helps to unblock
pores and deep cleanse skin.

MASSAGE OIL

Sensual Massage Blend for Him

Ylang-ylang essential oil is exotically fragrant and intensely **uplifting** with calming properties. It blends well with **relaxing** and emotionally **grounding** sandalwood. Mix the oils with a nourishing base oil, light a candle or two, and treat your loved one to a massage.

Ingredients

Makes 1 fl oz (30 ml)
Jojoba oil 2 tbsp
Ylang-ylang essential oil 6 drops
Sandalwood essential oil 6 drops
Nutmeg essential oil 2 drops

How to **make**

Combine all the ingredients in a bowl, then transfer the blend to a sterilized dark-glass bottle and seal with a cap or dropper, ready for use. Store the blend in a cool, dark place. It will keep for up to 3 months.

Best **uses**

As a massage oil Massage into the skin on the body (avoiding the face). Allow the oil to absorb into the skin before getting dressed.

MASSAGE OIL

Sensual Massage Blend for Her

For a more feminine blend, mix rose absolute or essential oil with patchouli essential oil. Beautifully floral rose opens the heart and **soothes** nerves and feelings of anxiety, while patchouli has a sweet, earthy scent that is **grounding** and **calming**.

Ingredients

Makes 1 fl oz (30 ml)
Jojoba oil 2 tbsp
Rose absolute or rose essential oil 8 drops
Patchouli essential oil 4 drops
Vetiver essential oil 2 drops
Geranium essential oil 2 drops

How to **make**

Combine all the ingredients in a bowl. Transfer to a sterilized dark-glass bottle and seal with a cap or dropper, ready for use. Store the blend a cool, dark place. It will keep for up to 3 months.

Best **uses**

As a massage oil Massage into the skin on the body (avoiding the face). Allow the oil to absorb into the skin before getting dressed.

Enjoy a sensual massage with this sweetly scented blend of oils.

BLEND
VARIATION

Cedarwood essential oil is thought to be an aphrodisiac for men; try mixing it with bergamot, neroli, and frankincense. Other feminine sensual oils include jasmine, clary sage, and orange.

Have a favorite blend *of oils prepared in advance to use whenever the mood takes you.*

MASSACE OIL

BLEND
VARIATION
For an alternative immune-strengthening blend, add lemon, thyme, and tea tree essential oils to a diffuser to refresh a room and protect against infection.

Immune-Boosting Blend

Immunity is the final line of **defense** against disease. Poor nutrition, lack of exercise, stress, and other lifestyle issues all put extra pressure on the body's ability to function well, which can lead to an accumulation of toxins that can cause disease. Niaouli, lavender, and rosemary essential oils help **support** a compromised immune system and are strongly **antimicrobial**, helping the body fight off infection.

Ingredients

Makes 1 fl oz (30 ml)

Grapeseed oil 2 tbsp

Lavender essential oil 2 drops

Niaouli essential oil 2 drops

Rosemary essential oil 2 drops

How to **make**

Combine all the ingredients in a bowl, then transfer the blend to a sterilized dark-glass bottle and seal with a cap or dropper, ready for use. Store the blend in a cool, dark place. It will keep for up to 3 months.

Best **uses**

As a massage oil Massage into the skin on the body (avoiding the face). Allow the oil to absorb into the skin before you get dressed.

Harness the antiseptic
properties of lavender essential oil.

MASSAGE OIL   BATH OIL

Regenerating Blend

Essential oils can be used to encourage **skin-cell regeneration,** which is useful in the case of cuts, burns, scars, and stretch marks. Myrrh essential oil is ideal for slow-to-heal wounds and weepy eczema, while **anti-inflammatory** helichrysum can help speed up the wound-**healing** process, and frankincense encourages the growth of new cells—all of which help with skin healing and regeneration.

Ingredients

Makes 1 fl oz (30 ml)

Rosehip seed oil 1 tbsp

Calendula macerated oil 1 tbsp

Frankincense essential oil 6 drops

Helichrysum essential oil 4 drops

Myrrh essential oil 2 drops

How to **make**

For a massage oil, combine all the ingredients in a bowl. Transfer to a sterilized dark-glass bottle and seal with a cap or dropper. Store in a cool, dark place. Keeps for up to 3 months.

Best **uses**

As a massage oil Massage into the skin (avoiding the face). Allow the oil to absorb into the skin before dressing.

In the bath Mix the essential oils with 1 tablespoon combined rose-hip and calendula oil or 1 tablespoon whole milk. Disperse in a warm bath.

Safe usage Do not use the blend on broken skin. Take care not to slip when getting in and out of the bath.

This healing blend of essential oils has a generally rejuvenating effect on the skin.

A rich source of nourishing fatty acids, rose hip is ideal for skin healing.

MASSAGE OIL BATH OIL

Stimulating Blend

Essential oils can be used to **stimulate** the appetite, digestive system, circulation, and lungs. This dynamic blend is ideal if you're feeling generally below par: ginger **calms** the digestive system and restores appetite; black pepper stimulates circulation; and tea tree helps **boost immunity**.

Ingredients

Makes 1 fl oz (30 ml)
Almond oil 2 tbsp
Ginger essential oil 6 drops
Black pepper essential oil 4 drops
Tea tree essential oil 4 drops

How to **make**

For a massage oil, combine all the ingredients in a bowl, then transfer the blend to a sterilized dark-glass bottle and seal with a cap or dropper, ready for use. Store the blend in a cool, dark place. It will keep for up to 3 months.

Best **uses**

As a massage oil Massage into the skin (avoiding the face). Allow the blend to absorb into the skin before you get dressed.

In the bath Mix the essential oils with just 1 tablespoon almond oil or, if you want, 1 tablespoon whole milk. For a stimulating shower, mix the essential oils with a fragrance-free shower gel.

Safe usage Take care not to slip when getting in and out of the bath. ▶

DIFFUSER

Refreshing Blend

If you feel sluggish and overcome by nervous exhaustion, this **energizing** blend could be the perfect pick-me-up. Pine oil has a **refreshing** effect, stimulating the nervous system and, along with eucalyptus, **enhancing concentration**, and peppermint is **reviving** and uplifting.

Ingredients

Pine essential oil 2 drops
Peppermint essential oil 2 drops
Eucalyptus essential oil 1 drop

How to **make**

Add the essential oils to a diffuser, vaporizer, or oil burner, according to the manufacturer's instructions.

Best **uses**

In a diffuser Allow the oil blend to disperse and gently fragrance your chosen environment.

Safe usage Peppermint oil may be irritating to the skin. Don't use in concentrations above 2 percent, and avoid near babies and young children.

BLEND
VARIATION
Other stimulating essential oils
include vetiver, rosemary, and
lemongrass, all of which help
to invigorate mind and body.

Add a therapeutic oil blend to
*your bath to enjoy a pampering
and reviving soak.*

Home and Body Fragrances

Filling your home with aromatic essential oils, or using oils as favorite scents, allows you to enhance your environment and enjoy their therapeutic benefits throughout the day. Whether creating a personalized scent, dispersing a delicious aroma in a simple atomizer, or making a perfumed candle, the following recipes will help you create natural, uplifting fragrances for yourself and your home.

FRAGRANCE

Floral Body Mist

Body mists create a light alternative to more concentrated perfumes. Here, a **hydrating** base of aloe vera juice and rose floral water is blended with **exotically sweet** and **floral** ylang-ylang, the deep undertones of vetiver, and the fresh **herbal** notes of clary sage.

Ingredients

Makes 4 fl oz (120 ml)
Rose floral water 2½ fl oz (75 ml)
Aloe vera juice or gel 2 tbsp
Glycerine 1 tbsp
Ylang-ylang essential oil 10 drops
Bergamot essential oil 5 drops
Vetiver essential oil 5 drops
Clary sage essential oil 5 drops

How to **make**

1 Place the rose-floral water, aloe-vera juice or gel, and glycerine in a bowl. Add the oils and combine.

2 Transfer into a sterilized bottle with an atomizer and store in a cool, dark place. It keeps for up to 6 months.

Best **uses**

As a fragrance Shake well before use then apply a burst of fragrance. Since body mists are lighter than perfumes, reapply as required. Avoid spraying on clothes, fabrics or bedding since the oils may stain.

Try out different blends to find your perfect signature scent.

Light and fresh, *body mist scents can be worn confidently throughout the day.*

FRAGRANCE

DIFFUSER

Lemon and Lime Room Scent

Refresh and deodorize your living space with a **zesty** and **uplifting** blend of citrus oils. Use in an atomizer as a room spray or simply vaporize the oil blend in a diffuser to freshen and **scent** the air. The citrus oil combination in this blend has fresh, **sharp**, and **fruity** notes, as well as being uplifting and deodorizing, making this room fragrance an everyday must-have for the home and office.

Ingredients

Makes 2 fl oz (60 ml)

Vodka 2 tbsp

Lime essential oil 10 drops

Lemon essential oil 7 drops

Bergamot essential oil 6 drops

Mandarin essential oil 5 drops

Mineral water 2 tbsp

How to **make**

1 For a room spray, mix the vodka and the essential oils in a bowl. Add the mineral water and combine.

2 Transfer into a sterilized bottle with an atomizer. Store in a cool, dark place. It will keep for up to 6 months.

Best **uses**

As a room scent Shake well, then atomize into the room.

In a diffuser Add the essential oils on their own to a diffuser, vaporizer, or oil burner.

This zesty citrus blend instantly freshens a room.

The refreshing aroma of lime calms and clears the mind.

FRAGRANCE DIFFUSER

BLEND
VARIATION
Try lavender and pine essential
oils combined with the reassuring
woody fragrance of cedarwood
for an alternative calming
bedroom scent.

Relaxing Bedroom Blend

At the end of a long day we often need help to relax. This blend of oils can transport you to a place of **tranquillity**. The strongly **floral**, seductive fragrance of **jasmine** combines with frankincense, which deepens breathing and lifts feelings of anxiety. Use as a room spray, or simply vaporize in a diffuser to create a calm ambience. Light a candle or two and chill out after a long day.

Ingredients

Makes 2 fl oz (60 ml)

Vodka 2 tbsp

Jasmine absolute essential oil 8 drops

Frankincense essential oil 7 drops

Cardamom essential oil 6 drops

Mineral water 2 tbsp

How to **make**

1 For a room spray, mix the vodka and essential oils in a bowl. Add the mineral water and combine.

2 Transfer into a sterilized bottle with an atomizer. Store in a cool, dark place. It will keep for up to 6 months.

Best **uses**

As a room scent Shake well before use, then atomize into your living space.

In a diffuser Add the essential oils on their own to a diffuser, vaporizer, or oil burner.

Deeply relaxing, jasmine offers the perfect wind-down aroma for bedrooms.

FRAGRANCE

Uplifting Candle

Candles can be made from different types of wax, such as paraffin wax, soy wax, or beeswax, the most **traditional.** Not all oils work well in a candle; **experiment** using cheaper oils. Some highly colored oils will change the color of paler waxes.

How to **make**

1 Melt the candle wax in a bain marie saucepan. Alternatively, place the candle wax in a heat-proof glass bowl. Half-fill a saucepan with boiling water and place the bowl on top of the saucepan to make a bain marie. Melt the candle wax gently.

2 For the candle wick, insert the end of a prewaxed wick between two small wooden sticks held together with rubber bands. Using a wax button or a drop of wax, place the wick in the center of a clean, dry votive mold or glass and stick the wick onto the base. Add the oils to the wax, mix thoroughly, then transfer half of the wax into a pitcher or spouted vessel.

3 Pour the wax into the mold in three stages. First, half-fill the mold by slowly pouring the melted wax, taking care not to disturb the wick. Let set and cool. Reheat and stir the wax, then continue to part-fill the mold, allowing the wax to set and cool before filling it to the top level. By pouring in stages before the wax sets, the surface should be smooth.

Ingredients

Makes 1 x 3 oz (90 g) candle

Candle wax 3 oz (90 g)

Lemongrass essential oil 60 drops

Basil essential oil 40 drops

Lime essential oil 40 drops

Best **uses**

As a room fragrance Place the candle in a safe place, away from fabrics and with sufficient ventilation, and fragrance your chosen room with this uplifting blend.

BLEND VARIATION

Add favorite floral scents, such as jasmine and rose, for a summery candle; or warming spicy oils, such as cinnamon and clove, for a cozy winter scent.

Creating your very own scented candles is a cost-effective and fun way to fragrance your home.

Pampering and Beauty

Bring the spa experience into your own home with revitalizing and rejuvenating essential-oil products and treatments. Simple recipes for moisturizing and refreshing bath products, nourishing and hydrating oils and scrubs for the face and body, and pampering hand and foot treatments will enable you relax, unwind, and enjoy the therapeutic benefits of essential oils in your own home.

BATH OIL

Soothing Muscle Soak

The essential oils in this blend work together to **improve circulation**, helping to repair muscle fibers and **relieve pain**. Mineral-rich Epsom salts reduce fatigue and **soothe** aches and pains, and the arnica and comfrey herbs help muscles recover from overexertion.

Ingredients

Makes 17½ fl oz (530 ml)
Comfrey herb 1 tbsp
Arnica montana herb 1 tbsp
Water for the infusion 16 fl oz (500 ml)
Lavender essential oil 2 drops
Rosemary essential oil 2 drops
Black pepper essential oil 1 drop
Epsom salt 1 tbsp

How to **make**

1 Make the comfrey and arnica infusion by steeping the herbs for 10 minutes in a teapot with 16 fl oz (500 ml) boiled water. Strain the liquid.

2 Add the essential oils to the Epsom salt and combine.

3 Add the Epsom salt and essential oil mixture to the strained herbal infusion and stir until dissolved.

Mineral-rich salt soothes skin and eases aching muscles.

Best **uses**

As a bath infusion Add the infusion mixture to the bath immediately and bathe as usual.

Safe usage Do not use on broken or freshly shaved skin.

BATH OIL

Energizing Mineral Bath

Has your get-up-and-go disappeared? Use this combination of herbs, salts, and essential oils to give you renewed vigor. The **stimulating** and **invigorating** benefits of tea tree and black pepper essential oils will **energize** you for the hours ahead, and a rosemary and peppermint herbal infusion mixed with Epsom salts helps reduce fatigue and give you some added oomph!

Ingredients

Makes 17½ fl oz (530 ml)

Peppermint dried herb 1 tbsp

Rosemary dried herb 1 tbsp

Water for the infusion 16 fl oz (500 ml)

Peppermint essential oil 2 drops

Tea tree essential oil 2 drops

Black pepper essential oil 1 drop

Epsom salt 1 tbsp

How to **make**

1 Make the rosemary and peppermint infusion by brewing the herbs for 10 minutes in a teapot with 16 fl oz (500 ml) boiled water. Strain the liquid.

2 Add the essential oils to the Epsom salts and combine.

3 Add the salt and essential oil mixture to the strained herbal infusion and stir until dissolved.

Best **uses**

As a bath infusion Add the infusion mixture to the bath immediately and bathe as usual.

Safe usage Do not use on broken or freshly shaved skin.

Stimulating and cooling, the essential oil of peppermint is instantly invigorating.

Lie back and enjoy this invigorating mineral-bath soak.

BLEND VARIATION

Cedarwood essential oil lifts feelings of lethargy. Try blending with juniper, jasmine, cypress, or mimosa and a herbal infusion for a similarly energizing soak.

BATH OIL

Rose Bath Bombs

Create bath bombs to suit your mood or the time of day. Here, **calming** rose and **balancing** geranium provide a perfect relaxing evening soak. Experiment with different dried flowers, such as lavender, and your favorite essential oils.

Ingredients

Makes 20
Baking soda 14 oz (400 g)
Citric acid 7 oz (200 g)
Dried rose petals 1 tsp
Cocoa butter or vegetable oil 1 tsp
Geranium essential oil 10 drops
Rose absolute essential oil 5 drops
Water 1 tsp

Best **uses**

In the bath Add the fragrant bath bomb to a warm bath and let it dissolve while you recline and relax.

How to **make**

1 Lightly grease the ice-cube molds (a spray oil is ideal for this). Measure out the dry ingredients in a bowl and mix with your hands (wearing gloves).

2 Melt the cocoa butter in a bain-marie (see p188), and add the essential oils. Add the melted cocoa butter to the dry ingredients and mix.

3 Add water with an atomizer and bind the mixture with your hands until it resembles damp sand and sticks together without fizzing. If it is crumbly, add a bit more water.

4 Firmly press into the molds and allow to set for at least 1 hour. Remove from the mold and use when you like. Keeps for up to 3 months.

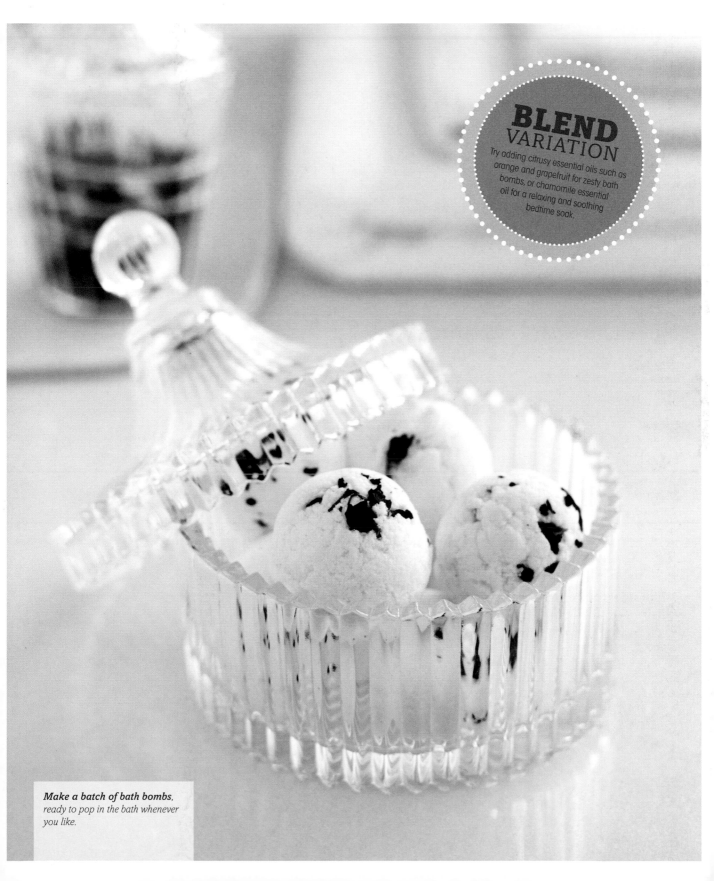

BLEND VARIATION

Try adding citrusy essential oils such as orange and grapefruit for zesty bath bombs, or chamomile essential oil for a relaxing and soothing bedtime soak.

Make a batch of bath bombs, ready to pop in the bath whenever you like.

BATH OIL

Moisturizing Bath Melts

Quick and simple to make, these skin-softening bath melts contain a combination of **nourishing** shea butter, **moisturizing** cocoa butter, and coconut oil, blended with **balancing** geranium essential oil. The melts also work well in a warm shower since the heat from the water softens the butters, allowing you to massage the melt gently into the skin for a deeply moisturizing dry-skin treatment.

Ingredients

Makes 10
Shea butter 1 oz (25 g)
Cocoa butter 1 oz (25 g)
Coconut oil 1 tbsp
Geranium essential oil 10 drops

How to **make**

1 Put the shea butter and cocoa butter in a glass bowl and melt in a bain-marie (see p188).

2 Add the coconut oil to the warm, melted butters; add the essential oil and combine. Pour into soap molds or miniature cupcake cases.

3 Leave to cool and set. You could decorate your melts by pressing dried flowers into the surface as they cool. Keep them cool and dry in their cases and store in the fridge until needed. They keep for up to 3 months.

Best **uses**

In the bath Add the bath melt to a warm bath. Alternatively, use it in a warm shower, allowing it to soften in the heat of the water then rubbing it into your skin for a moisturizing treat.

Safe usage Take care not to slip when getting in and out of the bath.

Enjoy an indulgent bath and feel silky smooth with these skin-replenishing bath melts.

BLEND
VARIATION
Vanilla extract creates a musky and skin-softening bath melt. Or try adding your favorite floral oils to a melt for a fragrant and relaxing treat.

Easy to make, bath melts are a lovely addition to a soak. Try oil blends that promote restful sleep.

BATH OIL   FOOTBATH

Lemon Balm and Lavender Bath Infusion

Try this mixture of herbs, petals, and fragrant oil to **soothe** body and mind. With its sweet, herbal scent, lavender oil is widely used for **relaxing**, while rose is **uplifting** and soothing. Lemon balm, a common garden plant, is wonderfully **calming**.

Ingredients

Makes 17½ fl oz (530 ml)

Lemon balm dried herb 1 tbsp

Dried rose petals 1 tbsp

Water for the infusion 16 fl oz (500 ml)

Lavender essential oil 10 drops

Epsom salt 1 tbsp

How to **make**

1 Make the infusion by steeping the lemon balm and rose petals for 10 minutes in a teapot with 16 fl oz (500 ml) boiled water. Strain the liquid.

2 Add the lavender essential oil to the Epsom salt and combine to make a paste.

3 Strain the infused liquid into a bowl. Add the oil and salt paste to the strained infusion and stir until the salt is dissolved.

Best **uses**

In the bath Add the infusion mixture to the bath immediately and unwind and relax.

As a footbath Add the infusion mixture to a warm footbath to soothe tired and aching feet.

BLEND
VARIATION

Bath infusions can be made with
a variety of dried flowers, herbs, and
favorite oils. Try combining cooling
oils such as bergamot, or
stimulating oils and herbs
such as rosemary.

Combining an herbal infusion
with therapeutic essential oils
relaxes the mind and body.

BLEND
VARIATION
Create body-scrub variations with
other skin-replenishing essential oil
blends, such as fragrant neroli or
balancing petitgrain.

Skin-softening oats provide a
gentle and cleansing base for this
aromatic body scrub.

SKIN CARE

Exfoliating Body Scrub

Using a body scrub is a great way to boost the **circulation** and remove dead skin cells, leaving the skin soft, smooth, and invigorated. Almond oil is richly nourishing and great for **moisturizing** dry skin. Combined with **skin-softening** oats and calming Roman chamomile and lavender essential oils, this soothing scrub conditions and softens skin, giving a silky feel.

Ingredients

Makes 1½ fl oz (45 ml)
Rolled oats 1 tbsp
Dried lavender flowers 1 tsp
Almond oil 2 tbsp
Lavender essential oil 4 drops
Roman chamomile essential oil 4 drops

How to **make**

1 Grind the oats and lavender flowers into a powder with a mortar and pestle or in a blender.

2 Mix the almond oil and essential oils together.

3 Mix the ground oats and flowers with the premixed oils until they form a paste (add more almond oil if dry and more ground oats if wet). Store in a sterilized jar with a tight-fitting lid. It will keep for up to 3 months.

Best **uses**

As a scrub Gently massage the scrub into clean skin, and rinse off with warm water. Pat your skin dry with a clean towel.

Safe usage Do not use on broken or freshly shaved skin.

Natural and nourishing, this fragrant scrub leaves skin feeling soft and invigorated.

MASSAGE OIL

Toning Body Oil

This **detoxifying** blend of essential oils promotes a healthy lymphatic system and tones and firms skin. Rosemary and peppermint combine a **diuretic** effect with **stimulating** and **decongesting** properties, while lemon stimulates the lymphatic system. Mandarin essential oil also has a diuretic action, and when massaged into the skin can help reduce the appearance of stretch marks.

Ingredients

Makes 1½ fl oz (45 ml)

Wheat germ oil 2 tbsp

Rosehip seed oil 1 tbsp

Peppermint essential oil 8 drops

Rosemary essential oil 5 drops

Lemon essential oil 4 drops

Mandarin essential oil 3 drops

How to **make**

Combine all the ingredients in a bowl, then transfer the blend to a sterilized dark-glass bottle and seal with a cap or dropper, ready for use. Store the blend in a cool, dark place. It will keep for up to 3 months.

Best **uses**

As a massage oil Massage into the skin with upward circular movements, paying particular attention to any areas of dry skin. For maximum effect, dry brush skin with a soft-bristled body brush to remove dead skin cells before using the oil.

This dynamic, toning group of essential oils can help tackle areas of stubborn cellulite.

BLEND VARIATION
Create body oils to suit your needs: try frankincense and rose essential oils for a nourishing blend, or sandalwood and neroli for an uplifting, destressing blend.

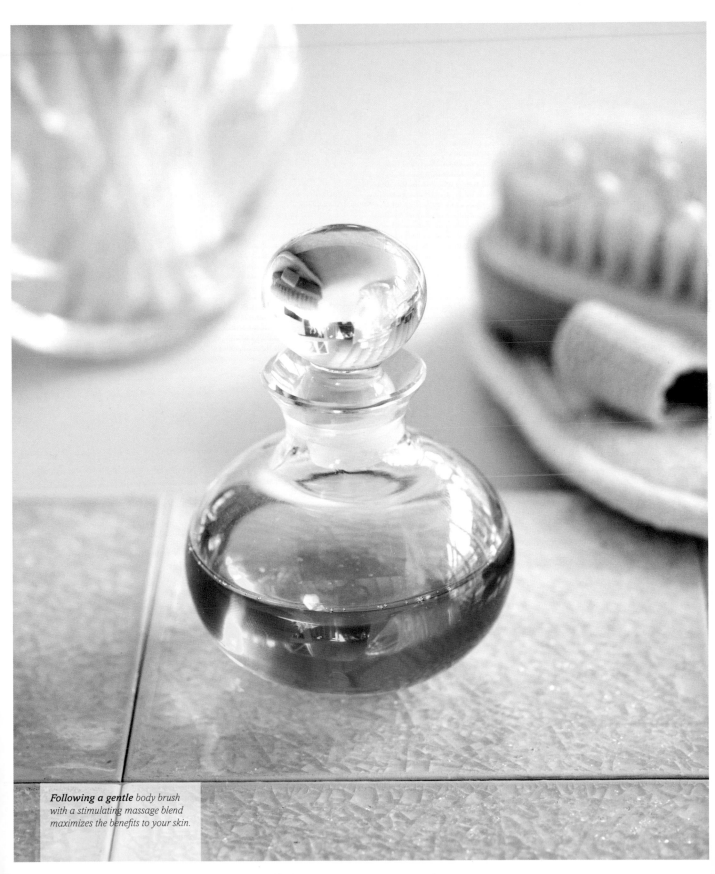

Following a gentle body brush with a stimulating massage blend maximizes the benefits to your skin.

HAIR CARE

Hair and Scalp Tonic

Stimulating and **cleansing** rosemary is excellent for hair and scalp conditions, including hair loss and dandruff, while cider vinegar helps to smooth the hair shaft and give added shine for healthy-looking hair. Combined with a herbal infusion, this **invigorating** hair tonic provides a fragrant rinse that not only leaves hair feeling **soft** and looking **glossy,** but can also help relieve a dry, flaking scalp.

Ingredients

Makes 7½ fl oz (220 ml)

Dried nettle leaves 1 tbsp

Water for infusion 7 fl oz (200 ml)

Cider vinegar 1 tsp

Sage essential oil 1 drop

Lemon essential oil 1 drop

Rosemary essential oil 1 drop

Cedarwood essential oil
1 drop

How to **make**

1 Make an infusion by steeping the nettles for 10 minutes in a teapot with 7 fl oz (200 ml) boiling water. Strain out the nettles.

2 Add the cider vinegar and the essential oils. Pour the mixture into a sterilized glass bottle. It will keep for up to 3 months.

Despite their sting, nettles have a host of benefits, and can help to cleanse and strengthen hair.

Best **uses**

As a hair tonic Shake the bottle before use. Before shampooing, pour a cupful of the tonic over wet hair in the shower or bath. Massage into the hair or comb through, then follow with your usual shampoo. Continue to dry and style as usual.

Safe usage *Avoid sage oil in pregnancy and when breast-feeding.*

This refreshing hair tonic will leave you with glossy locks and a healthy-feeling scalp.

HAIR CARE

Conditioning Hair Oil

Coconut oil and shea butter are widely used in hair care thanks to their **nourishing** properties and their ability to add body, **luster**, and **shine** to lank hair. Cypress essential oil helps to **revive** dull-looking and dry hair, lavender is soothing and **healing**, and lemon **moisturizes** the scalp. Apply the oil with a destressing scalp massage, working gently into any areas of tension.

Ingredients

Makes 1½ fl oz (45 ml)

Coconut oil solid 2 tbsp

Shea butter 3 tsp

Cypress essential oil 3 drops

Lavender essential oil 2 drops

Lemon essential oil 1 drop

How to **make**

1 Melt the coconut oil and shea butter together in a bain-maire (see p188). Remove from the heat and add the essential oils.

2 Pour into a sterilized glass jar. Let cool and then seal with a lid. It will keep for up to 3 months.

Best **uses**

As a hair conditioner Depending on the length of your hair, a coin-sized amount of oil should be enough for one application. Massage into the hair, paying particular attention to the scalp, then wrap hair in a warm towel and leave for 30–60 minutes, or overnight. To remove the oil, rub shampoo through the hair before it comes into contact with any water, then rinse out shampoo with warm water. Repeat to make sure the last traces of oil have been removed. Let hair dry naturally.

Nourishing coconut gives shine and luster to dry, damaged hair.

SKIN CARE

Argan and Avocado Facial Scrub

Frankincense oil has been used for centuries to **tone** and **firm** the skin, and is combined here with ground rice, a lovely natural exfoliator with a gentle scrubbing action. Mixed with **regenerative** argan oil and fatty acid-rich avocado oil, this facial scrub not only polishes, but also **replenishes** the skin. Use twice a week to achieve smooth, glowing skin.

Ingredients

Makes 1 fl oz (30 ml)

Ground rice 1 tsp

Kaolin clay 1 tsp

Argan oil 1 tbsp

Avocado oil 1 tbsp

Rose essential oil 1 drop

Frankincense essential oil 1 drop

How to **make**

1 Mix the ground rice, kaolin clay, and the argan and avocado oils together to form a paste (add more of the oils if too dry and more kaolin if the mixture seems too wet).

2 Add the essential oils. Use immediately.

Best **uses**

As a facial scrub Gently massage the scrub into clean skin, avoiding the delicate area around the eyes, then remove with warm water. Pat your skin dry with a clean towel.

Making a facial scrub a regular part of your beauty regimen keeps your skin supple and smooth.

BLEND
VARIATION
Experiment to find your favorite facial-scrub blend: try palmarosa, lemon, cypress, or other skin-friendly essential oils.

This rejuvenating *facial scrub is
a richly nourishing treat for
tired-looking skin.*

BLEND
VARIATION
Try other hydrating and refreshing essential oils for different "flavored" spritzes, such as palmarosa, bergamot, and lemon.

Carry this facial spray with you on long trips and revive and *hydrate skin with a quick spritz.*

STEAM INHALATION

Cleansing Facial Steam

One of the best ways to treat clogged facial pores is by giving them a **warm** steam facial. This sweats your skin, which opens pores and helps push any dirt out. Here, **antiseptic** tea tree, **skin-balancing** palmarosa, and **healing** lavender will help give your skin a deep cleanse.

Ingredients

Makes Enough for 1 facial steam
Palmarosa essential oil 2 drops
Tea tree essential oil 1 drop
Lavender essential oil 1 drop

How to **make**

Fill a bowl halfway with hot water, making sure the bowl is set securely on a table. Add the essential oils.

Best **uses**

As an inhalation Wash your face with a mild cleanser and rinse well. Keeping hair away from the face, drape a towel over your head and place your face over the bowl of steaming hot water. If at any point you feel the steam is too hot on your skin, move your face farther away. Remain over the steam for about 10 to 15 minutes, or until the steam cools. Rinse your skin with lukewarm water and then pat it dry.

SKIN CARE

Facial Spritz

Rose-floral water can be used as a simple, beautifully **fragrant** skin remedy. The water contains some of the essential oil, which **calms** skin and reduces redness. Also useful for a **hydrating** boost, this mix is suitable for all skin types. Keep in the fridge for an ultra-refreshing spritz.

Ingredients

Makes 3 fl oz (90 ml)
Mineral water 2½ fl oz (75 ml)
Rose floral water 1 tbsp
Aloe vera juice 1 tsp
Glycerine 1 tsp
Rose essential oil 5 drops

How to **make**

1 Combine the mineral water and rose-floral water together.

2 Add the aloe vera juice and glycerine. Add the drops of essential oil.

3 Transfer to a sterilized bottle with an atomizer and store in the fridge. It will keep for up to 3 months.

Best **uses**

As a skin spray Spritz the face or body after cleansing, or whenever you need a refreshing, hydrating boost. Perfect for traveling.

Facial massage oils work wonderfully to revive dull skin by balancing and improving skin tone.

Store facial blends in sterilized glass bottles and ideally keep in the fridge to maximize their shelf life.

MASSAGE OIL

Apricot and Rose Facial Oil

Facial oils are simple to make and effective **moisturizers**. Here, beautifully **light** apricot oil makes an ideal facial massage oil for normal skin types, blending well with rose-hip base oil, which helps tissue **regeneration** for facial lines and scars.

Ingredients

Makes 1 ½ fl oz (45 ml)

Apricot kernel oil 2 tbsp

Rosehip seed oil 1 tbsp

Rose absolute or essential oil 2 drops

Cypress essential oil 2 drops

Clary sage essential oil 2 drops

Patchouli essential oil 1 drop

How to **make**

1 Combine the apricot and rosehip seed oils in a bowl. Add the essential oils to the mixture.

2 Transfer into a sterilized dark-glass bottle and seal with a cap or dropper, ready for use. Store in a cool, dark place. It keeps for up to 3 months.

Best **uses**

As a facial massage oil Apply a few drops to the fingertips and massage into the face and neck, using upward sweeping motions and avoiding the delicate eye area. Use at night, or under your everyday moisturizer if your skin is in need of additional hydration.

MASSAGE OIL

Tea Tree and Lemon Facial Oil

Suitable for combination and oily skin types, grape-seed and jojoba carrier oils help to restore normal oil production. **Astringent** lemon and **balancing** cedarwood essential oils tone and **balance** problem skin, and tea tree is strongly **antiseptic**, working on pimples and blackheads.

Ingredients

Makes 1 ½ fl oz (45 ml)

Grapeseed oil 2 tbsp

Jojoba oil 1 tbsp

Tea tree essential oil 4 drops

Lemon essential oil 2 drops

Cedarwood essential oil 1 drop

Rosemary essential oil 1 drop

How to **make**

1 Combine the grapeseed and jojoba oils in a bowl. Add the essential oils to the mixture.

2 Transfer into sterilized dark-glass bottles and seal with a cap or dropper. Store in a cool, dark place. Keeps for up to 3 months.

Best **uses**

As a facial massage oil Apply a few drops to the fingertips and massage into the face and neck, using upward sweeping motions and avoiding the delicate eye area. Use at night after washing the skin.

Safe usage *Avoid exposure to the sun for 12 hours after using lemon essential oil.*

HAND
CREAM

BLEND
VARIATION
For a different blend and aroma,
substitute lemon and lime with
other skin-nourishing essential
oils, such as carrot, neroli,
sandalwood, jasmine,
or geranium.

Moisturizing Nail Balm

A daily hand and nail massage with this **refreshing** balm, concentrating on
the cuticles, will **brighten** dull nails and help stop them from flaking and
breaking. A combination of **nourishing** shea butter, cocoa butter, and coconut
oil, along with **protective** beeswax, helps to improve cuticles and moisturize and
strengthen nails, while lemon and lime essential oils **tone** and **revitalize**.

Ingredients

Makes 1 fl oz (25 ml)

Jojoba oil 1 tsp

Shea butter 1 tsp

Cocoa butter 1 tsp

Coconut oil solid 1 tsp

Beeswax ½ tsp

Lemon essential oil 5 drops

Lime essential oil 4 drops

How to **make**

1 Put the jojoba oil, shea butter,
cocoa butter, coconut oil, and
beeswax in a glass bowl. Heat in a
bain-marie until melted (see p188).

2 Remove from the heat. Add the
essential oils and combine.

3 Pour into a sterilized glass jar, let
cool, then seal with a lid. It will
keep for up to 3 months.

Best **uses**

As a nail balm Gently massage
into the nails and cuticles as part of
a daily hand-care regimen. If your
nails feel dry or brittle during the day,
apply more frequently as required.

*The jojoba is native
to the southern United
States and northern
Mexico.*

*Jojoba seeds look
similar to coffee beans,
but are larger and less
uniform.*

HAND
CREAM

Rejuvenating Hand Cream

Revive the skin on your hands, which is overexposed to the elements and often neglected, with this rich, protective cream that nourishes the hands and nails. The **soothing** and softening olive oil, **regenerative** hemp oil, nourishing cocoa butter, and **protective** beeswax moisturize and repair dry hands, while the **healing** and restorative essential oils are **uplifting** for the mind and increase well-being.

Ingredients

Makes 4 fl oz (120 ml)

Olive oil 1 tbsp

Hemp oil 1 tbsp

Cocoa butter 1 tsp

Beeswax 1 tsp

Emulsifying wax 1 tbsp

Mineral water 2 fl oz (60 ml)

Glycerine 1 tsp

Petitgrain essential oil 8 drops

Lemon essential oil 4 drops

Bergamot essential oil 4 drops

Myrrh essential oil 2 drops

How to **make**

1 Place the olive oil, hemp oil, cocoa butter, beeswax, and emulsifying wax in a glass bowl. Heat in a bain-marie until melted (see p188).

2 Heat the water to 176°F (80°C). Add the glycerine. Add the hot oil mixture to the hot water and mix with a handheld electric mixer. Add the essential oils and continue to mix.

3 Pour into a sterilized glass jar, let cool, and seal with a lid. It will keep for up to 3 months.

Best **uses**

As a hand cream Gently massage the cream onto dry hands, rubbing it into your nails and cuticles. Apply as often as required.

Treat your hands with this nourishing, rejuvenating, and beautifully scented hand cream.

Rich in vitamin E and fatty acids, hemp seeds produce a naturally skin-nourishing oil.

FOOTBATH

Footbath

Refresh and **soothe** aching feet with this footbath, which contains a **cooling** peppermint infusion as well as the essential oil with its pain-relieving and **anti-inflammatory** properties. Honey **softens** skin, while cider vinegar relaxes muscles and fights foot bacteria. Use before the foot balm, below.

Ingredients

Makes 17½ fl oz (530 ml)

Peppermint dried herb 1 tbsp

Water for infusion 16 fl oz (500 ml)

Peppermint essential oil 2 drops

Lemon essential oil 2 drops

Epsom salt 1 tbsp

Honey 1 tbsp

Apple cider vinegar 1 tbsp

How to **make**

1 Make a peppermint infusion by brewing the herbs for 10 minutes in a teapot with 16 fl oz (500 ml) freshly boiled water. Strain the liquid.

2 Add the essential oils to the Epsom salts and combine.

3 Add the honey and cider vinegar to the strained peppermint infusion and mix until dissolved.

4 Add the mineral salt and essential oil mixture to 1–2 cups of the infusion and stir until dissolved.

Best **uses**

As a footbath Add the infusion mixture to a warm footbath and soak your feet immediately.

Safe usage *Do not use on broken or freshly shaved skin.*

FOOTBATH

Foot Balm

A combination of **restorative** essential oils, such as myrrh, **nourishing** vegetable oils, and **protective** and **moisturizing** beeswax, helps to soften hard skin to remedy dry or cracked heels. **Deodorizing** lemon essential oil helps lift odors, making this a widely helpful foot treatment.

Ingredients

Makes 3 fl oz (90 ml)

Beeswax 2 tbsp

Castor oil 1 tbsp

Hemp seed oil 1 tbsp

Sunflower oil 2 tbsp

Myrrh essential oil 2 drops

Lavender essential oil 2 drops

Lemon essential oil 2 drops

How to **make**

1 Put the beeswax and vegetable oils in a glass bowl. Heat in a bain-marie (see p188) until melted.

2 Add the essential oils, mix, and allow to cool, stirring occasionally.

3 Scoop the mixture into a sterilized glass jar and seal with a lid. It will keep for up to 3 months.

Best **uses**

As a foot balm First exfoliate areas of dry skin on your feet with a pumice stone, then wash your feet thoroughly and pat dry. Massage the balm into the skin, paying particular attention to dry or cracked areas.

BLEND
VARIATION

Create a foot balm with essential oils of your choice: other restorative oils include helichrysum, palmarosa, frankincense, and cedarwood.

Enriching for the skin, this deliciously scented foot balm is a pampering treat for feet.

Healing
Remedies

Harness the healing powers of essential oils to provide relief from a range of common complaints. Learn how to use oils in therapeutic massages and baths, clearing inhalations, soothing compresses, and skin-healing ointments and creams.

Digestive Problems

Lifestyle factors such as diet, as well as **stress** and emotional upset, can all affect the **healthy functioning** of the digestive system, leading to blockages and other problems. Essential oils treat digestive upsets **holistically**, both addressing the root causes, such as anxiety, and providing relief for symptoms. If a condition persists or is acute, consult your doctor.

Bloating and Constipation

The unpleasant feeling of being bloated occurs when your abdomen is stretched, puffy, and uncomfortable. It's common to feel this way during a holiday period or celebrations. You can avoid feeling overfull by cutting down on carbonated drinks, monitoring portion sizes, sitting down to eat, and getting regular exercise. Constipation can be caused by poor diet and stress, and symptoms can be relieved by making dietary and lifestyle changes. Try increasing your daily intake of fiber to at least ¾–1 oz (18–30 g) a day. Fresh fruit, vegetables, and cereals are all high in fiber. You can also try including some bulking agents in your diet, such as oat bran, which helps to make stool softer and easier to pass. Drink plenty of water too, exercise regularly, and keep active. The following remedies can help ease digestive complaints.

Settling Carrot and Orange Compress

The combination of carrot seed, orange, and fennel in this warming compress has a tonifying and soothing effect on the digestive system. Orange essential oil calms unsettled digestion and helps food move through the digestive tract, in turn relieving constipation and trapped gas, and easing indigestion. Carrot seed is mildly diuretic so it helps to reduce fluid retention, and soothing fennel eases nervous indigestion caused by emotional upset, or indigestion after a rushed meal. This remedy is not suitable in pregnancy.

Ingredients

Makes 1 compress
Almond oil 1 tsp
Orange essential oil 3 drops
Fennel essential oil 2 drops
Carrot seed essential oil 2 drops

How to **make**

1 Fill a bowl with hot water. Add the essential oils to the base oil, then add to the water.

2 Soak a washcloth in the bowl, then remove the washcloth and squeeze out the excess water.

3 Wrap the washcloth in a towel or plastic wrap to insulate it. Put the compress on the abdomen. Leave the washcloth in place while it cools to body temperature, then repeat 3 times.

Stimulating Spearmint Massage

Abdominal massage is an effective way to treat constipation and is easily self-administered. Cooling spearmint essential oil is extremely soothing for digestion since it helps calm nausea and indigestion and can also improve a sluggish system.

Ingredients

Makes 1 fl oz (30 ml)
Grape-seed oil 2 tbsp
Spearmint essential oil 5 drops
Pine essential oil 5 drops
Rosemary essential oil 5 drops

How to **make**

1 Combine all the ingredients together in a bowl. Transfer to a sterilized dark-glass bottle and seal with a cap or dropper.

2 Massage clockwise into the abdomen. Allow the oil to absorb into the skin before you get dressed. Store the remaining oil in a cool, dark place. Keeps for up to 3 months.

Soothing Dill Bath Soak

This stomach-settling bath blend makes use of the antispasmodic properties of marjoram, together with the stimulating effect of black pepper and soothing dill to relieve trapped gas and pep up a sluggish digestion. It helps food move along the digestive tract.

Ingredients

Makes ½ fl oz (15 ml)
Base oil or whole milk 1 tbsp
Black pepper essential oil 3 drops
Dill essential oil 3 drops
Marjoram essential oil 3 drops

How to **make**

1 Combine all the ingredients together in a bowl.

2 Disperse the blend immediately in a warm bath and enjoy a relaxing and soothing soak.

Indigestion

Indigestion can be felt as pain or discomfort in the upper abdomen, or as a burning sensation behind the breastbone. The symptoms of indigestion often appear shortly after eating or drinking, and may be caused by stomach acid coming into contact with the sensitive stomach lining. The stomach acid breaks down the lining, leading to irritation and inflammation. In most cases, indigestion is related to eating and is often followed by heartburn, or reflux (see below), although it can be triggered by other factors such as smoking, drinking alcohol, pregnancy, stress, or taking certain medications. Try this massage to ease symptoms.

Cardamom Massage

Essential oils that are antispasmodic, calming, and warming, such as coriander, mandarin, and cardamom, can help to relieve indigestion.

Ingredients

Makes 1 fl oz (30 ml)
Almond oil 2 tbsp
Mandarin essential oil 5 drops
Coriander essential oil 3 drops
Cardamom essential oil 2 drops

How to **make**

1 Combine all the ingredients together in a bowl. Transfer to a sterilized dark-glass bottle and seal with a cap or dropper.

2 Gently massage into the chest and abdomen. Allow the oil to absorb into the skin before you get dressed. Store the remaining oil in a cool, dark place. Keeps for up to 3 months.

Reflux

Acid reflux is a condition where stomach acid comes back up into the mouth and causes an unpleasant, sour taste. It can also be accompanied by symptoms such as gas and bloating, and indigestion and heartburn. Reflux can be caused by a number of things, such as eating big portions and high-fat meals, eating too many acidic foods, and chronic stress. Try this soothing massage to help calm the symptoms.

Peppermint and Ginger Massage

Essential oils can help relieve the symptoms of reflux when massaged onto the chest and abdomen. You may also find that a slice of lemon or fresh ginger, or a sprig of fresh peppermint infused in a glass of hot water is helpful.

Ingredients

Makes 1 fl oz (30 ml)
Sunflower oil 2 tbsp
Peppermint essential oil 7 drops
Ginger essential oil 5 drops
Dill essential oil 3 drops

How to **make**

1 Combine all the ingredients together in a bowl. Transfer to a sterilized dark-glass bottle and seal with a cap or dropper.

2 Gently massage into the abdomen, chest, and upper back. Allow the oil to absorb into the skin before you get dressed. Store the remaining oil in a cool, dark place. Keeps for up to 3 months.

Dill *has a calming effect on digestion.*

Nausea and Vomiting

Nausea is the unpleasant sensation that can precede vomiting, or the feeling can be there without vomiting. Vomiting occurs when the stomach contents are forcefully expelled through the mouth. Nausea and vomiting may be due to a variety of causes, such as eating or drinking too much, hormonal changes in the first trimester of pregnancy, or an infection. These causes may need little or no treatment. However, if there is no obvious cause for prolonged bouts of vomiting, talk to your doctor since it is important to identify the underlying cause. Try the remedies here to ease nausea.

Warming Cardamom Compress

If the abdomen is tender and painful to touch, gently applying a warm compress can be soothing and just as effective as an abdominal massage.

Ingredients

Makes 1 compress
Almond oil 1 tsp
Cardamom essential oil 2 drops
Black pepper essential oil 2 drops

How to **make**

1 Fill a bowl with warm water. Add the essential oils to the base oil and then to the water.

2 Soak a washcloth in the bowl, then remove the washcloth and squeeze out the excess water.

3 Wrap the washcloth in a towel or piece of plastic wrap to insulate it. Place the compress on the abdomen. Leave the washcloth in place while it cools to body temperature, then repeat the process 3 times.

Ginger Diffusion

Ginger is a classic remedy for overcoming nausea and stomach upsets, whether caused by overindulgence, pregnancy hormones, or motion sickness. Here, ginger essential oil is partnered with Roman chamomile. A slightly gentler oil than German chamomile, Roman chamomile is suitable for young children and for those who have a delicate constitution.

Ingredients

Makes enough for 1 diffusion
Ginger essential oil 6 drops
Roman chamomile essential oil 3 drops
Peppermint essential oil 3 drops

How to **make**

1 Add the essential oil blend to a diffuser, vaporizer, or oil burner.

2 Gently scent your chosen environment.

***Ginger** can quell feelings of nausea.*

Diarrhea

Diarrhea is frequent, watery bowel movements. It can be caused by eating foods that irritate the gut, by a bowel infection, or by nerves and stress. Keep well hydrated if you have diarrhea. These remedies can soothe the intestinal lining.

Stomach-Calming Massage Blend

Blend antispasmodic essential oils, such as cypress and ginger, with pain-relieving lavender for this therapeutic blend.

Ingredients

Makes 1 fl oz (30 ml)
Sunflower oil 2 tbsp
Cypress essential oil 6 drops
Ginger essential oil 5 drops
Lavender essential oil 3 drops

How to **make**

1 Combine all the ingredients together in a bowl. Transfer to a sterilized dark-glass bottle and seal with a cap or dropper.

2 Massage clockwise into the abdomen. Allow the oil to absorb into the skin before you get dressed. Store the remaining oil in a cool, dark place. Keeps for up to 3 months.

Mandarin and Geranium Compress

Mandarin can settle digestion and is effective for overcoming feelings of nausea. Here it's combined with geranium and black pepper, which help to stimulate and support the digestive system. This compress will help soothe an unsettled stomach and restore normal bowel movements. The heat also relaxes the abdominal muscles.

Ingredients

Makes 1 compress
Almond oil 1 tsp
Mandarin essential oil 3 drops
Geranium essential oil 2 drops
Black pepper essential oil 2 drops

How to **make**

1 Fill a bowl with hot water. Add the essential oils to the base oil, then to the water.

2 Soak a washcloth in the bowl, then remove the washcloth and squeeze out the excess water.

3 Wrap the washcloth in a towel or piece of plastic wrap to insulate it. Place the compress on the abdomen. Leave the washcloth in place while it cools to body temperature, then repeat the process 3 times.

Appetite Loss

There are a number of reasons why you might lose your appetite. Some conditions are temporary, or sometimes, appetite loss can indicate a serious condition such as anorexia nervosa which is an eating disorder where a person keeps their body weight as low as possible. A condition such as anorexia requires specialized treatment. Always consult your doctor if you experience an unexplained loss of appetite. The bath soak below can help to stimulate appetite.

Peppermint Soak

Ginger and peppermint stimulate the appetite. Added to a warm bath, they are absorbed into the skin and their scent inhaled. Peppermint and ginger herbal teas also help to stimulate appetite.

Ingredients

Makes ½ fl oz 15 ml ()
Base oil or whole milk 1 tbsp
Peppermint essential oil 5 drops
Ginger essential oil 2 drops

How to **make**

1 Combine all the ingredients together in a bowl.

2 Disperse the blend immediately in a warm bath and enjoy a relaxing soak.

Mouth, Gum, and Tooth Problems

Most oral disease is caused by bacterial infection. When bacteria forms in the mouth it produces a sticky, colorless film on the teeth called plaque, which hardens into tartar. Plaque and tartar irritate and inflame gums, which can destroy the gums and tissues. Research has linked gum disease to cardiovascular health and diabetes, so a healthy mouth is thought to promote good health.

Bad breath (halitosis) has many causes, but is usually due to poor oral hygiene. If bacteria builds up in the mouth, it breaks down pieces of food lodged in

the teeth and creates a bad odor. The following remedies help to improve oral hygiene.

Soothing Gum Oil

Myrrh essential oil helps to reduce gum inflammation, while clove has a numbing effect to help relieve pain and soreness.

Ingredients

Makes ½ fl oz (15 ml)
Olive oil 1 tbsp
Clove essential oil 1 drop
Myrrh essential oil 1 drop
Peppermint essential oil 1 drop

How to **make**

1 Combine all the ingredients together in a bowl. Transfer to a sterilized small glass jar.

2 Gently rub the oil blend into the gums, then rinse out with water.

Oregano Gargle

To combat halitosis, try a gargle with antibacterial oils.

Ingredients

Makes ½ fl oz (15 ml)
Sunflower oil 1 tbsp
Peppermint essential oil 1 drop
Oregano essential oil 1 drop

How to **make**

1 Mix the oil blend with cold water.

2 Wash the solution around the mouth for 3–5 minutes, then spit it out. Rinse with water. Use 3 times daily.

Safe usage *Do not swallow. Not suitable in pregnancy.*

Respiratory Complaints

While it is hard to avoid all cold viruses, there are steps you can take to **boost immunity**. Once a cold has set in, early treatment can also help to minimize its severity. Chronic conditions, such as asthma, require careful medical management, but there are ways to help control them. Essential oil's **decongesting**, **antiviral**, and **calming** properties can ease respiratory complaints.

Colds and Sinusitis

A cold is a mild viral infection of the nose, throat, sinuses, and upper airways. This viral infection is very common and usually clears up on its own within a week or two. The main symptoms of a cold include an initial sore throat, stuffy or runny nose, sneezing, and coughing.

Sinusitis is another common condition in which the lining of the sinuses becomes inflamed, and this usually follows a viral infection such as a cold. Symptoms of sinusitis include a green or yellow nasal discharge, stuffy nose, pain and tenderness around the cheeks, eyes, or forehead, a sinus headache, and a temperature. The symptoms often improve within two to three weeks.

While you can't "cure" a cold virus, there are several ways in which you can use essential oils to bring relief to colds and blocked sinuses.

Frankincense Throat and Chest Rub

Frankincense essential oil helps to soothe the mucous membranes and calm breathing, and can also ease coughs, sore throats, and bronchitis. It is blended here with other soothing oils to create a warming upper-body rub to help combat colds and congestion.

Ingredients

Makes 1 fl oz (30 ml)
Sunflower oil 2 tbsp
Frankincense essential oil 7 drops
Sandalwood essential oil 5 drops
Lavender essential oil 3 drops

How to **make**

1 Mix all the ingredients together in a bowl. Transfer to a sterilized dark glass bottle. Seal with a cap or dropper.

2 Gently massage into the chest, throat, and upper back. Allow the oil to absorb before you get dressed.

Clearing Eucalyptus Diffusion

Eucalyptus has wonderful clearing properties that help to relieve blocked sinuses. Using a diffuser to disperse this essential oil in the air is an effective way to ease congested sinuses. Sit near the diffuser for the most direct effect.

Ingredients

Makes enough for 1 diffusion
Cedarwood essential oil 4 drops
Eucalyptus essential oil 4 drops
Ravensara essential oil 4 drops

How to **make**

1 Add the essential oil blend to a diffuser, vaporizer, or oil burner.

2 Gently scent your chosen environment.

Cajeput and Tea Tree Inhalation

Steam inhalations are very effective at treating sore throats and relieving congestion.

Ingredients

Makes enough for 1 inhalation
Cajeput essential oil 6 drops
Tea tree essential oil 4 drops
Lavender essential oil 4 drops

How to **make**

1 Add the essential oils to a bowl of hot water. Cover your head with a towel, making a tent over the bowl, then inhale deeply.

2 Allow the steam to soothe the throat for 5–10 minutes, taking a break from the steam if needed.

Asthma

Asthma is a common long-term condition that can cause coughing, wheezing, breathlessness, and tightness in the chest. The severity of the symptoms varies from person to person. In most people, the condition can be controlled well for most of the time, although some experience more persistent problems.

Occasionally, asthma gets gradually or suddenly much worse. This is known as an asthma attack, and these more severe attacks may require immediate hospital treatment and can even be life threatening, although this is unusual.

No single cause for asthma has been identified, however there are several factors that may trigger an asthma attack. Inhaled or ingested allergens, such as dust mites and certain foods, can trigger an attack. Exercise and emotional stress can also produce asthmatic symptoms. Learning to manage the condition and to avoid potential allergens is key to preventing attacks. The following remedies use oils to help calm mild symptoms, so they can be used alongside usual medical treatments. Consult your doctor before using these remedies, and always seek urgent medical help if you experience a severe asthma attack.

Eucalyptus and Lemon Inhalation

Sometimes asthma symptoms can be triggered by the presence of an infection such as a cold or flu virus. An inhalation using clearing essential oils can be useful to help ease asthma symptoms in these circumstances.

Ingredients

Makes enough for 1 inhalation
Lemon essential oil 4 drops
Eucalyptus essential oil 4 drops
Peppermint essential oil 4 drops

How to **make**

1 Place the oil drops directly on a tissue or handkerchief.

2 Keep the tissue with you and inhale by wafting the tissue under the nose. Do not cover the nose with the tissue.

Frankincense Diffusion

Asthma symptoms can sometimes worsen if a person has had an emotional upset or specific trauma. In these circumstances, a diffusion with calming

Eucalyptus has clearing properties.

essential oils such as frankincense, sandalwood, and lavender can be effective in easing the symptoms.

Ingredients

Frankincense essential oil 7 drops
Sandalwood essential oil 5 drops
Lavender essential oil 3 drops

How to **make**

1 Add the essential oil blend to a diffuser, vaporizer, or oil burner.

2 Gently scent your chosen environment.

Calming Chamomile Massage

If asthma symptoms are typically brought on by exposure to allergens, such as dust mites or certain foods, have an already-prepared massage blend on hand, made up of soothing essential oils such as chamomile, and an oil such as helichrysum, which has an antispasmodic action.

Ingredients

Makes 30ml (1fl oz)
Sunflower oil 2 tbsp
Helichrysum essential oil 4 drops
Lavender essential oil 4 drops
Roman chamomile essential oil 4 drops

How to **make**

1 Combine all the ingredients together in a bowl. Transfer to a sterilized dark-glass bottle and seal with a cap or dropper.

2 Gently massage into the chest, throat, and upper back. Allow the oil to absorb into the skin before you get dressed. Store the remaining oil in a cool, dark place. Keeps for up to 3 months.

Circulatory problems

Circulatory problems can be caused by poor diet, smoking, having a sedentary lifestyle, and stress. Improving **lifestyle factors** such as diet and building a regular **exercise regimen** can help to address problems. Essential oils can **stimulate** sluggish circulation and may help to provide the **motivation** to change your lifestyle.

Varicose Veins and Hemorrhoids

Varicose veins develop when the small valves inside the veins stop working properly. In a healthy vein, blood flows smoothly to the heart, and the blood is prevented from flowing backward by a series of tiny valves that open and close to enable it to pass through. If these valves weaken or are damaged, the blood can start to flow backward and then collect in the vein, eventually causing the vein to become swollen and enlarged (known as varicose). Pregnancy, being overweight, and old age are all factors that can increase the chances of developing varicose veins.

Hemorrhoids are related to varicose veins. These are swellings containing enlarged blood vessels that are found inside or around the rectum and anus. In many cases, hemorrhoids don't cause symptoms, and some people don't even realize that they have them. The following compress can help to ease and relieve symptoms such as pain or itching.

Soothing Cypress Compress

Cypress essential oil has a toning effect on the veins and is a useful oil for circulatory problems since it helps to regulate the flow of blood, making it particularly useful for conditions such as varicose veins. Here it is combined with detoxifying lemon and geranium essential oils, and juniper essential oil, which has an astringent action that is helpful for shrinking varicose veins and hemorrhoids.

Ingredients

Makes 1 compress
Sunflower oil 2 tsp
Cypress essential oil 3 drops
Lemon essential oil 3 drops
Juniper essential oil 3 drops
Geranium essential oil 1 drop

How to **make**

1 Fill a bowl with cold water. Add the essential oils to the sunflower oil, then add to the water.

2 Soak a washcloth in the bowl, then remove the washcloth and squeeze out the excess water.

3 Place the compress over the varicose veins, or for hemorrhoids, sit on the compress with a towel underneath. Leave in place for 10 minutes.

High Blood Pressure

Hypertension is another term for high blood pressure. Blood pressure is measured in millimeters of mercury (mmHg), and it is recorded as two figures: systolic pressure—the pressure of the

Essential oils can be used to stimulate or calm circulation.

blood when your heart pushes blood out, and diastolic pressure—the pressure of the blood when your heart rests in between beats, which reflects how strongly your arteries are resisting blood flow.

It is perfectly normal for the systolic blood pressure to increase during exertion or emotional stress, but in a healthy body it will return to normal quite quickly. A number of lifestyle and dietary changes can be made to help reduce the risk of hypertension, for example increasing exercise, reducing salt intake, quitting smoking, and reducing stress and stimulants. A relaxing massage can help combat the cumulative effects of stress and tension.

If you have been diagnosed with high blood pressure, talk to your doctor before using any complementary remedy to make sure that your condition is being monitored medically. Continue to take your usual prescribed medication alongside remedies unless directed otherwise by your doctor.

Lavender and Marjoram Massage

Essential oils that have a hypotensive action (meaning they help to lower blood pressure), as well as calming and sedating effects, can be used to alleviate mild hypertension. Here, lavender, marjoram, and ylang-ylang essential oils are combined to make a therapeutic massage blend that can be used to help combat mild hypertension.

Ingredients

Makes 1 fl oz (30 ml)
Almond oil 2 tbsp
Lavender essential oil 6 drops
Marjoram essential oil 6 drops
Ylang-ylang essential oil 3 drops

How to **make**

1 Combine all the ingredients together in a bowl. Transfer to a sterilized dark-glass bottle and seal with a cap or dropper.

2 Gently massage into the body. Allow the oil to absorb into the skin before you get dressed. Store remaining oil in a cool, dark place. Keeps for up to 3 months.

Sluggish Circulation

There are many different symptoms that can indicate poor circulation. For example, cold extremeties such as the feet and toes and fingers and hands, water retention, and cramps, all suggest that general circulation is sluggish. Other than the daily discomfort that poor circulation can cause, there are some potentially more serious consequences. Simple dietary and lifestyle changes can help improve the circulation. For example, if you sit at a desk all day, make sure that you take regular breaks and move around, stop eating junk food, and try to quit smoking. The following massage can help to stimulate circulation.

Stimulating Rosemary Massage

Some essential oils are stimulating and can help to improve circulation by dilating the capillaries to increase blood flow. This in turn stimulates the flow of lymph, which helps to control the passage of fluids around the body. Poor lymphatic drainage results in a buildup of fluid in the tissues.

Ingredients

Makes 1 fl oz (30 ml)
Almond oil 2 tbsp
Rosemary essential oil 3 drops
Thyme essential oil 3 drops
Black pepper essential oil 3 drops
Ginger essential oil 3 drops
Clove essential oil 1 drop

How to **make**

1 Combine all the ingredients together in a bowl. Transfer to a sterilized dark-glass bottle and seal with a cap or dropper.

2 Gently massage into the body. Allow the oil to absorb into the skin before you get dressed. Store remaining oil in a cool, dark place. Keeps for up to 3 months.

Rosemary *helps improve poor circulation.*

Fluid Retention and Urinary Tract Infections

Swelling and puffiness, known as edema, indicate **fluid retention**, which can have a number of causes. Infections in the urinary tract can cause bladder inflammation. Certain essential oils have **diuretic**, anti-inflammatory, and **antiseptic** properties that can help ease symptoms.

Swelling

Swelling is typically the result of inflammation or a buildup of fluid that can occur internally, or that can affect your outer skin and muscles. Using essential oils that have detoxifying properties helps to flush out excess fluids and reduce inflammation. Consult your doctor if you have any unexplained swelling.

Geranium Compress

A number of essential oils work as circulatory tonics that can help to reduce swelling and fluid retention and are effective used in massage, in a bath, or as a compress, as in the remedy here.

Ingredients

Makes 1 compress
Almond oil 1 tbsp
Geranium essential oil 5 drops
Cypress essential oil 4 drops
Yarrow essential oil 3 drops
Lemon essential oil 3 drops

How to **make**

1 Fill a bowl with cold water. Add the essential oils to the almond oil, then add to the water.

2 Soak a washcloth in the bowl, then remove the washcloth and squeeze out the excess water.

3 Place the compress on the affected area. Leave the washcloth in place while it reaches body temperature, then repeat the process 3 times.

Detox Massage

The lymphatic system is responsible for removing the waste products created by the body's organs and tissues. The blend of detoxifying essential oils used in this massage supports the action of the lymphatic system. Grapefruit specifically encourages lymphatic drainage and acts as a diuretic when it is massaged directly into the skin, helping to combat areas of puffiness caused by water retention. Rosemary helps to stimulate lymphatic circulation, helping the body to remove waste products and also relieving water retention. These two potent oils are combined here with black pepper, which works as a mild diuretic. To maximize the effect of this detox massage, use the oils in combination with a body brush to stimulate the circulation.

Ingredients

Grape-seed oil 2 tbsp
Grapefruit essential oil 5 drops
Rosemary essential oil 5 drops
Black pepper essential oil 5 drops

How to **make**

1 Combine all the ingredients together in a bowl. Transfer to a sterilized dark-glass bottle and seal with a cap or dropper.

2 Gently massage into the skin in upward circular movements. Allow the oil to absorb into the skin before you get dressed. Store the remaining oil in a cool, dark place. Keeps for up to 3 months.

Black pepper helps to flush out waste products.

Urinary-tract Infection

Urinary-tract infections (UTIs) are very common. They can be painful and uncomfortable, but they usually pass within a few days, though sometimes you may need a course of antibiotics. UTIs are more common in women than in men. Children can also get UTIs, but this is less common.

A UTI develops when part of the urinary tract becomes infected, usually by bacteria, which can enter the urinary tract through the urethra or, more rarely, through the bloodstream. There is usually no obvious reason why the urinary tract becomes infected, although some women find they develop a UTI after having sex. Since UTIs are far less common in men than in women, they need to be tested to find an underlying cause.

Cystitis is inflammation of the bladder, usually caused by an infection. Most cases are thought to occur when bacteria that live harmlessly in the bowels or on the skin enter the bladder through the urethra. It's a common type of UTI, particularly in women, and is usually more of a nuisance than a cause for serious concern. Mild cases will often get better by themselves within a few days. However, some people experience episodes of cystitis frequently and may need regular or long-term treatment. There's also a chance that cystitis could lead to a more serious kidney infection, so it's important to seek medical advice if your symptoms don't improve over a few days, or if you have a fever, severe pain, or blood or pus in the urine. Try the following remedies to help ease symptoms and bring relief.

Bergamot Sitz Bath

Because UTIs are caused by infection, essential oils with antibacterial activity are recommended to help fight the infection and support your recovery. Here, antiviral and antibacterial bergamot is combined with astringent chamomile and soothing lavender. The oils are added to a shallow "sitz" bath, which is waist height only and ideal for treating UTIs.

Ingredients

Makes enough for 1 sitz bath
Bergamot essential oil 4 drops
German chamomile essential oil 3 drops
Lavender essential oil 2 drops

How to **make**

1 Fill the bath to waist height. Adjust the temperature depending on how long you want to remain in the bath. For a bath of up to five minutes, run hot water at a temperature of 104–113°F (40–45°C). If you want to stay in the bath for up to 15 minutes, keep the water at 91–95°F (33–35°C). Alternatively, fill a bowl with warm water, add the essential oils, then soak a clean washcloth in the water. Remove and squeeze out the excess water, then gently wash the affected area with the washcloth. After washing, carefully pat the area dry.

2 If using the oils in a shallow bath, add the essential oils to the bath once run, then soak as required.

Tea Tree Wash

The antiseptic properties of tea tree essential oil are especially useful for treating UTIs. Try this simple wash to ease discomfort. Always make sure your washcloths and towels are clean before using and are washed immediately after every use.

Ingredients

Makes enough for 1 wash
Almond oil 1 tsp
Tea tree essential oil 3 drops
Bergamot essential oil 3 drops

How to **make**

1 Fill a large bowl with warm water. Add the essential oils to the almond oil, then add to the water.

2 Soak a clean washcloth in the water, then remove the washcloth and wring it out.

3 Gently wash the affected area with the washcloth, carefully patting the area dry afterward.

Antiseptic and soothing essential oils are useful for easing the symptoms of UTIs.

Muscle and Joint Problems and General Aches and Pains

Healthy muscles and joints help ensure strength and maneuverability. Old age can put a strain on joints and muscles, but **activity** helps maintain **flexibility**. Aches and pains can be due to muscle tension or other causes. Try oils that are **anti-inflammatory**, detoxifying, and **pain-relieving**.

Backaches, Neck Pain, and Sciatica

Back pain is a common problem that affects most people at some point in life. It may be triggered by bad posture, by bending awkwardly, or by lifting heavy loads and objects incorrectly. In most cases, back pain improves over a period of weeks or months, although some experience recurrent long-term pain.

Neck pain, or a stiff neck, is a common problem and usually nothing to worry about. You can get a painful or stiff neck if you sleep awkwardly, use a computer for a prolonged period of time, or strain a muscle because of bad posture. The pain and stiffness usually get better after a few days or weeks. Anxiety and stress can also cause tension in the neck muscles that can lead to neck pain. If pain is acute or long lasting, consult your doctor.

A stiff neck accompanied by other symptoms such as fever, headache, or intolerance to bright lights should be seen to by a doctor immediately.

Sciatica is the name for pain that is caused by irritation or compression of the sciatic nerve, which is the longest nerve in the body. It runs from the back of the pelvis, through the buttocks, and all the way down the legs, ending at the feet. When this nerve is compressed or irritated, it can cause pain, numbness, and a tingling sensation that radiates from the lower back down one leg to the foot and toes. While sciatica pain can also be accompanied by general back pain, the pain of sciatica usually affects the buttocks and legs more than the back. Try the following pain-relieving remedies.

Muscle-Relaxing Massage

Essential oils and massage can be extremely effective in treating backaches and neck pain where the pain is due to tension or muscular fatigue. Regular massage with oils and essential oil baths can help to prevent backaches by reducing stress, relaxing tight muscles, and improving general well-being, which helps to relieve persistent tension. The following massage blend can also be added to a bath for a relaxing soak, combining the essential oils with just a tablespoon of arnica oil, or alternatively with a tablespoon of whole milk or vodka.

Ingredients

Makes 1 fl oz (30 ml)
Arnica macerated oil 2 tbsp
Rosemary essential oil 5 drops
Marjoram essential oil 5 drops
Ginger essential oil 5 drops

Soothing lavender
helps to relieve pain.

How to **make**

1 Combine the ingredients in a bowl. Transfer to a sterilized dark-glass bottle. Seal with a cap or dropper.

2 Massage into the back and neck. Allow the oil to absorb into the skin before you get dressed. Store the remaining oil in a cool, dark place. Keeps for up to 3 months.

Soothing Lavender Compress

Lavender is mildly analgesic and anti-spasmodic, so it can soothe sciatic pain.

Ingredients

Makes 1 compress
Almond oil 1 tsp
Lavender essential oil 5 drops
Coriander essential oil 2 drops
Black pepper essential oil 5 drops

How to **make**

1 Fill a bowl with warm water. Add the essential oils to the almond oil, then add to the water.

2 Soak a washcloth in the bowl, then remove it and squeeze out the excess water.

3 Wrap the cloth in a towel or plastic wrap to insulate it. Place compress on affected area. Leave it in place while it cools to body temperature, then repeat the process 3 times.

Headaches and Migraines

Headaches are one of the most common health complaints. In many cases they can be easily treated with small lifestyle changes, such as getting more rest and drinking fluids so that you stay well hydrated. Tension headaches are often described as a constant ache that affects both sides of the head, and these are commonly linked to stress, poor posture, skipping meals, and dehydration. Migraines are less common than headaches. They're usually felt as a severe, throbbing pain at the front or side of the head. Other symptoms of migraines may include nausea, vomiting, and increased sensitivity to light or sound. A soothing compress or head massage can bring relief.

Calming Peppermint and Lavender Compress

With its gently stimulating and analgesic properties, peppermint is an established treatment in aromatherapy for tension headaches, working in a similar way to drugs such as acetaminophen. Its cooling action clears and refreshes the mind. Relaxing lavender helps to bring relief to headaches caused by anxiety and stress.

Ingredients

Makes 1 compress
Almond oil 1 tsp
Peppermint essential oil 3 drops
Lavender essential oil 2 drops

How to **make**

1 Fill a bowl with warm water. Add the essential oils to the almond oil, then add to the water.

2 Soak a washcloth in the bowl, then remove the washcloth and squeeze out the excess water.

3 Place the compress on the forehead. Leave the washcloth in place while it cools to body temperature, then repeat the process 3 times.

Warming Marjoram Compress

Marjoram essential oil has both a sedative and analgesic effect, so in addition to relieving pain, it can also help to reduce the anxiety and tension that lead to headaches and migraines.

Ingredients

Makes 1 compress
Almond oil 1 tsp
Lavender essential oil 3 drops
Marjoram essential oil 2 drops

How to **make**

1 Fill a bowl with warm water. Add the essential oils to the almond oil, then add to the water.

2 Soak a washcloth in the bowl, then remove the washcloth and squeeze out the excess water.

3 Wrap the washcloth in a towel or piece of plastic wrap to insulate it. Place the compress on the temples. Leave the washcloth in place while it cools to body temperature, then repeat the process 3 times.

Rosemary and Eucalyptus Temple Massage

Tension headaches caused by mental effort can be treated with rosemary. Eucalyptus is useful for soothing headaches caused by sinus congestion or allergic reactions. Here, the two oils are combined with refreshing peppermint and relaxing lavender.

Ingredients

Makes 1 fl oz (30 ml)
Almond oil 2 tbsp
Rosemary essential oil 5 drops
Peppermint essential oil 3 drops
Lavender essential oil 2 drops
Eucalyptus essential oil 2 drops

How to **make**

1 Combine all the ingredients together in a bowl. Transfer to a sterilized dark-glass bottle and seal with a cap or dropper.

2 Massage gently into the temples in a circular motion. Store the remaining oil in a cool, dark place. Keeps for up to 3 months.

Arthritis

Arthritis is caused by joint inflammation. The two most common types are rheumatoid arthritis and osteoarthritis. Rheumatoid arthritis is a chronic autoimmune disease that causes swelling, pain, and stiffness in joints, commonly affecting the hands, wrists, and feet. Osteoarthritis makes joints painful and stiff. It occurs when there is damage in and around joints. Most joints can be affected with arthritis, but the condition commonly causes problems in the knees, hips, and the small joints of the hands. Massage and bath soaks can ease the stiffness caused by arthritis.

Circulation-Boosting Massage

Warming, relaxing, and pain-relieving oils such as marjoram help relieve the pain of arthritis. Black pepper and ginger stimulate circulation, in turn revitalizing tired, aching joints. Black pepper also has anti-inflammatory properties, making it an ideal oil for soothing arthritis. Ginger also has an anti-inflammatory effect and is naturally reviving and stimulating when applied locally. Try using this massage oil blend locally to bring relief to affected areas.

Ingredients

Makes 1 fl oz (30 ml)
Almond oil 2 tbsp
Marjoram essential oil 6 drops
Black pepper essential oil 5 drops
Ginger essential oil 4 drops

How to **make**

1 Combine all the ingredients together in a bowl. Transfer to a sterilized dark-glass bottle and seal with a cap or dropper.

2 Massage into the affected joints. Allow the oil to absorb into the skin before you get dressed. Store the remaining oil in a cool, dark place. Keeps for up to 3 months.

Soothing Yarrow Soak

Nutmeg and yarrow oils help to reduce inflammation. Adding these oils to a warm bath combines the soothing effects of warm water with the oils' benefits.

Ingredients

Makes ½ fl oz (15 ml)
Base oil or whole milk 1 tbsp
Nutmeg essential oil 3 drops
Yarrow essential oil 3 drops
Lavender essential oil 5 drops

How to **make**

1 Combine all the ingredients together in a bowl.

2 Disperse immediately in the bath and enjoy a relaxing soak.

Muscular Aches and Pains

Muscular aches and pains are common and can involve several muscles. Muscle pain can also involve ligaments, tendons, and fascia (the soft tissues that connect muscles, bones, and organs). It's usually related to tension, overuse, or injury from exercise or movement. Muscle pain may be a sign of another condition. For example, certain infections and disorders, such as lupus, affect connective tissues and cause muscle pain. Another cause of muscular aches and pains is fibromyalgia, a condition that causes tenderness in the muscles and surrounding tissue, sleep difficulties, fatigue, and headaches. A targeted massage or compress can reduce pain.

"Unknotting" Massage

An essential oil massage can help to stimulate the circulation, relieve pain, and reduce inflammation. The blend here, with pain-relieving plai and stimulating black pepper, can also be added to a bath with 1 tablespoon of whole milk or base oil.

Ingredients

Makes 1 fl oz (30 ml)
Arnica macerated oil 1 tbsp
Almond oil 1 tbsp
Plai essential oil 5 drops
Lemongrass essential oil 2 drops
Black pepper essential oil 3 drops

How to **make**

1 Combine all the ingredients together in a bowl. Transfer to a sterilized dark-glass bottle and seal with a cap or dropper.

2 Massage into the affected area. Allow the oil to absorb into the skin before you get dressed. Store the remaining oil in a cool, dark place. Keeps for up to 3 months.

Hot Ginger Compress

Alternating hot and cold compresses can be an effective way to deal with aches and pains. This warming ginger blend boosts circulation and soothes sore, aching muscles.

Arnica is effective for reducing bruising.

Ingredients

Makes 1 compress
Almond oil 1 tsp
Ginger essential oil 7 drops
Lavender essential oil 4 drops
Rosemary essential oil 4 drops

How to **make**

1 Fill a bowl with warm water. Add the essential oils to the almond oil, then add to the water.

2 Soak a washcloth in the bowl, then remove the washcloth and squeeze out the excess water.

3 Wrap the washcloth in a towel or plastic wrap to insulate it. Put compress on affected area. Leave it while it cools to body temperature, then repeat the process 3 times.

Sprains and Strains

Sprains are torn ligaments, which connect bone to bone, and strains are injuries to tendons, which connect muscle to bone. Sprains are more serious. They can be inflamed, painful, and hot to touch. The initial treatment for both is PRICE: "protection, rest, ice, compression, elevation." Try the following soothing remedies.

Anti-inflammatory Lemongrass Compress

Try this cold compress on a sprain. This compress uses pain-relieving lemongrass and the anti-inflammatory oils ginger and black pepper.

Ingredients

Makes 1 compress
Almond oil 1 tsp
Black pepper essential oil 5 drops
Lemongrass essential oil 2 drops
Ginger essential oil 5 drops

How to **make**

1 Fill a bowl with cold water. Add the essential oils to the almond oil, then add to the water.

2 Soak a washcloth in the bowl, then remove the washcloth and squeeze out the excess water.

3 Place the compress on the affected area. Leave it while it warms to body temperature, then repeat the process 3 times.

Analgesic Rosemary Massage

A massage with analgesic and anti-inflammatory oils promotes healing. Here, arnica is also used, a traditional remedy to reduce bruising and swelling.

Ingredients

Makes 1 fl oz (30 ml)
Arnica oil 1 tbsp
Almond oil 1 tbsp
Marjoram essential oil 5 drops
Rosemary essential oil 5 drops
Thyme essential oil 5 drops

How to **make**

1 Combine all the ingredients together in a bowl. Transfer to a sterilized dark-glass bottle and seal with a cap or dropper.

2 Massage into the affected area. Allow the oil to absorb into the skin before you get dressed. Store the remaining oil in a cool, dark place. Keeps for up to 3 months.

Skin and Hair

Our skin has a protective function, forming a **barrier** against our external environment. Sometimes, though, skin can become irritated, clogged, or affected by hormonal changes, or can become damaged by the weather or by being broken. Essential oils can **tone**, balance, and **soothe** a wide range of skin problems, and can also help to **nourish** and hydrate skin.

Acne

Acne is a common skin condition caused by chronic inflammation of the hair follicles and sebaceous glands. It affects many people at some point, but is most common in adolescence. Acne causes pimples to develop usually on the face, back, and chest. The pimples can range from blackheads and whiteheads to deep, inflamed, pus-filled pustules and cysts, which can be severe and long lasting, sometimes leading to scarring. It's very important to keep skin clean using a mild cleanser. Be careful not to scrub the skin too hard since it could cause irritation. These skin-soothing remedies can help calm problem skin.

Lavender Massage

Skin-regenerating oils help promote healing and minimize scarring. Lavender is antiseptic and calming on the skin. Here it is combined with palmarosa, which is gently astringent and anti-inflammatory, helping to soothe dry, inflamed skin.

Ingredients

Makes ½ fl oz (15 ml)
Wheat-germ oil 1 tsp
Rosehip seed oil 1 tsp
Calendula macerated oil 1 tsp
Palmarosa essential oil 3 drops
Lavender essential oil 1 drop

How to **make**

1 Combine all the ingredients together in a bowl. Transfer to a sterilized dark-glass bottle and seal with a cap or dropper.

2 Massage into the skin on the body or face. Allow the oil to absorb into the skin before you get dressed. Store the remaining oil in a cool, dark place. Keeps for up to 3 months.

Lemon and Bergamot Facial Sauna

Essential oils can help bring acne and pimples under control by helping to clear infection and reduce inflammation. The oils can also help mentally, reducing the stress and anxiety that can often accompany skin conditions. For a deep-pore cleanse, try this essential oil facial steam. The skin-clarifying and toning effects of lemon are combined with the antiseptic and skin-balancing properties of petitgrain, and soothing and antibacterial bergamot.

Ingredients

Makes 1 facial sauna
Bergamot essential oil 3 drops
Lemon essential oil 2 drops
Petitgrain essential oil 1 drop

How to **make**

1 Add the essential oils to a bowl of hot water. Cover your head with a towel, make a tent over the bowl of hot water, and then lean forward over the bowl.

2 Allow the steam to act on the face for 5 minutes, taking a break from the steam if necessary. Wash your skin with cool water and pat dry with a clean towel.

Lemon essential oil cleanses and tones problem skin.

Palmarosa Massage

The essential oils geranium and palmarosa have skin-balancing properties that naturally help to reduce the amount of sebum produced by the oil glands. Combining these essential oils with skin-conditioning base oils helps create a nourishing and toning massage oil that can help calm outbreaks.

Ingredients

Makes ½ fl oz (15 ml)
Jojoba oil 1 tsp
Grape-seed oil 2 tsp
Palmarosa essential oil 3 drops
Geranium essential oil 2 drops

How to **make**

1 Combine all the ingredients together in a bowl. Transfer to a sterilized dark-glass bottle and seal with a cap or dropper.

2 Massage into the skin on the body or face. Allow the oil to absorb into the skin before you get dressed. Store the remaining oil in a cool, dark place. Keeps for up to 3 months.

Tea Tree Hot Compress

Tea tree essential oil is renowned for its antiseptic properties, making it an excellent choice for treating problem-skin conditions. Added to a hot compress, it can help soothe and cleanse skin. If you want, you can also apply it undiluted on pimples as an antiseptic ointment.

Ingredients

Makes 20 to 30 treatments
Grape-seed oil 1 tbsp
Tea tree essential oil 3 drops
Cajeput essential oil 2 drops
Lavender essential oil 1 drop

How to **make**

1 Fill a bowl with warm water. Add a few drops of the essential oil blend. Transfer the remaining blend to a sterilized glass jar and store in a cool, dark place. The blend keeps for up to 3 months.

2 Soak a washcloth in the bowl, then remove the washcloth and squeeze out the excess water.

3 Wrap the washcloth in a towel or piece of plastic wrap to insulate it. Put it on the area requiring treatment. Leave the washcloth while it cools to body temperature, then repeat the process 3 times.

Athlete's Foot

Athlete's foot is caused by fungi growing on the skin. The fungi thrive in warm, dark, moist places such as the feet, usually between the toes. Affected skin may be itchy, red, scaly, dry, cracked, or blistered. It's not usually serious, but should be treated to stop it from spreading to other parts of the body or to other people. Keep feet clean, carefully dry the feet, especially between the toes, and go barefoot when possible. Try the massage below to help combat this fungal infection.

Geranium Foot Massage

Antifungal essential oils, such as tea tree and geranium, are ideal for athlete's foot. Here, these oils are blended with lavender essential oil, which helps to heal skin conditions and rejuvenate skin.

Ingredients

Makes 1 fl oz (30 ml)
Neem oil 2 tbsp
Geranium essential oil 4 drops
Tea tree essential oil 4 drops
Lavender essential oil 3 drops

How to **make**

1 Combine all the ingredients together in a bowl. Transfer to a sterilized dark-glass bottle and seal with a cap or dropper.

2 Massage into clean, dry skin on the feet. Allow the oil to absorb into the skin before you get dressed. Store the remaining oil in a cool, dark place. Keeps for up to 3 months.

Bruising

Bruises are bluish or purple-colored patches. They appear on unbroken skin when tiny blood vessels under the skin, known as capillaries, break. The blood leaks into the tissues, causing discoloration, which fades through shades of yellow or green. Try these healing remedies.

Cooling Lavender Compress

Applying an ice-cold compress with healing oils as quickly as possible can help to reduce bruising.

Ingredients

Makes 1 compress
Almond oil 1 tsp
Yarrow essential oil 3 drops
Lavender essential oil 5 drops

How to **make**

1 Fill a bowl with ice and cold water. Add the essential oil blend to the almond oil, then add to the water.

2 Soak a washcloth in the bowl, then remove the washcloth and squeeze out the excess water.

3 Place the compress on the area requiring treatment. Leave the washcloth in place while it reaches body temperature. Repeat 3 times.

Arnica Massage

Arnica macerated oil, ideal for bruising, is blended here with regenerative and rejuvenating helichrysum and lavender oils for a massage blend that can help to reduce the appearance of bruises.

Ingredients

Makes 1 fl oz (30 ml)
Arnica oil 2 tbsp
Helichrysum essential oil 3 drops
Lavender essential oil 3 drops

How to **make**

1 Combine all the ingredients together in a bowl. Transfer to a sterilized dark-glass bottle and seal with a cap or dropper.

2 Gently massage the affected area. Allow the oil to absorb into the skin before getting dressed. Store the remaining oil in a cool, dark place. Keeps for up to 3 months.

Body Odor

Body odor is the unpleasant smell that can occur when the body sweats. The sweat doesn't smell, but bacteria on the skin break down the sweat into acids that produce the odor. Deodorizing oils help to regulate perspiration and reduce and control unwelcome body odor.

Lemon Deodorant

Deodorants work to cover the smell of body odor. The essential oils grapefruit and lemon combine fantastic deodorizing properties with an appealing aroma to keep you smelling fresh throughout the day.

Ingredients

Makes 3½ fl oz (100 ml)
Witch hazel 3 fl oz (90 ml)
Glycerine 1 tsp
Aloe juice 1 tsp
Palmarosa essential oil 5 drops
Lemon essential oil 5 drops
Coriander essential oil 3 drops
Grapefruit essential oil 3 drops

How to **make**

1 Mix all the ingredients together in a bowl. Pour into a sterilized bottle with an atomizer.

2 Shake before use. Apply to clean underarms and use whenever it is required.

Safe usage Do not use on freshly shaved skin.

Pine-fresh Shower Gel

The best way to avoid developing unwelcome body odor is to keep the areas of your body that are prone to sweating, such as the armpits, feet, and genital area, clean and free of bacteria. Changing your clothes regularly and washing daily will also help to avoid a buildup of sweat and bacteria.

Ingredients

Makes 1 fl oz (30 ml)
Unscented shower gel 2 tbsp
Lemongrass essential oil 7 drops
Pine essential oil 7 drops
Vetiver essential oil 1 drop

How to **make**

1 Make a fresh and revitalizing shower gel by adding the essential oils to a fragrance-free shower gel.

2 Use the gel once or twice a day to keep skin clean and odor free.

Eczema and Psoriasis

Eczema is when skin becomes itchy, red, dry, and cracked. It is often long-term (chronic), although it can improve, especially in young children. Atopic eczema ("atopic" means a tendency to develop a sensitivity to allergens), also known as atopic dermatitis, is the most common

Aloe vera calms and cools irritated and inflamed skin.

type of eczema. It mainly affects children, but can affect adults, too. Its exact cause is unknown, but it often occurs in people who are prone to allergic reactions, or who have a family history of allergies, and it can be linked to stress. Psoriasis is an inflammatory skin disease that is linked to stress and diet. Sufferers develop red, crusty patches of skin, usually on the elbows, knees, scalp, and back.

Soothing essential oils can be used to treat eczema and psoriasis to help control itching and reduce inflammation.

Calming Chamomile Compress

Chamomile has been found to be very effective for treating eczema due to its anti-inflammatory and soothing effects that help to relieve and calm itchy and inflamed skin. Sandalwood and lavender are both soothing essential oils that are especially effective on dry, itchy skin. Apply this compress to affected areas to help balance and soothe the skin.

Ingredients

Makes 1 compress
Sunflower or almond oil 1 tsp
German chamomile essential oil 1 drop
Lavender essential oil 3 drops
Sandalwood essential oil 3 drops

How to **make**

1 Fill a bowl with cold water. Add the essential oils to the base oil, then add to the water.

2 Soak a washcloth in the bowl, then remove the washcloth and squeeze out the excess water.

3 Place the compress on the area requiring treatment. Leave the washcloth in place while it reaches body temperature. Repeat 3 times.

Lavender Bath Float

Create a relaxing bath float with this mix of skin-soothing oats and bran, dried flowers, and uplifting oils. Helichrysum is calming on itchy breakouts, and cistus is mildy astringent, helping to tone skin.

Ingredients

Makes 1½ oz (45 g)
Organic rolled oats 1 tbsp
Bran 1 tbsp
Dried lavender flowers 1 tbsp
Helichrysum 4 drops
Lavender essential oil 4 drops
Cistus essential oil 1 drop

How to **make**

1 Make an herb bag using a muslin cloth. Lay the cloth out and place 1 tablespoon each of organic rolled oats, bran, and dried lavender flowers on the cloth. Add the essential oils.

2 Gather the cloth around the bath mix and tie a ribbon around the corners to keep all the ingredients together.

3 Place the float in a warm bath and dab on the skin to soothe affected areas.

Stress-Busting Diffusion

Aromatherapy is especially effective in reducing stress and anxiety, making it helpful for dealing with stress-related cases of psoriasis and eczema. The calming oils in this diffusion will help to soothe the anxiety that can be caused by and might exacerbate skin conditions.

Ingredients

Makes 1 diffusion
Cedarwood essential oil 4 drops
Frankincense essential oil 3 drops
Geranium essential oil 2 drops

How to **make**

1 Add the essential oil blend to a diffuser, vaporizer, or oil burner.

2 Gently scent your chosen environment.

Eczema Ointment

Chamomile and rose cool and balance skin. Combined with an unscented base they can be applied to affected areas to take the heat out of itchy skin.

Ingredients

Makes ½ fl oz (15 ml)
Fragrance-free lotion 1 tbsp
Roman chamomile essential oil 3 drops
Rose absolute essential oil 2 drops

How to **make**

1 Mix the essential oils into the lotion or ointment.

2 Dab onto affected areas of skin.

Stretch Marks

Stretch marks are caused by excessive and rapid weight gain, for example during pregnancy, which stretches skin and causes the fibers in the deeper layers to tear. This leaves wavy reddish stripes that gradually turn white. The marks usually appear on the thighs, breasts, abdomen, and buttocks. Massage tones skin, which may limit the effects and severity of stretch marks. Once they appear they are permanent, although they do fade over time.

Skin-toning Massage

A massage with nourishing oils improves skin tone, encourages the renewal of skin cells, and makes skin look and feel smoother. Here, moisturizing base oils are blended with toning frankincense and skin-cell regenerating mandarin and neroli essential oils.

Ingredients

Makes 1 fl oz (30 ml)
Almond oil 1 tbsp
Wheat-germ oil 1 tsp
Apricot kernel oil 1 tsp
Avocado oil 1 tsp
Frankincense essential oil 7 drops
Mandarin essential oil 5 drops
Neroli essential oil 3 drops

How to **make**

1 Combine all ingredients in a bowl. Transfer to a sterilized dark-glass bottle and seal with a cap or dropper.

2 Gently massage affected area. Allow oil to absorb into the skin before you get dressed. Store the remaining oil in a cool, dark place. Keeps for up to 3 months.

Sunburn

Sunburn occurs when skin is damaged by the sun's ultraviolet rays. Skin

becomes red, sore, warm, tender, and, occasionally, itchy, and starts to flake and peel after a few days. It is extremely important to try to avoid getting sunburned in the first place since damaging the skin in this way increases the chances of developing serious health problems later, for example, skin cancer. If skin does become burned, try to keep the affected area cool and moist. Essential oil remedies that are calming and cooling are ideal.

Cooling Lavender Compress

Skin-healing oils, such as lavender and chamomile essential oils, and cooling peppermint essential oil are combined here to make a cooling compress that can be applied to help bring relief to tender, sunburned skin.

Ingredients

Makes 1 compress
Aloe vera juice 1 tbsp
Lavender essential oil 4 drops
Peppermint essential oil 1 drop
German chamomile essential oil 2 drops

How to **make**

1 Fill a bowl with cold water. Add the aloe vera juice and essential oil blend.

2 Soak a washcloth in the bowl, then remove the washcloth and squeeze out the excess water.

3 Place the compress on the affected area of skin. Leave the washcloth on the skin while it reaches body temperature. Repeat 3 times.

Cradle Cap

Cradle cap, also known as seborrheic dermatitis, is a condition that causes greasy, yellow, scaly patches on babies' scalps. It's a harmless condition that doesn't usually itch or cause any discomfort. Most cases clear up on their own over a period of weeks or months. The cause of cradle cap is unknown, but may be linked to an excess of sebum. Essential oils blended with base oils, or with an unscented baby shampoo, can help it clear up.

Gentle Scalp Massage

Massaging almond or olive oil into the scalp at night loosens crusts. Patchouli is astringent and tones skin; palmarosa is skin balancing; and lavender heals and soothes skin if crusts peel off. This blend is suitable for infants over 12 months; for babies 3–12 months, use just one drop of lavender; under 3 months just the base oil.

Ingredients

Makes 1 fl oz (30 ml)
Olive oil 2 tbsp
Lavender essential oil 1 drop
Palmarosa essential oil 1 drop
Patchouli essential oil 1 drop

How to **make**

1 Combine all the ingredients together in a bowl. Transfer to a sterilized dark-glass bottle and seal with a cap or dropper.

2 Gently massage into your baby's scalp. Leave in overnight, then use a soft-bristled baby brush to gently remove loose flakes in the morning before washing with a baby shampoo. Don't be tempted to pick at or remove flakes that aren't already lose since this could damage skin and lead to infection.

3 Store the oil in a cool, dark place. Keeps for up to 3 months.

Lavender Shampoo

Gently washing your baby's hair and scalp with a mild shampoo can help prevent a buildup of scales. In addition to its skin-healing properties, lavender is a gentle oil to use on your baby's scalp.

Ingredients

Makes 2 applications
Unscented baby shampoo 1 tbsp
Lavender essential oil 2 drops

How to **make**

1 Mix 2 drops of lavender essential oil in a fragrance-free shampoo.

2 Gently wash your baby's hair, being careful not to remove flakes that aren't loose. Rinse with just warm water.

Dandruff

The body continually sheds dead skin cells as new cells are formed.

In most cases, this is a gradual process that goes unnoticed. However, if the process speeds up, it can produce a buildup of dead skin cells that appear prominent and unsightly. Dandruff is a common skin condition that causes dry white or gray flakes of dead skin to appear on the scalp or attached to hair. The scalp may feel dry and itchy. It's not always clear why this happens, but possible causes include seborrheic dermatitis, which is a common skin condition that causes oily skin. Certain factors can make dandruff worse, for example, an overuse of hair products, emotional stress, and washing hair too much or too little. The following treatments can help to condition the scalp.

Invigorating Scalp Massage

The stimulating action of a scalp massage can be used with essential oils to create an effective dandruff treatment. Thyme essential oil has an antifungal action that is useful for treating conditions such as dandruff, while tea tree helps to balance oils and keep the scalp healthy.

Ingredients

Makes 2 applications
Coconut oil solid 1 tbsp
Tea tree essential oil 3 drops
Lavender essential oil 2 drops
Thyme essential oil 2 drops

How to **make**

1 Melt the coconut oil solid in a bain-marie (see p188), then add the essential oils and pour the blend into a sterilized glass jar. Massage half the oil blend into the scalp. Do this before bed, then cover the pillow with a towel to keep the oil blend from staining the pillowcase.

2 Leave the oil on overnight and then rinse it out in the morning, applying shampoo before wetting and rinsing the hair.

Peppermint Hair Rinse

Combining essential oils with dried herbs creates a natural hair tonic that can add shine and help to tone and balance oils on the scalp and control flaky dandruff. Adding soothing peppermint to stimulating rosemary can help to condition the scalp and combat dandruff.

Ingredients

Makes 1½ fl oz (45 ml)
Dried peppermint 1 tbsp
Dried rosemary 1 tbsp
Cider vinegar 1 tbsp
Peppermint essential oil 2 drops
Rosemary essential oil 1 drop

How to **make**

1 To make the infusion, put the dried herbs in a teapot and add 7 fl oz (200 ml) boiling water. Let infuse for about 10 minutes, then strain the water.

2 Add the essential oils to the cider vinegar, then to the herbal infusion.

3 Use the infusion as a final hair rinse after shampooing. Finish with a final rinse of warm water only.

Thyme has antifungal properties.

Allergic Reactions

Our immune system is designed to **protect** the body against harmful foreign substances. Sometimes, however, the body develops a **sensitivity** to a substance that doesn't pose a threat and reacts as though it is harmful, releasing the substance histamine, which triggers an allergic reaction. Essential oils can help **calm** allergic responses and **soothe** symptoms.

Allergies and Hay Fever

An allergy is the body's reaction to a particular food or substance, known as an allergen. Allergic reactions are most common in children. The severity of a reaction can vary. Most are mild, but occasionally a severe reaction, called anaphylaxis, or anaphylactic shock, can occur, which is a medical emergency and requires urgent treatment. Allergic reactions can usually be kept under control with careful management. Common allergens include dust mites, medication, food such as nuts, shellfish, fruit, cow's milk, and animal fur.

Hay fever is a common allergic reaction to pollen in the warmer months. Many types of pollen are released by plants at different times of the year, causing symptoms such as sneezing, a runny nose, and itchy eyes. Remedies with calming oils can help control symptoms.

Clearing Eucalyptus Inhalation

Essential oils can help open the airways. Here, the sharp aroma of eucalyptus blends with ravensara for an effective decongestant. The addition of calming lavender helps to quell the stress and anxiety caused by allergic reactions.

Ingredients

Makes 1 inhalation
Eucalyptus radiata essential oil 5 drops
Lavender essential oil 3 drops
Ravensara essential oil 2 drops

How to **make**

1 Add the essential oils to a bowl of hot water. Cover your head with a towel, make a tent over the bowl of hot water, and then lean forward over the bowl. For children or asthma sufferers, don't cover the head with a towel.

2 Inhale the steam for 5 minutes, taking a break if needed.

Chamomile Nose Balm

Essential oils provide a simple yet effective way to reduce hay fever and allergy symptoms. Using calming oils such as chamomile in a balm can trap pollen and soothe irritated skin.

Ingredients

Makes 20 to 30 applications
Beeswax 1 tbsp
Sunflower oil 1 tbsp
German chamomile essential oil 1 drop
Lavender essential oil 1 drop
Peppermint essential oil 1 drop

How to **make**

1 Gently melt the wax and sunflower oil in a bain-marie (see p.188).

2 Add the essential oils and mix together. Pour into a sterilized jar and let cool, then seal with a lid.

3 Apply the balm around the nose as required to soothe irritated skin.

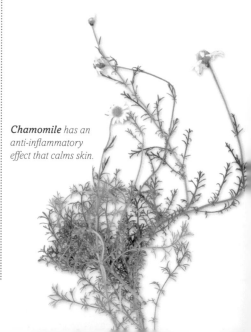

Chamomile has an anti-inflammatory effect that calms skin.

Mind and Well-being

Stress is a common modern-day malady and it can have profound effects on mental health. Addressing overly hectic lifestyles can help to **combat stress**, and essential oils can be a great support here since their numerous therapeutic benefits work **holistically** to **soothe** and calm emotions, ease anxiety and tension, and **balance moods**, creating an enhanced sense of well-being.

Anxiety

We all experience anxiety at some point in life. The feeling of unease or worry that can be mild or severe is a normal response to the stresses of life. For example, you may feel worried about an exam, or anxious about a medical test or an interview. Feeling anxious at stressful times is normal, but if it becomes hard to control worries, and feelings of anxiety become constant, talk to your doctor. Using oils in a diffuser creates a reassuring and calm environment.

Lemon Balm Diffusion

There are a number of relaxing oils for reducing anxiety that can be used in a massage, in the bath, or diffused into a room to create a peaceful environment.

Ingredients

Makes 1 diffusion
Lemon balm essential oil 5 drops
Lemon essential oil 3 drops
Cypress essential oil 3 drops
Bergamot essential oil 2 drops

How to **make**

1 Add the essential oil blend to a diffuser, vaporizer, or oil burner.

2 Gently scent your chosen environment.

Depression

Difficult events and experiences can leave us feeling in low spirits. If this low feeling persists we can develop depression.

Some common causes of depression include relationship problems, bereavement, sleep problems (which may arise from stress and other concerns), stress at work, bullying, and chronic illness and pain. Sometimes it's possible to feel down without there being an obvious reason. Depression can also come on at specific points in life or at specific times, for example after the birth of a child or during the winter months.

A low mood that lasts for two weeks or more can be a sign of depression. Other symptoms of depression include: not getting any enjoyment out of life, feeling hopeless, feeling tired or lacking energy, not being able to concentrate on everyday tasks such as reading the news or watching television, comfort eating or losing one's appetite, sleeping more than usual or being unable to sleep, and having suicidal thoughts or thoughts about harming yourself. It's always important to talk to your doctor about how you are feeling if you are experiencing any of the above symptoms and a low mood persists for an extended period of time.

Therapeutic essential oils can be very beneficial for helping to lift feelings of depression and bring a feeling of calm that can release anxiety and tension.

Calming Diffusion

Essential oils can be wonderful remedies for providing emotional support. In this diffusion, calming frankincense helps to lift the spirits and is especially helpful when you are feeling tired or overwhelmed, while mandarin soothes frayed nerves, promoting relaxation, and uplifting neroli helps to balance emotions and is effective for relieving stress.

Ingredients

Makes 1 diffusion
Frankincense essential oil 5 drops
Neroli essential oil 3 drops
Mandarin essential oil 2 drops

How to **make**

1 Add the essential oil blend to a diffuser, vaporizer, or oil burner.

2 Gently scent your chosen environment.

Grief and Shock

Times of emotional crisis and upset often involve some kind of loss or bereavement. This may be the loss of a loved one, or the end of a marriage or important relationship.
Most people grieve when they lose something or someone important to them. Grieving can feel unbearable at times, but it's a necessary process to work through. There are many different reactions to loss, and no one right reaction, but grief usually does consist of a few key emotions: these include anxiety and helplessness, and anger and sadness. Eventually, you adjust to a loss and though your feelings can remain intense, they tend to become less frequent. Essential oils can be especially helpful at times of loss or trauma, helping to lift spirits and ground emotions.

Neroli "Rescue" Remedy

Neroli essential oil is considered to be the "rescue remedy" of essential oils and is particularly helpful during times of grief and shock. Here, its effects are supported by uplifting bergamot and calming petitgrain essential oils. Disperse this blend of oils in your environment to help calm emotions and ease feelings of anxiety.

Ingredients

Makes 1 diffusion
Neroli essential oil 5 drops
Petitgrain essential oil 3 drops
Bergamot essential oil 2 drops

How to **make**

1 Add the essential oil blend to a diffuser, vaporizer, or oil burner.

2 Gently scent your chosen environment.

Soothing Rose and Geranium Massage

Essential oils with uplifting and euphoric properties are very useful for helping to deal with grief. Geranium is uplifting and calming at the same time, which makes it useful for warding off the feelings of depression that often accompany grief. Frankincense essential oil also helps to lift the spirits, and the calming aroma of rose promotes relaxation and helps to reduce feelings of anxiety and releases tension, helping to create a sense of well-being that can interrupt the grief.

Ingredients

Makes 2 tbsp of massage oil
Almond oil 2 tbsp
Frankincense essential oil 4 drops
Rose absolute or essential oil 3 drops
Geranium essential oil 1 drop

How to **make**

1 Combine all the ingredients together in a bowl. Transfer to a sterilized dark-glass bottle and seal with a cap or dropper.

2 Massage into the skin (avoiding the face). Allow the oil to absorb into the skin before you get dressed. Store the remaining oil in a cool, dark place. Keeps for up to 3 months.

Uplifting Jasmine Bath

This combination of oils provides a revitalizing bath soak that can create a feeling of well-being. Jasmine essential oil or absolute helps to increase optimism, combating the feelings of listlessness, while sandalwood promotes restful sleep and helps to restore vitality.

Ingredients

Makes 1 tbsp
Almond oil or whole milk 1 tbsp
Sandalwood essential oil 4 drops
Jasmine absolute or essential oil 4 drops
Grapefruit essential oil 2 drops

How to **make**

1 Combine all the ingredients together in a bowl.

2 Disperse the blend immediately in the bath and enjoy a reviving and soothing soak.

Stress and Insomnia

Stress is one of the major health problems in the Western world and is responsible for many

of our illnesses. It has numerous causes and can affect us in a number of different ways, both mentally and physically. The body's natural response to stress is controlled by the autonomic nervous system and involves the release of the hormones adrenaline and cortisol, which also control the "fight or flight" mechanism— the body's built-in reaction to dangerous or threatening situations. While a certain amount of stress is good for us, helping to keep us motivated and interested in tasks, if stress starts to affect our moods, digestion, and sleep, it becomes more of an issue. Try these relaxing and soothing remedies to help yourself wind down and let go of tension.

De-stressing Clary Sage Massage

Using therapeutic essential oils in a massage blend is an excellent way to help the body to manage chronic stress, promote relaxation, and improve the quality of sleep if stress is causing insomnia. You can also enjoy this oil blend in a soothing bedtime bath by adding the essential oils to 1 tablespoon of either base oil or whole milk, and dispersing immediately in the bath, then enjoy a relaxing pre-bedtime soak.

Ingredients

Makes 2 tbsp
Almond oil 2 tbsp
Clary sage essential oil 5 drops
Frankincense essential oil 5 drops
Geranium essential oil 5 drops

How to **make**

1 Combine all the ingredients together in a bowl. Transfer to a sterilized dark-glass bottle and seal with a cap or dropper.

2 Massage into the skin (avoiding the face). Allow the oil to absorb into the skin before you get dressed. Store the remaining oil in a cool, dark place. Keeps for up to 3 months.

Litsea and Bergamot Calming Diffusion

Litsea essential oil is a useful stress buster. Its naturally soothing properties calm the rapid heartbeat that can accompany stress and panic, helping you think more rationally. Bergamot is grounding and helps balance the mind. The addition of uplifting orange adds to the calming effect of this blend.

Ingredients

Makes 1 diffusion
Litsea essential oil 6 drops
Orange essential oil 4 drops
Bergamot essential oil 4 drops

How to **make**

1 Add the essential oil blend to a diffuser, vaporizer, or oil burner.

2 Gently scent your chosen environment.

Ylang-ylang Bedtime Spray

If stress and anxiety keep you awake at night, or you find it difficult to switch off at bedtime and you wake up groggy in the morning, try this wonderfully relaxing pillow spray. Calming chamomile and rose essential oils are joined by the uplifting, sweetly scented ylang-ylang, which helps calm breathing, and grounding vetiver, which has a profoundly calming effect when you feel overwhelmed by stress.

Ingredients

Makes 1 fl oz (30 ml)
Ylang-ylang essential oil 6 drops
Rose essential oil 6 drops
Vetiver essential oil 2 drops
Roman chamomile essential oil 1 drop

How to **make**

1 Mix the essential oils with 2 tablespoons cold water and pour into a sterilized bottle with an atomizer.

2 Spritz your room before bedtime. Shake before use, and avoid spraying directly onto fabric.

Geranium helps to calm a busy, stressed mind.

Women's Health

Women's hormones go through a number of changes throughout life, causing physical and **emotional** symptoms, many of which can be helped by essential oils. Premenstrual fluid retention can be alleviated using oils and massage, and premenstrual syndrome can be **soothed** with **calming oils.** Uplifting oils can alleviate depression after birth and during menopause.

Premenstrual Symptoms

Many women experience a mix of emotional and physical symptoms in the days before menstruation. For some women, these symptoms are mild and occur for just a couple of days before menstruation begins. For others, symptoms can be wider ranging, more pronounced, and can start as early as two weeks before the onset of menstruation.

Physical premenstrual symptoms include fluid retention and bloating, fatigue, breast tenderness, lower-back ache, and abdominal discomfort. Emotional symptoms include general anxiety, irritability, stress, and a low mood, or unpredictable mood swings. Therapeutic essential oils are a great help for premenstrual complaints as their holistic nature helps to treat the whole range of symptoms, relieving physical complaints and providing emotional support by calming and balancing emotions.

Juniper Compress for Fluid Retention

Essential oils with a mild diuretic action, such as juniper, geranium, and fennel, are effective for flushing out toxins and reducing the uncomfortable fluid retention and puffiness commonly experienced before menstruation. In addition to their physical benefits, the oils relieve emotional premenstrual symptoms, too. Juniper helps revive flagging spirits and calms nervous tension, and geranium balances the emotions, which can ward off mood swings. A hot or cold compress using this essential oil blend makes a soothing and effective premenstrual remedy. Avoid this blend in pregnancy.

Ingredients

Makes 1 compress
Almond oil 1 tsp
Calendula macerated oil 2 tsp
Wheat-germ oil 1 tsp
Juniper essential oil 5 drops
Fennel essential oil 5 drops
Geranium essential oil 5 drops

How to **make**

1 Fill a bowl with hot or cold water, whichever is your preference. Add the oil blend.

2 Soak a washcloth in the bowl, then remove it and squeeze out the excess water.

3 If the washcloth is hot, put a towel or piece of plastic wrap over it to insulate it, if you wish. Put the compress on the area requiring treatment. Leave in place while it reaches body temperature. Repeat 3 times.

Premenstrual Rose and Geranium Bath

Premenstrual syndrome (PMS) can be stressful and tiring as hormonal changes lead to sudden mood swings, or bring on a general low mood, and feelings of tension and anxiety can feel overwhelming. Try this soothing and grounding essential oil bath soak for a premenstrual stress-reducing tonic that will leave you feeling more grounded, calm, and uplifted.

Ingredients

Makes 1 tbsp
Base oil or whole milk 1 tbsp
Rose essential oil 5 drops
Clary sage essential oil 2 drops
Geranium essential oil 2 drops

How to **make**

1 Combine all the ingredients together in a bowl.

2 Disperse the oil blend immediately in a hot bath, and then enjoy a reviving and uplifting soak that can leave you feeling revived.

Pregnancy

Many essential oils aren't advised in pregnancy (see Safe usage in the A–Z for each oil), but some are safe and help with relaxation and some pregnancy symptoms. For example, juniper, mandarin, rose, rosemary, marjoram, and neroli are popular pregnancy oils. See page 37 for a list of oils that are safe in pregnancy.

Skin-Nourishing Pregnancy Massage

Enjoy a backache-relieving massage or a calming facial massage. Stick to 1 percent dilutions since your sense of smell is heightened in pregnancy. The following blend nourishes skin and improves elasticity. Used daily from the fifth month of pregnancy, it can help prevent stretch marks. It is best not to use essential oils until you are past the first trimester (unless you have had advice from a qualified aromatherapy practitioner).

Ingredients

Makes 1 fl oz (30 ml)
Almond oil 1 tbsp
Wheat-germ oil 1 tbsp
Mandarin essential oil 2 drops
Lavender essential oil 2 drops
Neroli essential oil 2 drops

How to **make**

1 Combine the ingredients in a bowl. Transfer to a sterilized dark-glass bottle. Seal with a cap or dropper.

2 Gently massage the skin. Allow the oil to absorb into the skin before dressing Store remaining oil in a cool, dark place. Keeps for up to 3 months.

Postpartum and Menopause

Hormonal swings after birth can affect mood, leading to the baby blues, and sometimes longer-lasting postpartum depression. Similarly, hormonal changes in menopause can affect mood, causing irritability and depression. Menopause also has a range of physical symptoms, one of the best-known being hot flashes, characterized by a sudden feeling of heat sweeping over the body. Calming and relaxing essential oils can help to ease symptoms and lift the spirits.

Soothing Blend for Hot Flashes and Irritability

This cooling blend of oils is ideal for hot flashes and general irritability. Bergamot is particularly helpful when the body is overheated. Roman chamomile calms and soothes, while rose and geranium enhance well-being.

Ingredients

Makes 3 fl oz (90 ml)
Bergamot essential oil 5 drops
Rose absolute oil 5 drops
Geranium essential oil 2 drops
Roman chamomile essential oil 2 drops

How to **make**

1 Add the oils to 3 fl oz (90 ml) water. Transfer to an atomizer bottle.

2 Spritz the face to cool hot flashes, or spray a room to create a calming environment. Alternatively, add the blend to a diffuser and gently scent your chosen environment.

Hormone-Balancing Fennel Massage

Cooling fennel is blended with soothing rose and geranium oils here to create a gentle balancing and grounding blend. Avoid this blend in pregnancy.

Ingredients

Makes 2 tbsp
Almond oil 2 tbsp
Fennel essential oil 3 drops
Rose absolute oil 5 drops
Geranium essential oil 5 drops

How to **make**

1 Combine all the ingredients together in a bowl. Transfer to a sterilized dark-glass bottle and seal with a cap or dropper.

2 Gently massage the body (avoid the face). Allow the oil to absorb into the skin before getting dressed. Store the remaining oil in a cool, dark place. Keeps for up to 3 months.

Rose has a calming and uplifting aroma.

Men's Health

As with women, men can encounter specific health issues. Prostate health is important for men, and the effects of stress can feature prominently. Essential oils have clear benefits for these areas. Remedies that work **holistically** on **body** and **mind** help to counter the negative effects of stress, and antiseptic and diuretic oils target prostate problems **alongside medical treatments.**

Heart Health and Stress

Cardiovascular disease is one of the leading causes of death for men in the US and is a growing health concern worldwide. General heart health can be improved by exercising regularly, eating a healthy, balanced diet, quitting smoking, and finding ways to reduce and manage everyday stress. See pages 222–23 for other remedies for circulation. Essential oils have numerous properties that can help with problems that are associated with the cardiovascular system, such as high blood pressure and sluggish circulation.

Bergamot and Neroli Bath Oil Blend

This bath oil remedy can also be used as a massage blend, added to a shower gel, or the essential oils can be added to a diffuser. Here, relaxing essential oils are used in a warm bath to help release tension in the body and combat the effects of stress and anxiety.

Ingredients

Makes ½ fl oz (15 ml)
Almond oil 1 tbsp
Bergamot essential oil 5 drops
Neroli essential oil 2 drops
Sandalwood essential oil 5 drops

How to **make**

1 Combine all the ingredients together in a bowl.

2 Disperse the oil blend immediately in the bath and enjoy a relaxing soak.

Prostate Problems

Problems with the prostate are increasingly common in older men. The prostate gland can become enlarged, which can sometimes be due to bacterial infection. Anti-inflammatory and antiseptic essential oils can help calm swelling and kill off bacteria. It's also important that men get the prostate checked regularly so that changes in size are spotted and any necessary treatment given.

Prostate Massage

Antiseptic and anti-inflammatory frankincense blends well with myrrh and antibacterial rosemary. Massage around the genital area regularly to stimulate circulation and improve prostate health.

Ingredients

Makes ½ fl oz (15 ml)
Almond oil 1 tbsp
Rosemary essential oil 1 drop
Frankincense essential oil 1 drop
Myrrh essential oil 1 drop

How to **make**

1 Combine all the ingredients together in a bowl. Transfer to a sterilized dark-glass bottle and seal with a cap or dropper.

2 Gently massage into the area around and below the genitals. Allow the oil to absorb into the skin before getting dressed. Store the remaining oil in a cool, dark place. Keeps for up to 3 months.

Bergamot helps to relieve anxiety and ease tension.

First Aid

Essential oils are a valuable addition to a home first-aid kit. Along with the bandages and Band-Aids, oils act as antiseptics for cuts and wounds and can **soothe** and **calm** irritated skin, bites and stings, and minor burns and scalds. Oils such as tea tree can be applied undiluted to protect wounds from infection, while **cooling** and **warming oils** can counter the effects of weather.

Blisters

Blisters on the skin often occur after an injury, burning, scalding, repetitive rubbing, or an insect sting. They can be painful and also very annoying. A blister develops when there is an accumulation of fluid underneath the skin. When the blister bursts, the revealed tissue beneath may be sore and become infected.

Tea Tree and Lavender Ointment

Regular application of lavender essential oil directly onto the affected area can help reduce swelling and prevent infection and ease pain.

Ingredients

Makes 1 application
Tea tree essential oil 1 drop
Lavender essential oil 1 drop

How to **make**

1 Apply the essential oils directly to the blister with a cotton swab.

2 Cover the blister carefully with a Band-Aid to reduce the chance of an infection.

Heat Exhaustion and Fever

Heat exhaustion is when too much heat or sunlight causes lethargy, dizziness, nausea, vomiting, and a headache. A person with heat exhaustion should be moved to a cool place and given water.

Fever is the body's defence against infections. Seek medical help if a temperature rises quickly.

Cooling Compress

Cool the body with this compress.

Ingredients

Makes 1 compress
Witch hazel 1 tbsp
Peppermint essential oil 2 drops
Lavender essential oil 3 drops

How to **make**

1 Fill a bowl with cold water. Add the essential oils to the witch hazel and then to the water.

2 Soak a washcloth in the bowl, remove, and wring out.

3 Place the compress on the skin. Leave in place while it reaches body temperature. Repeat 3 times.

Insect Bites and Stings

The severity of bites and stings depends on the type of insect and a person's sensitivity. A serious allergic reaction will require immediate medical help.

Lavender Compress

This soothing compress reduces itching.

Ingredients

Makes 1 compress
Witch hazel 1 tbsp
Lavender essential oil 3 drops
Roman chamomile essential oil 1 drop

How to **make**

1 Fill a bowl with cold water. Add the essential oils to the witch hazel and then to the water.

2 Soak a washcloth in the bowl, remove, and wring out.

3 Place the washcloth on the skin. Leave it in place while it reaches body temperature. Repeat 3 times.

Treatment Reference Charts

Essential oils are versatile and the choice can be overwhelming, which can make it hard to decide which oils have the right properties for your specific needs. The quick reference charts below are designed to help you rapidly pinpoint the essential oils particularly suited to your needs. The chart on pages 244–6 lists essential oils for common complaints, while the charts on page 247 recommend essential oils for mind and well-being and essential oils for cosmetic use.

Common **Complaints**

Everyday common complaints include chronic conditions that require long-term management, such as arthritis, depression, and stress; occasional problems, such as headaches or diarrhea; less common first-aid situations; skin complaints, such as eczema, athlete's foot, and dandruff; and menstrual and menopausal complaints. This chart helps you to identify at a glance which essential oils are especially recommended to help with specific concerns. Always consult your doctor about symptoms and use essential oils as complementary treatments alongside medications when necessary. For information on each essential oil, check the A–Z listings on pages 40–145.

HEALING **OILS**

Certain essential oils have specific properties that make them ideal for treating a particular complaint. The remedies in this chapter show you how to use oils in massage, compresses, inhalations, and ointments to treat a range of conditions.

Common Complaint	Recommended Essential Oils
Allergies	Yarrow, Helichrysum, Lavender, Chamomile
Appetite loss	Buchu, Galangal, Dill, Tarragon, Cinnamon, Lemon, Lemongrass, Fennel, Wintergreen, Litsea, Peppermint, Nutmeg, Ginger
Arthritis	Yarrow, Lemon verbena, Mugwort, Birch leaf, Frankincense, Cedarwood, Cypress, Wintergreen, Helichrysum, Star anise, Juniper, Lavender, Nutmeg, Marjoram, Parsley, Black pepper, Benzoin, Plai, Ginger
Asthma	Frankincense, Caraway, Lemon, Eucalyptus, Lavender, Roman chamomile, Niaouli, Lemon balm, Peppermint, Myrtle, Sandalwood, Clove
Athlete's foot	Galangal, Cedarwood, Lemongrass, Palmarosa, Eucalyptus, Wintergreen, Star anise, Lavender, Manuka, Tea tree, Cajeput, Oregano, Geranium, Patchouli, Summer savory, Tagetes, Thyme
Backaches and neck pain	Tarragon, Coriander, Camphor, Grapefruit, Bay laurel, Lavender, Niaouli, Marjoram, Geranium, Allspice, Black pepper, Rosemary, Ginger
Bites and stings	Lime, Lavender, Manuka, Roman chamomile, Lemon balm, Peppermint, Allspice, Patchouli, Summer savory
Blisters	Lavender, Tea tree
Body odor	Galangal, Tarragon, Petitgrain, Lemon, Grapefruit, Coriander, Cypress, Lemongrass, Palmarosa, Cardamom, Star anise, Manuka, Litsea, Pine, Sage, Vetiver

Common Complaint	Recommended Essential Oils
Bruising	Yarrow, Lavender
Constipation	Orange, Fennel, Marjoram, Peppermint, Pine, Black Pepper, Rosemary
Coughs and colds	Frankincense, Cedarwood, Lemon, Cypress, Eucalyptus, Fennel, Helichrysum, Lavender, Tea tree, Peppermint, Marjoram, Pine, Ravintsara, Rosemary, Clary sage, Thyme
Cradle cap	Palmarosa, Lavender, Patchouli
Dandruff	Birch, Cedarwood, Lime, Lemon, Wintergreen, Juniper, Bay laurel, Lavender, Tea tree, Peppermint, Geranium, Rosemary, Sage, Thyme
Depression	Frankincense, Ylang-ylang, Cedarwood, Cinnamon, Neroli, Bergamot, Mandarin, Orange, Lemongrass, Helichrysum, Jasmine, Litsea, Basil, Geranium, Tuberose, Ravintsara, Clary sage, Benzoin
Diarrhea	Neroli, Mandarin, Cypress, Eucalyptus, Fennel, Chamomile, Peppermint, Black pepper, Ginger
Eczema and psoriasis	Yarrow, Frankincense, Cedarwood, Cistus, Cumin, Helichrysum, Juniper, Lavender, German chamomile, Lemon balm, Geranium, Sandalwood, Benzoin, Fenugreek
Fluid retention	Yarrow, Buchu, Dill, Cedarwood, Cistus, Lime, Lemon, Grapefruit, Mandarin, Orange, Cypress, Carrot seed, Juniper, Geranium, Parsley seed, Rosemary
Grief	Frankincense, Cistus, Neroli, Petitgrain, Bergamot, Geranium, Rose
Headaches and migraines	Rosewood, Grapefruit, Coriander, Lemongrass, Eucalyptus, Bay laurel, Lavender, Lemon balm, Peppermint, Marjoram, Rosemary, Ginger
Heat exhaustion and fever	Lime, Bergamot, Lavender, Lemon balm, Peppermint, Vetiver
High blood pressure	Ylang-ylang, Cumin, Lavender, Marjoram, Clary sage, Valerian
Hot flashes	Bergamot, Roman chamomile, Geranium, Rose, Clary sage

Essential oils make useful additions to your home medicine cabinet.

Using oils *therapeutically in steam inhalations can be an excellent way to relieve congestion.*

Common Complaint	Recommended Essential Oils
Insomnia	Yarrow, Dill, Neroli, Petitgrain, Bergamot, Lemon, Orange, Star anise, Bay laurel, Lavender, Roman chamomile, Nutmeg, Myrtle, Marjoram, Allspice, Tuberose, Sandalwood, Valerian, Vetiver
Mouth and gum care	Cistus, Myrrh, Cardamom, Fennel, Tea tree, Peppermint, Nutmeg, Clove
Muscular aches and pains	Eucalyptus, Lavender, Peppermint, Nutmeg, Rosemary, Clove, Thyme, Ginger
Nausea and vomiting	Buchu, Lemon verbena, Galangal, Dill, Mandarin, Cardamom, Litsea, Roman chamomile, Lemon balm, Peppermint, Nutmeg, Parsley seed, Allspice, Black pepper, Rose, Clary sage, Fenugreek, Ginger
Premenstrual syndrome	Fennel, Juniper, Marjoram, Geranium, Rose, Clary sage
Prostate health	Frankincense, Myrrh, Rosemary
Reflux and indigestion	Dill, Mandarin, Coriander, Cardamom, Fennel, Chamomile, Peppermint, Basil, Parsley, Ginger
Sprains and strains	Lemongrass, Marjoram, Black pepper, Rosemary, Thyme, Ginger
Stress and anxiety	Frankincense, Ylang-ylang, Cedarwood, Neroli, Petitgrain, Bergamot, Lemon, Mandarin, Orange, Jasmine, Lavender, Litsea, Chamomile, Lemon balm, Basil, Marjoram, Geranium, Patchouli, Rose, Rosemary, Clary sage, Sandalwood, Vetiver
Sunburn	Bergamot, German chamomile, Lavender, Tea tree
Urinary-tract infections	Lavender, German chamomile, Peppermint
Varicose veins/ hemorrhoids	Lemon, Cypress, Helichrysum, Juniper, Geranium

Each essential oil has a range of therapeutic properties.

Add essential oils *to balms and creams to create healing remedies and nourishing cosmetic products.*

Mind and **Well-being**

An important and key element of aromatherapy is its ability to treat holistically, looking beyond isolated symptoms and treating both body and mind. For example, when oils are used to promote relaxation or to energize, they can also help the body to deal with other specific complaints. The chart, right, suggests key oils for mental and physical well-being.

Mind and Well-being	Recommended Essential Oils
Calming and soothing	Ylang-ylang, Cypress, Palmarosa, Helichrysum, Lavender, Chamomile, Patchouli, Rose, Clary sage, Sandalwood
Concentration and focus	Cardamom, Peppermint, Basil, Thyme
Energizing	Lemongrass, Juniper, Pine, Rosemary, Clove, Thyme
Relaxation	Ylang-ylang, Neroli, Orange, Lavender, Rose, Sandalwood, Vetiver
Stimulating and invigorating	Citronella, Basil, Black pepper, Rosemary, Ginger
Uplifting	Lime, Neroli, Petitgrain, Bergamot, Lemon, Grapefruit, Orange, Lemongrass, Palmarosa, Litsea, Lemon balm, Peppermint, Geranium, Rose
Warming	Cinnamon, Nutmeg, Marjoram, Black pepper, Clove

Sandalwood has calming and restorative properties.

Cosmetic **Treatments**

Essential oils can play a key role in cosmetics, where their properties prove extremely useful for balancing and enhancing skin. The chart, right, helps you choose oils and tailor blends to suit your particular skin type. When using oils cosmetically, make sure you first dilute them in a base oil or combine them with a cream or lotion base. The recipes in chapter five show you how to create cosmetic products using essential oils.

Skin Conditions	Recommended Essential Oils
Dry and mature skin	Frankincense, Ylang-ylang, Neroli, Palmarosa, Jasmine, Lavender, Chamomile, Patchouli, Rose, Sandalwood
Dry/oily hair	Cedarwood, Grapefruit, Tea tree, Rosemary
Oily and acne-prone skin	Ylang-ylang, Petitgrain, Bergamot, Lime, Neroli, Lemon, Mandarin, Cypress, Palmarosa, Juniper, Bay laurel, Lavender, Tea tree, Niaouli, Geranium, Rose, Rosemary, Clary sage, Sandalwood
Scars/stretch marks	Frankincense, Neroli, Mandarin, Palmarosa, Jasmine, Lavender, Patchouli, Sandalwood, Vetiver, Plai
Sensitive skin	Neroli, Helichrysum, Lavender, Chamomile, Sandalwood

Juniper has an astringent effect, ideal for cleansing skin prone to acne.

Glossary

Absolute Concentrated aromatic oils extracted from a single plant source by solvent extraction. None of the solvent remains after the process. Absolutes can be used like essential oils.

Adaptogen A substance that can relax or stimulate to help balance body systems, especially in times of stress.

Adrenaline *See epinephrine*

Analgesic A substance that reduces or eliminates pain.

Antibacterial A substance that inhibits bacterial growth.

Antidepressant A medication or compound that alleviates depression.

Antifungal Inhibits the growth of mold and fungi.

Antihistamine A substance or medication that counters allergic reactions. Commonly used in the treatment of hay fever, hives, itching, and insect bites and stings.

Anti-inflammatory A substance that prevents or reduces inflammation.

Antimicrobial A substance that reduces or resists microbes, commonly used to refer to substances that are active against a wide range of bacteria, viruses, and fungi.

Antioxidant Substances that inhibit the oxidation of other molecules. Oxidation is a chemical reaction that can produce free radicals, which damage body tissues. It is also a process that can cause oils and fats to become rancid.

Antispasmodic Provides relief from muscle spasms and cramps.

Antiviral Capable of killing some viruses.

Aphrodisiac Something that arouses or increases sexual desire.

Aromatherapy The therapeutic use of essential oils. Aromatherapy can involve inhalation or application of essential oil blends to the skin.

Aromatic Refers to the unique aroma emitted by a plant or substance.

Astringent A substance that produces a localized tightening effect on body tissues. Used in preparations to tone the skin and close pores, or to reduce secretions and bleeding from abrasions. Astringents also help to close wounds and ulcers.

Base oil An oil used to dilute essential oils before a massage.

Carrier oil *See Base oil*

Compound A substance formed when two or more chemical elements bond together.

Compress A wet cotton pad or washcloth pressed onto the body to relieve pain or inflammation, or to stop bleeding. Can be used hot or cold.

Concentrated Essential oils are concentrated because they are the essence of a large volume of plants distilled into a small amount of oil. For example, it takes around 300lb (136kg) of rose petals to produce 1oz (30ml) of rose essential oil.

Concrete The first products of solvent extraction; a concrete is a semisolid mix of plant waxes and essential oils that are used to make solid perfumes.

Decongestant A substance or process that reduces congestion in the nasal passages or lungs.

Detoxifying Aids the body in eliminating waste and impurities.

Diffusion/diffuser In aromatherapy, the process by which concentrated essential oil molecules are dispersed/diluted into the air. This can be via a device, such as an electronic diffuser, or a process, such as using a room spray, which releases fragrance molecules into the air.

Dilution The process of making something less concentrated.

Diuretic Increases urine production and output.

Dopamine A neurotransmitter that helps control the brain's reward and pleasure centers.

Elixir In aromatherapy, a blend of essential oils in a base oil. Usually refers to a mixture used on the face for the purposes of improving skin tone.

Emollient Any substance that prevents water loss from the skin. Most natural oils perform this function.

Emulsifier A substance that holds oil and water together, necessary for the production of lotions and creams.

Epinephrine A hormone, commonly called adrenaline, released by the body when a person feels a strong emotion, such as excitement, fear, or anger. It causes the heart to beat faster and prepares the body for a "fight or flight" response.

Esters Chemical compounds derived from an acid. One of a number of constituents of essential oils. Most esters have fruity aromas.

Exfoliate To remove surface layers of the skin, especially dead skin cells, by using an abrasive agent.

Expectorant Encourages mucus to be expelled from the lungs.

Expression The "cold press" method by which essential oils are extracted from citrus peels.

Extraction In aromatherapy, any one of a number of methods by which essential oils are obtained from plant materials. *See also Expression, Steam distillation,* and *Solvent extraction.*

Holistic Treatment of the whole person, taking into account mental and social factors, rather than just the symptoms of a disease.

Hypotensive Having low blood pressure.

Infusion When the active constituents of a plant are extracted into a solvent such as water, alcohol, or oil. The process can be aided by heat and/or time. *See also Macerate.*

Irritant A substance that can irritate the skin or mucous membranes.

Macerate A type of infusion made by steeping chopped-up parts of a plant in a base oil to extract the plant's therapeutic properties.

Neurotransmitter Chemicals released by the brain that act like messengers, carrying information and instructions to other parts of the body.

Ointment An oily substance that is rubbed on the skin for medicinal or cosmetic purposes.

Olfactory Refers to the sense of smell. The olfactory system collects aromatic compounds from the environment and translates these into neural signals that help our brains identify individual aromas.

Organic A method of farming and growing using practices that strive to work with nature and seasonal cycles, promote ecological balance, and conserve biodiversity. Organic farmers and growers, for instance, do not use synthetic pesticides and fertilizers.

Photo-allergy A skin reaction, often slow to develop (1–3 days), caused when the sun's UV rays change a substance such as an essential oil into one that the immune system considers foreign. The reaction can spread beyond the sun-exposed area.

Photosensitive Referring to any substance that can increase skin damage on exposure to UV rays. *See also Photo-allergy* and *Phototoxicity.*

Phototoxicity A skin reaction, often immediate, caused by the interaction of a substance with UV rays, which produces free radicals that damage skin. This is the most common type of photosensitive reaction; rashes tend to be limited to the sun-exposed area.

Regenerative Supports healing and the regeneration of cells and tissues.

Sedative A substance that has a tranquilizing effect, reducing irritability and overexcitement.

Sensitizer Something that causes an allergic reaction. Often an initial application will not produce an effect, but used over time it may induce a severe inflammatory response.

Solvent extraction A method of extracting essential oils from delicate plant materials that cannot withstand heat. With this method, the oil is infused in a solvent. The solvent is then removed, leaving behind a waxy substance, a "concrete," from which a thick essential oil known as an absolute is extracted. *See also Concrete* and *Absolute.*

Steam distillation A process by which steam is used to extract an essential oil from plant material. Steam flows into a container that holds the raw plant material. The heat encourages the release of the oil into the steam, which passes into another container where the steam is condensed back into water. The essential oil is then separated out from the water.

Steam inhalation The process of inhaling steam deep into the lungs. Adding essential oils to hot water creates an aromatic steam that, once in the lungs, has a range of medicinal effects.

Sustainability Refers to the way we produce and use goods, specifically to systems that are regenerative and that work to conserve the natural balance of ecosystems.

Synergy When several elements work together to produce an effect that is greater than the sum of each part. Synergy usually refers to compounds in a single essential oil, but the way an oil blends with other oils to produce a therapeutic or aromatic effect is also sometimes referred to as synergy.

Terpenes One of the naturally occurring constituents of essential oils. A large and diverse class of organic compounds, often strong smelling, produced by a variety of plants, particularly conifers.

Therapeutic Having a healing effect on the body and/or mind.

Toxic Something that can cause damage to living organisms.

Vaporizer A device used to disperse an essential oil mist into the air. *See also Diffusion.*

Volatile In aromatherapy, refers to volatile aromatic compounds: the molecules that make up individual essential oils. They are very light and mobile and quickly disperse into the air, even at room temperature.

Index

Resources

Neal's Yard Remedies

www.nealsyardremedies.com
www.us.nyrorganic.com
Supplier of essential oils and essential
oil products.
Email: inquiries.us@nyrorganic.com
Tel: 888-NYR-0909

National Association of Holistic Aromatherapists (NAHA)

www.naha.org
Has a registry of qualified
aromatherapy practitoners.

Tisserand Institute

www.tisserandinstitute.org
Studies the research on the safety
and use of essential oils.

Pompeii Organics

www.pompeiiorganics.com
Carries over 60 Certified Organic
essential oils, hydrosols, and carriers.

Aromatics International

www.aromatics.com
Sells high-quality therapeutic GC/MS
tested essential oils.

Acknowledgments

The authors at Neal's Yard Remedies would like to thank:
our great editor, Claire Cross, from DK. Our wonderful essential oil suppliers and experts
who work so hard to get fairly traded, organic, and amazing quality oils, and share their
expertise freely, especially Patrick Collin, Walter De Boeck, Denzil Phillips, and Ulli Wentzler.
Also the inspiring and dedicated tutors on our aromatherapy courses, especially Victoria
Plum and Elaine Tomkins.

Dorling Kindersley would like to thank the great team at Neal's Yard Remedies
for their expertise and guidance throughout.

**The publisher would like to thank the following for their kind
permission to use their photographs:**
(Key: a-above; b-below/bottom; c-centre; f-far; l-left; r-right; t-top)

Beniculturali (bc). 13 SuperStock: Eye Ubiquitous (bc). 16 Dorling Kindersley: Barnabas
Kindersley (ca). 18 Science Photo Library: Eye of science (c). 40-41 123RF.com: Elena
Lifantseva. Paperbark Co., Fragonia p43, 45 Alamy Stock Photo: Blickwinkel (l). 47 Alamy
Stock Photo: Valery Voennyy (r). 49 123RF.com: Ekasak Chuenchob (crb). 54-55 Alamy
Stock Photo: imageBROKER. 57 123RF.com: Arcticphotoworks (r). 59 123RF.com: Igor
Dolgov. 66-67 123RF.com: Varaporn Chaisin. 69 123RF.com: Vitaly Suprun / suprunvitaly (r).
71 Dorling Kindersley: Mockford and Bonetti / Villa Giulia and Beniculturali (r). 72
SuperStock: Eye Ubiquitous. 79 123RF.com: Arthit Buarapa (crb). 82-83 123RF.com: Joemat
(c). 87 Alamy Stock Photo: Emilio Ereza (l). 90-91 Alamy Stock Photo: Tim Gainey. 97 Alamy
Stock Photo: Yooniq Images (crb). 103 Alamy Stock Photo: Stephanie Jackson - Aust
wildflower collection (tr). Alan Buckingham, Peppermint p107, Parsley p114, 119 Alamy
Stock Photo: imageBROKER (l). Alan Buckingham, Tuberose p120 122 Alamy Stock Photo:
WILDLIFE GmbH (tr). 124-125 Alamy Stock Photo: Steffen Hauser / botanikfoto. 135 Dorling
Kindersley: John Glover / Unwins (tr). 143 123RF.com: Anna Bogush. 144 123RF.com: Pittawut
Junmee (crb). 154 Getty Images: Image Source (cla). 155 123RF.com: Mohammed
Anwarul Kabir Choudhury (cla). 166 Dorling Kindersley: Alan Buckingham (br). Getty
Images: Image Source (tr). 218 Getty Images: felipedupouy.com / Photodisc (bc)

All other images © Dorling Kindersley
For further information see: www.dkimages.com

Recipe and ingredient photography William Reavell
Recipe styling Jane Lawrie
Photoshoot prop styling and art direction
    Isabel de Cordova
Design/illustration help Steve Marsden
Proofreading Anna Davidson
Indexing Hilary Bird

Disclaimer

*Essential oils contain natural therapeutic properties and should be treated with
respect. This book is not intended as a medical reference book, but as a source of
information. Do not use essential oils for conditions if you are undergoing any other
course of medical treatment without seeking professional advice. The reader is advised
not to attempt self-treatment for serious or long-term problems, during pregnancy, or
for children without consulting a qualified aromatherapist. Neither the authors nor the
publisher can be held responsible for any adverse reactions to the recipes or remedies,
recommendations, and instructions contained herein, and the use of any essential oil
is entirely at the reader's own risk.*